D0389528

From the *New York Times* and *Wall Street Journal*
Bestselling Author on Strategic Thinking

STRATEGIC

— THE SKILL TO —
SET DIRECTION, CREATE ADVANTAGE,
AND ACHIEVE EXECUTIVE EXCELLENCE

RICH HORWATH

Copyright © 2024 by Rich Horwath. All rights reserved.

Published by John Wiley & Sons, Inc., Hoboken, New Jersey.
Published simultaneously in Canada.

No part of this publication may be reproduced, stored in a retrieval system, or transmitted in any form or by any means, electronic, mechanical, photocopying, recording, scanning, or otherwise, except as permitted under Section 107 or 108 of the 1976 United States Copyright Act, without either the prior written permission of the Publisher, or authorization through payment of the appropriate per-copy fee to the Copyright Clearance Center, Inc., 222 Rosewood Drive, Danvers, MA 01923, (978) 750-8400, fax (978) 750-4470, or on the web at www.copyright.com. Requests to the Publisher for permission should be addressed to the Permissions Department, John Wiley & Sons, Inc., 111 River Street, Hoboken, NJ 07030, (201) 748-6011, fax (201) 748-6008, or online at http://www.wiley.com/go/permission.

Trademarks: Wiley and the Wiley logo are trademarks or registered trademarks of John Wiley & Sons, Inc. and/or its affiliates in the United States and other countries and may not be used without written permission. All other trademarks are the property of their respective owners. John Wiley & Sons, Inc. is not associated with any product or vendor mentioned in this book.

Limit of Liability/Disclaimer of Warranty: While the publisher and author have used their best efforts in preparing this book, they make no representations or warranties with respect to the accuracy or completeness of the contents of this book and specifically disclaim any implied warranties of merchantability or fitness for a particular purpose. No warranty may be created or extended by sales representatives or written sales materials. The advice and strategies contained herein may not be suitable for your situation. You should consult with a professional where appropriate. Further, readers should be aware that websites listed in this work may have changed or disappeared between when this work was written and when it is read. Neither the publisher nor authors shall be liable for any loss of profit or any other commercial damages, including but not limited to special, incidental, consequential, or other damages.

For general information on our other products and services or for technical support, please contact our Customer Care Department within the United States at (800) 762-2974, outside the United States at (317) 572-3993 or fax (317) 572-4002.

Wiley also publishes its books in a variety of electronic formats. Some content that appears in print may not be available in electronic formats. For more information about Wiley products, visit our web site at www.wiley.com.

Library of Congress Cataloging-in-Publication Data is Available:

ISBN 9781394215331 (Cloth)
ISBN 9781394215348 (ePub)
ISBN 9781394215355 (ePDF)

Cover Design: Wiley
Cover Images: Compass Rose © warmworld / Adobe Stock;
Contour Map © Olga Kurbatova / Getty Images
Author Photo: © Aaron Gang

SKY10055395_091523

To the leaders I have been blessed to work with, learn from, and laugh with—your insights form the foundation of this story.

CONTENTS

INTRODUCTION

"Cloudy weather, cloudy."

The Lockheed Electra plane flew through the overcast sky under a blanket of rain, having already traveled more than 22,000 miles of the planned 29,000-mile journey.

"KHAQQ calling *Itasca*. We must be on you, but we cannot see you. Fuel is running low. Been unable to reach you by radio. We are flying at 1,000 feet."

The U.S. Coast Guard cutter *Itasca* was stationed just offshore of Howland Island, a whisper of land 1.5 miles long by .5 miles wide in the South Pacific, approximately 2,000 miles southwest of Hawaii.

"KHAQQ calling *Itasca*. We received your signals but unable to get a minimum. Please take bearing on us and answer 3105 with voice."

The U.S. Coast Guard cutter *Itasca* attempted to get a bearing on the transmission and failed.

"KHAQQ to *Itasca*, we are on the line 157 337, will repeat message, we will repeat this on 6210 KCS. Wait. We are running north and south."[1]

Silence.

The two pilots aboard the aircraft were never heard from again.

Or were they?

A day later in Rock Springs, Wyoming, 16-year old Dana Randolph was tuned in to a shortwave band of his parent's radio and reported hearing a woman say, "This is Amelia Earhart. Ship on reef south of the equator. Station KHAQQ."[2]

The same day in St. Petersburg, Florida, 15-year-old Betty Klenck was also tuned into her family's radio shortwave band. She reported hearing a woman, sounding in distress, say, "This is Amelia Earhart."[3]

The most extensive air and sea search in naval history, covering 250,000 square miles of ocean, found . . . nothing.

On May 20, 1937, Amelia Earhart departed from Oakland, California, with Fred Noonan, in an attempt to become the first woman to fly around the world. Over the course of more than six weeks, they followed a route that included 28 stops in exotic locales such as Caripito, Venezuela; Natal, Brazil; Asaab, Ethiopia; Bangkok, Thailand; Bandoeng, Java (Indonesia); Darwin, Australia; and Lae Papau, New Guinea. They were scheduled to stop on Howland Island to refuel and complete the trip by flying to Honolulu and then returning to Oakland, California. Just prior to her final flight from New Guinea, Earhart said, "Not much more than a month ago, I was on the other shore of the Pacific, looking westward. This evening, I looked eastward over the Pacific. In those fast-moving days, which have intervened, the whole width of the world has passed behind us, except this broad ocean. I shall be glad when we have the hazards of its navigation behind us."[4]

Those last words, "the hazards of its navigation," are eerily prophetic. What few people know is that shortly before her fateful trip, she received the following letter from world-renowned navigation author, inventor, and instructor P.V.H. Weems:[5]

May 14, 1937
MISS AMELIA EARHART
c/o G.P. Putnam
2 W. 45th ST. NEW YORK, N.Y.
Dear Miss Earhart:

In case you could find time to come to Annapolis for a few weeks intensive work in celestial navigation, I believe you would be well re-paid for the efforts. I have just had Miss Amy Johnson here for two weeks. She did beautiful work and seems to be more than pleased with the results.

As I see the picture, both of you ladies are in the flying game of your life-time work. Aside from piloting, about which there is no question of your both having a great deal of ability, the only important contribution you can make to a flight is the ability to see the direct course as not to miss the objective.

As both of you know a great deal about dead-reckoning and radio, I recommend that you make a special effort to perfect yourself, not only in radio including the Morse Code, but also in celestial navigation, since radio and celestial navigation afford the only means for fixing your position above the cloud or over the water . . . .

I further believe you would save a great deal of expense and perhaps worry by practicing until you could lay out your own charts and do your own navigation all the way through. You can then take any reasonably dependable co-pilot with you and be sure of hitting your objective. In addition, it would give you a great deal more confidence and you could keep your plans more confidential when necessary . . .

Yours sincerely,
P.V.H. WEEMS.

Amelia Earhart's disappearance remains a mystery to this day. Several theories have emerged as to what happened to her: she crash-landed on the remote Gardner Island and died a castaway there; she landed in the Japanese-held Marshall Islands where she was taken prisoner and transferred to the island of Saipan. Another theory holds that she was then released from the Japanese island and repatriated to the United States under an assumed name. The U.S. government's official explanation was that the plane ran out of fuel and fell into the ocean.[6] While no proof of Earhart's true fate has been confirmed, and each of these theories has been disputed, what is indisputable is that she will be remembered as a courageous visionary with an indomitable spirit.

Earhart was a pioneer and trailblazer in aviation and a fearless role model for men and women alike. Her long list of achievements includes being the first woman to fly across the Atlantic Ocean, the first woman to fly solo across the Atlantic, the first woman to fly solo nonstop coast to coast, setting numerous speed records in domestic and international flights, published author, and recipient of awards including the National Geographic Society's gold medal from President Herbert Hoover, and the Distinguished Flying Cross awarded by the U.S. Congress.[7] However, floating out there like the insidious cloud cover on that fateful day, the question remains: Would Amelia Earhart have completed her amazing journey around the world if she had taken P.V.H. Weems's offer to enhance her navigational skills?

Navigate Your Business

To navigate is to direct or manage something on its course—in other words, to control the movement from one place to another.[8] To navigate means to determine one's position and direction and make a way over or through. Historically, the field of navigation is most prominent in air, sea, and space as the primary skill in successfully guiding planes, ships, and rockets to their intended destinations. More recently, the term "navigate" has been used in an array of contextual landscapes including politics, relationships, ecosystems, and business.

As Earhart's story demonstrates, the ability to navigate is critical to success. In Earhart's era, it was estimated that 50% of aircraft accidents were due to bad navigation. Navigational authority P.V.H. Weems noted, "Many flyers are really lost a good part of the time."[9]

Today, research indicates that "human error contributes to 80% of navigational accidents and that in many cases essential information that could have prevented the accident was available to but not used by those responsible for the navigation of the vessels concerned."[10] The business corollary of this issue is exemplified in a 10-year study of 103 companies that found that strategic blunders—the inability to navigate an organization's course—were the cause of the greatest loss of shareholder value a whopping 81% of the time.[11]

Whether you are navigating a vehicle or a business, it's imperative that you're able to effectively determine your current position and then set direction. A study of 250,000 executives showed that setting strategic direction is the most important role of a leader and the number-one factor that improved organizational health.[12] Despite the importance of leaders' ability to set direction, research by Gallup over the past 30 years with more than 10 million managers found only 22% of employees strongly agreed that the leaders of their organization have set clear direction for the business.[13]

During my strategic executive coaching work the past 20 years, the issue of how to best navigate the business has become a recurring theme for many highly effective leaders, as the following direct quotations demonstrate:

"One issue I'm wrestling with is how best to navigate that with the team."

"There are just some things that I don't know how to, I don't know how to navigate them."

"That's what I want healthcare to be like. That's what my family wants. Yes, it's fragmented. It's confusing to know how to navigate it, and how are we going to solve that?"

"As our market becomes even more competitive with nontraditional players entering, I'm just trying to constructively navigate."

When Disney brought back Bob Iger for his second stint as CEO, his return was described this way in the *Wall Street Journal*: "Walt Disney Co. has brought back the CEO responsible for its pivot to streaming. As he returns, Robert Iger has to navigate a competitive landscape that is far more challenging than when he left less than three years ago."[14]

The navigational role of a leader was further described by Hilton CEO Chris Nassetta in the following manner: "I have a philosophy in life, and that is keeping a steady hand on the wheel. Have a plan and work the plan and adapt the plan. The plan needs to change. Let me use driving vernacular. I don't take every exit, but I will change lanes and I will take exits that really make sense. My longevity has been the ability to just sort of filter noise out and know when to take an exit occasionally, when to change lanes, but not doing it so often that everyone around you is rattled and they can't see what tomorrow is going to be."[15]

The essential meta-skill of a leader is to navigate their business with a thorough understanding of their current situation, vision to see the future destination, and the ability to create the path to reach it. When you have the knowledge, tools, and skills to navigate your business, it produces both competence and confidence. How then do you acquire, maintain, and grow the ability to successfully navigate your business, moving from your current position, over and through obstacles, to reach your goals?

It requires you to be strategic.

Being Strategic

The primary definition of the term "strategic," according to Merriam-Webster's dictionary, is: "of, relating to, or marked by strategy."[16] Since that's about as helpful as an umbrella in a hurricane, I'd like to share the following definition:

Strategic: Possessing insight that leads to advantage.

We can break this definition of *strategic* down into its two core elements: insight and advantage. An insight is when you combine two or more pieces of information or data in a unique way to come up with a new approach, new offering, or new solution that moves the business forward. Simply put, an insight is a learning that leads to new value. Advantage is inherently an element of strategy. It commonly refers to a desired end in the form of gain, profit, benefit, or position of superiority.

When we use this definition of strategic, it helps us clarify what is and is not strategic. A person or plan can be strategic because both have the potential to possess insight that leads to advantage. The word "strategic" is plastered in front of a lot of other words to make them sound important, but their meanings don't hold up. Phrases such as "strategic objective" or "strategic imperative" are examples of terms that sound proper but don't pass the test of being able to house and leverage learnings. Eliminate the overuse of the term "strategic" and you'll clarify and simplify communication among your team.

Here's something you'll never hear in business: "Let's promote her to a senior leadership role . . . she's highly tactical." One of the greatest compliments a person can receive is to be referred to as "strategic." A survey of 10,000 senior executives asked them to select the leadership behaviors most critical to their organization's future success and they chose "strategic" 97% of the time.[17] Additional research with 60,000 managers and executives "found that a strategic approach to leadership was, on average, 10 times more important to the perception of effectiveness than other behaviors studied. It was twice as important as communication (the second most important behavior) and almost 50 times more important than hands-on tactical behaviors."[18]

Business leaders, academicians, and boards of directors echo these findings:

"To me, the single most important skill needed for any CEO today is strategic acuity."

—Indra Nooyi, former CEO, Pepsi[19]

"After two decades of observation, it is clear that mastery of strategy is not an innate skill. Most great CEOs learn how to become better strategic thinkers."

—David Yoffie, professor, Harvard Business School, and Michael Cusumano, professor, MIT Sloan School of Management[20]

"The #1 trait of active CEOs that makes them attractive board candidates is strategic expertise."

—Corporate Board of Directors Survey[21]

"The No. 1 capability boards are looking for in a CEO: strategic capability."

—Cathy Anterasian, Senior Partner, Spencer Stuart.[22]

As the research and thought leaders demonstrate, the importance of being strategic is universal. After all, who doesn't want to be seen as providing new value that leads to benefits, gains, or profits for their organization? For instance, label someone what many perceive as the opposite of strategic—tactical—and it won't be taken as a compliment. Another descriptor for the purely tactical is "unstrategic."

The Unstrategic

In recent years, zombies have amassed in quantity and popularity, securing a place for the undead in the supernatural landscape. The zombie's doppelgänger in the business arena is the unstrategic. The unstrategic are those individuals unable to raise themselves from their tactical tombs to contribute to the business at a higher strategic level. You wouldn't tolerate a zombie attempting to eat Mark from finance during the staff

meeting, yet the unstrategic can cause a similar—albeit less mortal—
outcome for your team. Which of these three sins of the unstrategic are
being committed in your organization?

1. **Wandering aimlessly.** The undead wander the landscape aimlessly,
   attracted by loud noises and bright lights. The unstrategic lack direction, which causes them to latch onto each and every new shiny
   opportunity that pops up. Fundamentally, they lack priorities and the
   appropriate filters to keep them focused. As Cal Henderson, co-
   founder of Slack, said, "What are the things that are the most strategically important, and am I allocating my time to them correctly? Am I
   spending the right percentage of my time on them? It's easy to get
   lost in the weeds."[23]

In my experience, facilitating strategy sessions with executive leadership teams to shape strategic direction, I've found it important to
address two obvious but often obscured questions: 1) What are you trying to achieve? 2) How will you achieve it? Look at your most recent
plan. Are these two questions answered immediately up front in the first
slide or two? If not, there's a good chance the answers are buried in
Excel spreadsheets or colorful graphs, and not known or recognized by
the team. Research shows that when teams believe their leader is competent in setting good strategic direction, they are 40% more committed
to successfully executing the strategy.[24]

2. **Doing everything.** The undead lack the discipline to select just one
   victim—they try to eat everyone. The unstrategic lack the discipline
   to say no. They try to be all things to all customers, both internally
   and externally. When Mary Barra took the reigns as CEO of General
   Motors, she compared her new approach with that of the previous
   leaders by saying, "We're here to win. We aren't going to win by being
   all things to all people everywhere. It's not the right strategy."[25]

The dirty secret of being strategic is that you have to say no to people, both internally and externally. Managers need to be deliberately
unresponsive to some types of customers so that they can be highly
responsive to others where they can provide maximum appreciable value.

The necessary role of trade-offs in strategy is to intentionally make some customers unhappy by focusing resources in areas destined to provide the most value to the customers most willing to pay for it. If you fail to prioritize what's important, then nothing is important.

3. **Killing meetings.** The undead continually utter gibberish due to their severely diminished brain activity. The unstrategic kill strategy meetings by taking conversations down rabbit holes, preventing progress, and causing widespread frustration among the other members of the group. Research has shown that executives spend an average of 21.5 hours per week in meetings, and a frightening 83% of executives said that these meetings are an unproductive use of time.[26] Why? It's often due to one or two members of the group who are unstrategic, taking the team off-topic until people lose interest and become numb to the epic waste of time.

   As a facilitator who has led hundreds of strategy sessions, I'd recommend several ways to address this issue. An effective preventative step is to educate the team on the difference between strategy and tactics, with examples of each. This helps people better understand which topics are strategic and which are tactical, enabling them to contribute appropriately. Another technique is to establish a "Tactical Parking Lot." Playing off the parking lot flipchart concept, the tactical parking lot allows the facilitator to quickly move any rabbit-hole tactical comments to the flipchart, resuming the group's strategic-level conversation.

Strategic Fitness

Consider your business for a moment: What are the predominant market trends and patterns and the resulting impact on your business? How have customers' thinking and actions changed during the past year? What type of nontraditional competitors are entering your market and what have your traditional competitors been doing to take your customers? Does your culture support your initiatives and are each and every functional group's strategies aligned? Do these answers make you want to reach for a bottle of aspirin? Wine? Scotch?

You're not alone.

A Gartner survey of 75 human resource leaders on how their managers were coping with their business found 68% reporting that they were overwhelmed. And only 14% of those companies have developed a plan to help their managers overcome the challenges of navigating their business.[27] Running a business today can be likened to trying to put together a jigsaw puzzle where the sizes and shapes of the pieces are constantly changing, and oh, by the way, you don't have all the pieces, either.

A magnetic compass typically contains a small, magnetized needle and always points north due to its attraction to a large magnetic deposit near the North Pole. When you consider the many different instruments used in navigation, the magnetic compass is arguably the simplest and most reliable. Based on more than 25 years of helping executive leadership teams develop their strategic capabilities to set direction, create advantage, and achieve their goals, I created the Strategic Fitness System, as represented by a compass (Figure I.1) to help leaders navigate their business and enhance their executive performance.

Figure I.1 Strategic Fitness System.

There are four areas of strategic fitness that contribute to navigation and development: Strategy, Leadership, Organization, and Communication.

Strategy Fitness refers to your ability to understand and develop strategy, set direction, allocate resources, make decisions, and create competitive advantage.

Leadership Fitness is built on a leader's philosophy, personal performance, mental training, and ability to master time and calendar.

Organization Fitness is determined by one's ability to create the appropriate business structure, evolve the business model, develop talent while planning for succession, and innovate.

Communication Fitness revolves around the facilitation of conversations, effective collaboration, bringing value to customers, and leading productive meetings.

While simple in structure, each area contains dozens of tools, techniques, and checklists to give you a methodical and comprehensive approach to mastering your business. The result: the ability to think, plan, and act strategically to successfully navigate your business.

What's Your Strategic Quotient (SQ)?

To navigate means to determine one's position and direction and make a way over or through. It may be helpful as part of this journey to determine your current position as it relates to your strategic capabilities. One option I've designed to assist in this process is the Strategic Quotient Assessment. The Strategic Quotient (SQ) is a measure of a person's strategic capabilities as exhibited through their mindset and behaviors.

The SQ is based on the 3A Framework of the three critical disciplines for being strategic. These three disciplines are:

• Acumen (Thinking): The generation of insights to create new value
• Allocation (Planning): Focusing resources through strategic trade-offs
• Action (Acting): Prioritizing and executing initiatives

The SQ is used to identify opportunities for development of a person's strategic capabilities, and, following a targeted intervention, to determine whether the individual understands and applies the disciplines of Acumen,

Table I.1 Primary and Secondary Dimensions of the Strategic Quotient.

ACUMEN (Thinking)	ALLOCATION (Planning)	ACTION (Acting)
• Context	• Resource Allocation	• Collaboration
• Insight	• Decision Making	• Execution
• Innovation	• Competition	• Personal Performance

Allocation, and Action. A person's score on the SQ may indicate the likelihood they can successfully apply and demonstrate these strategic capabilities. Table I.1 identifies the foundational elements of the Strategic Quotient.

The SQ Assessment is comprised of 50 statements to determine the performance level of how one thinks, plans, and acts strategically. Table I.2 contains sample statements from the SQ Assessment.

For additional information on taking the assessment and discovering your SQ score, visit www.StrategySkills.com.

As you move through the book, you'll find several additional techniques to facilitate your understanding and application of the material:

Rocket Burn: Due to the lack of atmosphere, a spacecraft coasts for the majority of its journey. Therefore, astronauts navigate at a few critical moments by setting their trajectory with precise burns of the rocket engines during the voyage. The rocket burns in this book will provide you with quick tips and techniques to successfully navigate your business and calibrate your learning trajectory.

Off Course: To navigate is to manage something along its course. In navigating a ship or plane, challenges in the form of weather conditions, other crafts, and human error can hinder one from reaching their destination. In these sections, we'll identify issues to be aware of and mitigate in order to enhance your ability to navigate the business.

Trail Blazes: Experienced hikers will recognize the term "blaze" as the most common type of trail marking to help guide one's adventure. Blazes are typically in the form of paint or carvings on trees along the trail. You'll discover a trail blaze page at the end of each chapter containing a summary of insights to ensure you're on the right path.

Ready? 3 . . . 2 . . . 1 . . . liftoff!

Table 1.2   SQ Assessment Sample.

	Never	Rarely	Sometimes	Often	Always
I record my assessment of the current business situation					
I meet with colleagues from other areas to align on strategy					
I update my business plan with new insights					
I take time at the completion of projects to record key learnings					
I schedule time in my calendar to think about the future of my business					

Trail Blazes

To navigate means to determine one's position and direction and make a way over or through.

A study of 250,000 executives showed that setting strategic direction is the most important role of a leader and the number-one factor that improved organizational health.

Strategic: Possessing insight that leads to advantage.

A survey of 10,000 senior executives asked them to select the leadership behaviors most critical to their organization's future success and they chose "strategic" 97% of the time.

The Unstrategic:
1. Wandering Aimlessly
2. Doing Everything
3. Killing Meetings

Four areas of Strategic Fitness:
1. Strategy Fitness
2. Leadership Fitness
3. Organization Fitness
4. Communication Fitness

The Strategic Quotient (SQ) is a measure of a person's strategic capabilities as exhibited through their mindset and behaviors.

The SQ is based on the 3A Framework of the three critical disciplines for being strategic. These three disciplines are:
- Acumen (Thinking): The generation of insights to create new value
- Allocation (Planning): Focusing resources through strategic trade-offs
- Action (Acting): Prioritizing and executing initiatives

PART I

Strategy Fitness

"Once we reach a certain level of expertise at a given discipline and our knowledge is expansive, the critical issue becomes: How is all this stuff navigated and put to use? I believe the answers to this question are the gateway to the most esoteric levels of elite performance."

—Josh Waitzkin, U.S. Junior Chess Champion, martial arts champion, and author

The distance around the earth is divided into 360 units called degrees. We can measure longitude from 0 to 180 degrees both east and west. Latitude is measured north and south from 0 to 90 degrees, from the equator. One degree is comprised of 60 units called minutes, and each minute is broken into 60 seconds. Wherever we are, we have 360 directions to select from to travel to a destination of our choice. While 360 potential directions may seem like a dizzying array of choices, there's great power in knowing that you always have different options to choose from.

CHAPTER 1

Strategy

"Good strategies promote alignment among diverse groups within an organization, clarify objectives and priorities, and help focus efforts around them. In essence, they act like a map and compass. They provide direction."

—Clayton Christensen, former professor,
Harvard Business School

The concept of strategy initially sprang from the need for people to defeat their enemies. The first treatises that discuss strategy are from the Chinese during the period of 400–200 BCE. Chinese general and philosopher Sun Tzu's *The Art of War*, written around the fifth century BCE, has received critical acclaim as the best work on military strategy, including those that have followed it centuries later. However, unlike the later theoretical treatises, the Chinese works took the form of narratives, including poems and prose accounts. An example of this prose form of strategy can be seen in the poem by Lao Tzu, the father of Taoism:

Once grasp the great form without a form
and you will roam where you will
with no evil to fear,
calm, peaceful, at ease.
The hub of the wheel runs upon the axle.
In a jar, it is the hole that holds water.
So advantage is had
from whatever there is;

but usefulness rises
from whatever is not.[1]

While at first glance it may be difficult to identify an element of strategy in the poem, a key principle found here is the importance of "not," because strategy demands trade-offs—choosing your "nots." The business parallel is the need for disciplined focus that comes from making strategic trade-offs: What products will we not offer? What customers will we choose not to serve? As Meg Whitman, former CEO of companies such as eBay and Hewlett Packard Enterprise, proclaimed, "Our strategy is as much the art of exclusion as it is the art of inclusion."[2]

The term "strategy" is derived indirectly from the classic and Byzantine (330 AD) Greek *strategos,* meaning "general," but no Greek ever used the word. The Greek equivalent for the modern concept would have been *strategike episteme* (general's knowledge) or *strategon sophia* (general's wisdom). "Strategy" retained this narrow meaning until Count Guibert, a French military thinker, introduced the term *La Strategique* in 1799, in the sense that is understood today. Strategy as a term entered the English language in 1810.[3]

Strategy Fitness refers to your ability to develop strategy, allocate resources, make decisions, and create competitive advantage. Strategy is a prerequisite for success whenever the path to a goal is obscure. Charting a clear path to a desired destination starts with a common understanding and language for strategy. Yet research with 400 talent management executives showed less than half believe their organizations have either a universal definition (44.3%) or a common language (46%) for strategy.[4] And research spanning a 25-year period on the term "strategy" uncovered 91 different definitions![5]

Strategy Is Not . . .

Essence (noun): the basic, real, and invariable nature of a thing.[6] If there was ever one thing that needed to be returned to its "basic, real, and invariable nature," that thing is strategy. Like a boat with no anchor flailing about in the open sea, strategy has become unmoored from its true meaning. It has become meaningless. In determining the essence of a thing, it's helpful to begin with what that thing is not. Think ABCs.

Strategy is not **A**spiration. How often have you seen a vision or goal masquerading as strategy? A vision is the future aspiration, what you'd like to be in 10 or 15 years. A goal is generally what you are trying to achieve. To become the market leader or the premier provider of your secret sauce or the world's most sustainable product are noble aspirations. Just don't confuse them with strategy.

Strategy is not **B**est practices. If you benchmark the competition and then adopt the best practices, you have not developed strategy. You have converged with the competition, not distanced yourself from it. Strategy serves to differentiate your offerings and your company from the competition by providing superior value to customers.

Strategy is not **C**autious. Find a strategy that's not last year's leftovers reheated and dolled up with some salt and pepper to make it palatable to the group going down the same path that they've been down a dozen times before. Find a strategy that isn't afraid to upset some of the customer base because it actually contains real trade-offs that are not designed to appeal to everyone, especially the unprofitable, high-maintenance customers you should have fired years ago. Find a strategy that doesn't bore the people expected to implement it because it contains nary a new insight. As Disney CEO Bob Iger said, "The riskiest thing we can do is just maintain the status quo."[7]

Off Course: Strategy is not Aspiration, Best practices, or Cautious.

The following are examples of strategies pulled from real companies:

"Become more profitable."
"Grow our audience."
"Be number one in the market."
"Execute integration and capture synergies."
"We're trying to find the people who were customers and didn't come back. That's a major strategy."

That last one still cracks me up. Make no mistake: bad strategy can literally kill a company. In a 25-year study of 750 bankruptcies, the researchers found that the number-one cause of bankruptcy was bad strategy.[8] Bad strategy often begins with imprecision in applying planning terms to our business. As the Chinese philosopher Confucius noted, "The beginning of wisdom is to call things by their right name."

A plan answers two fundamental questions:

1. What are you trying to achieve?
2. How will you achieve it?

GOST Framework

I created the GOST Framework™ (Figure 1.1) to help leaders and their teams develop a consistent approach to answering these two key questions and provide a common language for strategy.

A goal is WHAT *generally* you are trying to achieve, let's say reaching the top of a mountain. The objective is WHAT *specifically* you are trying to achieve, so in this example ascending 3,000 feet each day for four days until we reach the 12,000-foot summit. Objectives are often described with the acronym SMART: Specific, Measurable, Achievable, Relevant, and Time-bound.

The strategy is HOW *generally* you'll reach the goal and objective, in this case your general approach to reaching the top of the mountain—hiking straight up, zigzagging, or ascending a path on the opposite side. The tactics

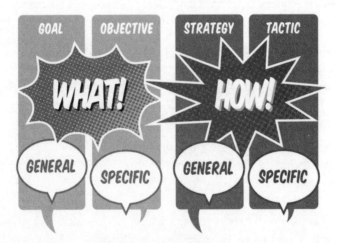

Figure 1.1 GOST Framework.

then are HOW *specifically* you'll achieve your goal—using ropes, pickaxes, or maybe an inflatable raft to paddle around to the other side.

Here is an example for the business application of the GOST Framework:

Goal:	Become the market leader in wearable biotechnology.
Objective:	Achieve 40% market share in the apparel category by Q4.
Strategy:	Neutralize competitor product entries through real-time innovation.
Tactic:	Key customers contribute to product engineering platform.

> **Rocket Burn:** The GOST Framework enables you to clearly and consistently answer the two foundational questions at the core of a plan:
>
> 1. What are you trying to achieve? [Goals & Objectives]
> 2. How will you achieve it? [Strategy & Tactics]

Ozan Varol, author of the book *Think Like a Rocket Scientist*, reinforces these definitions when he writes, "A strategy is a plan for achieving an objective. Tactics, in contrast, are the actions you take to implement the strategy. We often lose sight of the strategy, fixate on the tactics and the tools, and become dependent on them. But tools can be the subtlest of traps. Only when you zoom out and determine the broader strategy can you walk away from a flawed tactic."[9]

A common challenge is distinguishing between strategy and tactics. The complementary nature of strategy and tactics has defined their intertwined existence. In the military realm, tactics teach the use of armed forces in engagements, while strategy teaches the use of engagements to achieve the objectives of the war. The original meaning of "tactics" is "order"—literally the "ordering of formations on the battlefield."[10]

However, the current use of "strategic" and "tactical" stems from World War II. "Strategic" is associated with long-range aircraft and missiles, while "tactical" has referred to shorter-range aircraft and missiles. The term "strategic" then became associated with the completely incidental quality of long range, which bombers might need to attack industrial targets in some geographic areas. In turn, that caused "tactical" to take on the aura of short range.

Off Course: Putting the word "strategic" in front of other planning terms such as "goals" or "objectives" adds no value and only muddies the water. Keep goals, objectives, strategies, and tactics separate.

From a business perspective, a more accurate and useful distinction than time for strategy and tactics is general versus specific. Strategy is how *generally* to achieve a goal while tactics are how *specifically* to achieve a goal. If your team struggles with the difference between strategy and tactics, perhaps the "Rule of Touch" will help. If you can reach out and physically touch some aspect of the item in question, it is most likely a tactic. Strategy, on the other hand, is abstract, like leadership or love. In his writings that became the book *The Art of War,* Sun Tzu described the difference between strategy and tactics this way: "All the men can see the tactics I use to conquer, but what none can see is the strategy out of which great victory is evolved."[11]

Strategy Defined

Strategy can be defined as the intelligent allocation of resources through a unique system of activities to achieve a goal. Simply put, strategy is how you plan to achieve your goal. With this definition comes the caveat of competition—both direct and indirect—which will attempt to prevent you from reaching your goal. That is why plans must be fluid and strategy created and calibrated with a continuous flow of strategic thinking.

Based on strategy's definition as "the intelligent allocation of resources through a unique system of activities to achieve a goal," let's break strategy down into its three primary components:

1. **Allocation of Resources.** How you and your organization use your resources—time, talent, and budget—comprises your strategy. You may have a strategy written down in a PowerPoint deck, but observe how your people are spending their time, talent, and budget every day and you'll see your true strategy. Discipline is a key ingredient. Aimlessly investing a few hours each day on tasks that are

not directly supportive of your goals may seem productive but will destroy your chances of real success. If you have not clearly written out and communicated the strategy on a consistent basis, then where people channel their resources becomes a matter of chance. Good leaders don't leave strategy to chance.

2. **Unique System of Activities.** Perhaps the most common error in business planning is mistaking operational effectiveness for strategy. Operational effectiveness is the proverbial wolf in strategy's clothing. It means performing similar activities in a similar manner as competitors, trying to do them a little better or faster. However, employing operational effectiveness without strategy is like running the same race as competitors, only hoping to run a little faster. Creating strategy indicates that we are going to run a different course than our competitors are running—one that we ourselves have designed to win. A study of more than 200 companies found that 93% of the top 20% of financial performers have a strong form of differentiation at their core.[12] Do you? If your strategy does not include different activities or similar activities performed in different ways, then it's not going to create distinct value. Not until you get off the beaten path can the beating begin.

3. **Achieve a Goal.** In preparation for facilitating strategy workshops and executive coaching with senior executives, I review roughly 300 plans a year, and some are too complex, too long, or both. A good plan simply answers the two questions we introduced earlier: 1) What are you trying to achieve? 2) How will you achieve it? Your goal and objective represent the answer to the first question (what you are trying to achieve), and strategy and tactics answer the second question (how you will achieve it). While it may be tempting to start with the strategy in developing a plan, remember that you first have to determine your destination before you can identify how to get there.

Rocket Burn: Strategy is the intelligent allocation of resources through a unique system of activities to achieve a goal.

When to Change Strategy

We as human beings don't like to change. The Johns Hopkins School of Medicine reports several studies of people who underwent a type of heart surgery called CABG, or "coronary artery bypass grafting." The doctors met with patients immediately following the heart surgery and told them they must make changes in their lifestyles, including diet, exercise, and medication. Two years later, the percentage of patients who did not make any sustainable changes was 90%.[13] That's right—90% of patients made no changes despite being told that without those changes, they had a greater chance of dying.

If it's that difficult for people to make changes when their lives are at stake, what's the chance we'll change our business strategy when the time comes? And exactly how do we know when the right time is to change it? One thing is for sure: not changing strategy at the right time can start a death spiral for your business.

Research on 500 companies examined their stall points, or continued periods of revenue decline, and found that 70% of stall factors resulted from a choice about strategy. During these stall points, companies lose on average 74% of their market capitalization in the decade surrounding the stall point.[14] The ability to modify strategy at the right time can literally save or destroy a business. Here is a checklist of five moments when it is critical to reevaluate your strategy.

1. **Goals are achieved or modified.** Since goals are "what" you are trying to achieve and strategy is "how" you're going to get there, it makes sense that if the destination changes, so too should the path to get there. As you accomplish goals and new goals are established, changes in resource allocation are often required to meet them. In some cases, goals are modified during the course of the year to reflect changes in the market, competitive landscape, or customer profile. It's important to reflect on the strategy as these changes occur to see if it also needs to be modified.

   Ask yourself: Have goals been achieved or changed?

2. **Customer needs evolve.** The end game of business strategy is to serve customers' needs in a more profitable way than the competition. But as the makers of VHS tapes, printed encyclopedias, and pagers

will tell you, customer needs evolve. The leaders skilled in strategic thinking are able to continually generate new insights into the emerging needs of key customers. They can then shape their group's current or future offerings to best meet those evolving needs.

Ask yourself: Have customer needs changed?

3. **Innovation in the market.** The word "innovation" is used by almost everybody and consistently practiced by a very few. In the vast sea of articles and books on innovation, the simplest definition is "creating new value for customers." The new value may be technological in nature, but it can also be generated in many other ways. including service, experience, marketing, process, and so on. It may be earth shattering, or it may be incremental in nature. The key is to keep a tight pulse on the market, customers, and competitors to understand when innovation, or new value, is being delivered and by whom. Once that's confirmed, assess your goals and strategies to determine if they need to be adjusted based on this new level of value in the market.

Ask yourself: Is there innovation in the market?

4. **Competitors change perceived value.** For many years, fast food was fast food. There are burgers, tacos, chicken, pizza, and hot dogs– the standard fare. Within each category, there was greater similarity between competing offerings than distinction. Enter Chipotle, a company that has focused on a "Food with Integrity" campaign in which their healthy ingredients have played the starring role in their burritos, tacos, and bowls. Sourcing their food from farms rather than factories, they became the first national restaurant chain to voluntarily disclose the presence of GMOs (genetically modified organisms) in their food. Increasing the perceived value of an aspect of your offering—in Chipotle's case, ingredients–through marketing campaigns, social media, celebrity endorsers, and so on, is a real weapon or threat, depending on your position.

Ask yourself: Have competitors changed perceived value?

5. **Capabilities grow or decline.** A final consideration when determining whether to change strategies falls under your own roof. Having led strategic thinking and planning sessions for the past 25 years, I know how challenging it can be for organizations to honestly evaluate their capabilities and their effectiveness. A list of 17 strengths during the SWOT Analysis (strengths, weaknesses, opportunities, and

threats) is one indication. However, objective assessment of the group's capabilities relative to the competition is a starting point. If they have significantly grown, it may open up new avenues or strategies for increasing profits. If the capabilities have declined, it may call for new approaches, whether neutralizing strategies or exit strategies.

Ask yourself: What is the state of our capabilities?

3A Strategic Framework

While there are many skills an executive must be proficient at in order to successfully run a business, the research shared earlier shows that none are as important as their ability to develop strategy. How then do you ensure that strategy development isn't a weakness that torpedoes your career and your company? By becoming more effective at thinking, planning, and acting strategically.

Introduced earlier as the conceptual foundation of the Strategic Quotient Assessment, the 3A Strategic Framework (Figure 1.2) represents the key areas of being strategic:

Acumen (Thinking): Generating insights to create new value
Allocation (Planning): Focusing resources through trade-offs
Action (Acting): Prioritizing and executing initiatives

Acumen begins with ensuring that all of your people are accountable for contributing new ideas that lead to customer and organizational value. Elite leaders design insight networks that connect people and their ideas across functions and levels. Some have taken this a step further by assigning accountability to their direct reports for harnessing insights from their teams on a monthly basis and generating "Insight Updates" across the matrix. This means that everyone is contributing ideas on how the business can be more effective, efficient, and innovative. As Apple CEO Tim Cook said, "We want ideas coming from all 80,000 people, not five or three. A much smaller number of people have to decide and edit, and move forward, but we want ideas coming from everywhere."[15]

Allocation begins with active disengagement. Inventory the areas where your time, talent, and budget are currently being spent and then match those aggregates with your priorities. You'll be amazed at how

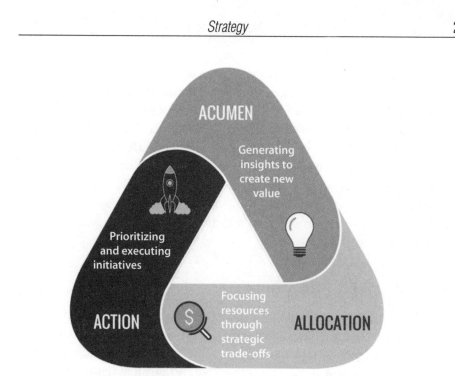

Figure 1.2 The 3A Strategic Framework.

much time and budget is continuing to be invested in areas that don't yield value. Then have the guts to pull the plug on things that aren't working—not slowly over nine months, but now! Research by the MIT Sloan School of Management shows that 80% of mid-level managers say their senior leaders fail to kill unsuccessful initiatives quickly enough.[16] How many tasks and initiatives are your team currently working on that add little value while sucking up the time and energy of your best people?

Action begins with a more strategic approach to your time. A Harvard Business School study of 60,000 CEO hours identified the CEO's largest time commitment is meetings, at 61% of their time.[17] Since meetings are on average the largest consumer of an executive's time, they need to be as productive and efficient as possible. Currently, they are not. A whopping 71% of executives say that their meetings are unproductive and inefficient.[18] To add insult to injury, half of all companies surveyed indicated senior leaders' meeting agendas were either exactly the same or completely ad hoc.[19] It's difficult to act strategically if your calendar manages you, instead of you managing your calendar.

The 3A Strategic Framework of Acumen, Allocation, and Action can be an effective mental model to trigger you to think, plan, and act strategically on a regular basis. It requires the discipline to prioritize learning, harness your team's best thinking, and set a course to continually overcome challenges in the pursuit of excellence. Being a senior leader should no longer be dictated by years on the job, but by the expertise and value a person brings. It's an honor to lead people, so approach it as such. Do it strategically with a hunger for new insights and you'll make the most of the opportunity. Do it tactically with complacency and you won't do it for long.

Strategy Development

Strategic thinking is the ability to generate insights that lead to advantage. Strategic planning is the channeling of those insights into an action plan that drives people's activities. The strategic plan should clearly describe where the business is today, where it's going, and how it's going to get there. Inherent in that description is what you choose to do and—equally important—what you choose *not* to do. Great strategy demands trade-offs, and trade-offs come from the ability to make decisions, and cut things off from your time, attention, and resources. As *Money* magazine research noted:"The higher you go, the more valuable strategic thinking becomes. Both 'strategy development' and 'business strategy' are skills that set executives apart. Moreover, even within that elite stratum, workers with those skills earn 9.1% and 8.2%, respectively, more than those without."[20]

Research demonstrates that 66% of organizations lack a coherent set of strategic thinking frameworks and 81% of managers say they do not have a consistent process for developing strategy.[21,22] An effective method for strategy development includes regular conversations guided by strategic thinking frameworks. These frameworks are shaped by a concise strategy process that helps leaders take a consistent approach to setting strategic direction and ensures that they are thinking holistically about the business. With more than 150 strategic thinking tools to choose from, it's important to select the few that are most relevant to your business so as to not overwhelm the team.

A few years back I was invited to Venice, Italy, to lead a strategic thinking workshop for executives from western Europe. Following the workshop, I traveled to Florence, Italy, and had the opportunity to visit the Accademia Gallery, home to perhaps the most famous of all sculptures, Michelangelo's *David*. After taking in this awe-inspiring work of art, I walked back down the hall to view some of Michelangelo's other sculptures, including the *Four Prisoners*. It was here that his unique approach to sculpting came shining through for me.

His approach involved the element of discovery. Whereas his counterparts would carve their figures into the stone, Michelangelo started with the belief that the figure was *already* in the stone before he touched it. His gift was to uncover the figure that lay waiting in the stone. Michelangelo's works such as *The Atlas* demonstrate this approach: the figure is only partially visible and the remainder lies embedded in the stone. His task was to uncover, or *free* the figure from the stone.

For thousands of years, strategists and sculptors have used similar techniques to create their works. Sculptors employ one of two techniques: modeling or carving. Modeling sculptors begin with an intense study of their subject and then mold soft materials such as clay or wax into specific shapes. Carving sculptors, on the other hand, create an art form by removing or chiseling material from a shapeless block of wood or stone, often without having a specific end result in mind.

The modeling technique of sculpture is analogous to the classical school of strategy development where intense analysis of the industry and competitive landscape is used to form the strategy. Similarly, the carving technique of sculpture is comparable to the evolutionary school of strategy development, where strategy emerges from the marketplace environment. Michelangelo's sculpture and your business strategy share the common element of both starting out buried in their compositions. However, once intense analysis and the accompanying synthesis occur, they both begin to emerge with clarity and vision.

Michelangelo's belief that the figure is embedded in the stone, requiring vision and skill to draw it forth, teaches us a valuable business premise: your business strategy lies embedded in the form that encompasses your customers, competition, company offerings, and marketplace opportunities. What is required of you is the strategic thinking necessary to free your strategy.

The process of developing strategy is quite similar to the process that a sculptor uses to navigate the process of creating a work of art. Therefore, we can describe the five phases of the best-of-breed strategy development process in concert with the five phases of sculpting.

1. Discovery: "Choosing the Tools"

A sculptor begins the process by selecting the material to work with (clay, marble, metal) and the appropriate tools (hammer, chisel, knives) with which to work. Similarly, the discovery phase of strategy development involves the selection of the people, process, and information to be used.

The discovery phase of the strategy development process entails designating the team, outlining the process being used, and disseminating the prework. The prework involves intelligence gathering on the market, customers, competitors, and the organization. Specific tasks include primary research with customers and employees in the form of one-to-one interviews, focus groups, and the Strategy Survey.

2. Strategic Thinking: "Playing in Space"

Once a sculptor has chosen the tools, they begin working ideas out in space by creating a maquette, or small 3-D model of the intended work. The strategic thinking phase provides the forum for the group to begin generating and capturing their business insights in model format.

The strategic thinking sessions, conducted with the strategy development team, are designed to generate new insights through a methodical and comprehensive examination of the four key areas of the business: market, customers, competitors, and company. In examining these areas, often the primary challenges identified can act as the seeds of strategy. The main reason so many strategic plans collect dust and are not actively used to drive daily activities is because they don't contain any new thinking on current challenges. The lack of insights in a plan is often due to the management team's failure to invest time in high-level strategy conversations guided by a thoughtful process.

3. Strategic Planning: "Building the Framework"

After creating the miniature 3-D model, the sculptor working in clay creates a skeletal structure or wire frame, known as an armature, to serve as the foundation of the sculpture. The strategic planning phase acts in the same manner, creating the framework for the strategy and all of its elements.

The strategic planning phase transforms the insights generated from strategic thinking into the strategic action plan that achieves the organization's goals and objectives and includes the appropriate timelines and budgets. The key is that the deliverable is a concise one- to three-page map or blueprint for the business.

4. Strategy Rollout: "Sculpting the Masterpiece"

Once the framework has been developed, the artist sculpts the figure, adding and taking away material as necessary. In the same way, the strategy rollout phase transforms the strategic plan into the activities and offerings that move the business forward.

The strategy rollout phase ensures that the key elements of the strategic action plan are clearly communicated throughout the organization and that an implementation plan is in place. The following steps support the strategy rollout:

1. Development of the communication plan
2. Dissemination of the strategic action plan through the chosen communication vehicles to employees
3. Collection and review of feedback regarding the strategic action plan components and the effectiveness of their communication to the organization
4. Incorporation and application of the strategic action plan to employees' daily activities and their corresponding metrics
5. Periodic pulse-taking to monitor progress and assess effectiveness and relevance of both strategy and tactics and their understanding by employees

5. Strategy Tune-up: "Polishing the Form"

Once the sculptor finishes the work, they must ensure that adjustments, such as proper lighting, and maintenance activities, including cleaning and polishing, are performed on a regular basis to keep the sculpture in its best form. Similarly, the strategy tune-up phase serves to keep the strategy in an evergreen state.

Comprised of a half- to full-day session on a quarterly basis, the strategy tune-up consists of periodic formal reviews of the business by the strategy development team to hone their work. The team methodically reviews the four key areas of the business—market, customers, competitors, and company—to identify changes and make any necessary adjustments to strategy and tactics.

Great strategy, like great works of art, requires vision, creativity, and hard work. Are you and your team bringing each of these elements to your business? If not, your success may stay buried in mounds of irrelevant activities, like the figure in *The Atlas* struggling to free his potential. Successfully generating insights from these regular strategy conversations are the springboard for the strategic plan.

Designing a StrategyPrint

One way to evaluate someone's strategic capabilities is to take a look at their plan. If the plan is long, complicated, and not crystallized into a useable one- to two-page document, then there is work to be done. The longer the plan, the less likely it is to be updated with new insights and remain a relevant compass for one's strategic direction. Brian Chesky, CEO of Airbnb, shares his perspective on the strategic plan: "If you can't fit it on a page, you're not simplifying it enough. I told my team they have to put the entire plan on a page this big (8.5" × 11") by next week—same size font."[23]

To help executive teams with this challenge of condensing their plans into useable documents, I developed the StrategyPrint®. The tool serves as a two-page blueprint for the business:

Page 1: Insights, People, and Priorities
Page 2: Action Plan

Page 1 is focused on insights, which are defined as learnings that lead to new value. Placing insights at the beginning acts as a behavioral trigger to move leaders to actively generate and capture them as a part of what they do. Categories of insights might include customer, team, business, and culture. A key step is to assign accountability for insights to ensure your team is aware of and actively engaged in discovering them.

Insights then shed light on priorities and the people to help achieve them. While priorities consist of the activities, initiatives, and projects that drive your business, it's critical also to take a strategic look at the people who contribute to their accomplishment. Key people may include customers, select members of the board of directors, peers, direct reports, suppliers, and vendors. What are the development activities you have in place to continue to build and nurture those relationships?

Page 2 channels your insights and priorities into an action plan. The action plan needs to answer these two questions identified earlier:

1. What are you trying to achieve?
2. How will you achieve it?

It's useful to answer those questions by identifying the goals and objectives (what you are trying to achieve), and the strategies and tactics (how you will achieve them). There are a number of other elements that can be customized to this area based on your business, but be sure to answer those two key questions.

At the heart of your plan are the activities, which act as the hub for purpose, people, and resources. A common sign an organization is missing the discipline to make trade-offs, which in turn acts as the filter within the strategy, is the proliferation of activities and tactics to the point that people are drowning in them. Consider your team: Is there a clear set of three to five priorities on which the majority of your activities are based?

To take a quick check on how well your team is applying the concepts and tools of strategy to the business, take the complimentary 20-question quiz, "Is Your Team Tactical or Strategic?" at https://www.strategyskills.com/is-your-team-strategic/.

Trail Blazes

Strategy Fitness refers to your ability to develop strategy by allocating resources, making decisions, and creating competitive advantage.

Strategy is not Aspiration, Best practices, or Cautious.

A plan answers two fundamental questions:
1. What are you trying to achieve?
2. How will you achieve it?

GOST Framework:
Goal: What you are trying to achieve [General]
Objective: What you are trying to achieve [Specific]
Strategy: How you are trying to achieve it [General]
Tactics: How you are trying to achieve it [Specific]

Strategy can be defined as the intelligent allocation of resources through a unique system of activities to achieve a goal. Simply put, strategy is how you plan to achieve your goal.

Five moments to consider changing strategy:
1. Goals are achieved or modified.
2. Customer needs evolve.

3. Innovation in the market.
4. Competitors change perceived value.
5. Capabilities grow or decline.

The 3A Strategic Framework represents three key areas of being strategic:
Acumen (Thinking): Generating insights to create new value
Allocation (Planning): Focusing resources through trade-offs
Action (Acting): Prioritizing and executing initiatives

Five Steps of the Strategy Process:
1. Discovery: "Choosing the Tools"
2. Strategic Thinking: "Playing in Space"
3. Strategic Planning: "Building the Framework"
4. Strategy Rollout: "Sculpting the Masterpiece"
5. Strategy Tune-up: "Polishing the Form"

A StrategyPrint is a two-page blueprint for the business containing insights on performance, people, priorities, and the action plan.

CHAPTER 2

Resource Allocation

"How resources are actually allocated and used determines strategic outcomes—not the words on paper or policies. The allocation of resources and execution of process determines strategic outcomes."
—Authors Joseph Bower and Clark Gilbert

A company is only as good as its people. People are only as good as their actions. And actions are only as good as the thinking behind them. If your team's modus operandi can best be described as "Fire, aim, ready!" perhaps it's time to take a step back and ask two important questions:

1. Are we thinking about what we're doing before we do it?
2. Are the majority of our actions proactive or reactive?

The answers to these questions indicate your approach to resource allocation, which in turn determines your strategy, and whether you will outperform or underperform your competition in delivering value to customers. Accomplished leader Meg Whitman offers this advice: "You must actively instill an awareness of the importance of conserving resources in your company. Whenever you attack waste, one of the first reactions you get is an outcry from folks who say that you are cutting into muscle, not fat, and that quality will suffer. People generally hate change. My response as a manager is that it's important to cut until you get that reaction. By forcing people to justify what they're doing and what they're spending on it, you're instilling a healthy discipline. Some will be able to justify what they spend; others will not, and they deserve to see their budgets trimmed."[1]

As noted earlier, studies have shown that the number-one cause of business failure is poor strategy. Resources are at the core of any strategy, so taking a thoughtful approach to how you and your team are allocating resources—not just at the corporate level but at the individual level—can provide a window into enhancing your performance. Resources consist of tangible (e.g., real estate, equipment, financial), intangible (brand equity, positioning, intellectual property), and human resource assets (knowledge, time, talent) and are considered relevant if they are not easily imitated, are durable, able to capture value, and offer competitive superiority.

The allocation of resources, and just as important, the reallocation of resources, is directly linked to your financial performance. In fact, research by McKinsey & Co. showed companies that regularly assess their allocation of resources and then reallocate resources from underperforming areas to areas with greater performance are worth 40% more after 15 years than those companies that cower in the status quo.[2]

Rocket Burn: Most executives reallocate resources once a year during the planning process, if at all. You can significantly outperform others if you reallocate resources *throughout* the year from underperforming areas to ones with greater performance.

The following concepts and tools can be effective in snapping teams out of the resource allocation status quo.

1. **Start with I.** If you've ever had a love interest end things with, "It's not you, it's me," maybe they were right. It does start with "me," even when it comes to resource allocation. It's common for leadership teams to begin their resource allocation and prioritization discussions with a quantitative look at group budgets, IT hours, keep-the-lights-on requirements, and new strategic initiatives. However, it can be more powerful to have leaders begin with a deep dive into their individual resource allocation—time, talent, budget—and the patterns at their level. The areas that senior leaders invest their time sends a Bat Signal about what's important to their colleagues and direct reports.

It's also enlightening and sometimes shocking to see how their time investment is aligned or misaligned with their goals and priorities. If a senior leader is more prone to acting on fire drills than with a disciplined approach to how they allocate their resources, it's likely their entire team will feel that heat and act in kind. I refer to this issue as a game of "Leader Dominoes," where even the smallest action/reaction by a senior leader tips the first domino, which falls into their direct reports and sparks an often unnecessary chain reaction.

One exercise you may find useful that I employ in my strategic coaching work with executives is the Time Assessment. For one week, leaders or their executive assistants track where their time is invested in 30-minute blocks. At the end of the week, the categories of time investment are listed, along with the total time in each. This data is then graphed to provide a visual assessment of their resource allocation and finally overlaid onto their goals and priorities. Adjustments can then be made to recalibrate areas receiving too much time that are not in sync with priorities and increasing investment in activities that are better aligned with goals.

2. **Prune to grow.** When you were a kid, how often did your mom or dad say, "Hey, stop doing that!" Well, maybe it's time to revisit that parental wisdom. When you allocate or reallocate resources in your business, you are typically either planting, growing, or pruning. Planting involves moving resources to a new area that can produce value. Growing includes using your resources to maximize value to the organization and/or customers. Pruning is the act of removing resources from an activity, initiative, or area with the intent of applying them to a more favorable situation. We tend to spend the majority of our time on resource allocation in the planting and growing phases. However, creating a cadence of discipline to prune resources throughout the year can have a dramatically positive impact on your business.

Managers are always making their case for more resources in the form of FTEs, capital, or budget. Not acquiescing to that request may be in everyone's best interest. Laboratory research published in *MIT Sloan Management Review* demonstrated that when test subjects were provided with fewer instead of more resources, they became more innovative.[3]

When we're faced with resource constraints—less time, fewer people, reduced budget—it forces us out of the status quo to search for ways to do things differently.

Case in point: master film director Steven Spielberg had no working shark when he started filming the classic movie *Jaws*. Despite the fact that the shark was supposed to be featured prominently in the opening scene, he didn't wait around, but filmed without it, leading to a more heightened scare effect—what you can't see below the water is more frightening than what you can see.[4] As the Finnish proverb states, "If the heavy armor does not move with four people pushing it, take one man away and let us see if three can do it!"

3. **See the system.** A hallmark of a great leader is the ability to expand their view of resource allocation beyond their group and take an enterprise-wide view of where resources should be channeled. The leadership teams that are able to shift resources across business units for the betterment of the organization significantly increase their chances of success versus the leadership teams that guard their resources like one of the Seven Kingdoms in *Game of Thrones*. A key component of the ability to take this bigger-picture view is the invest-ment in developing stronger relationships with your colleagues at the senior level to create deeper wells of trust. An effective technique for nurturing these relationships is to ensure that you're meeting with your colleagues in a one-to-one format at least once a quarter to share insights, offer feedback, and discuss potential resource shifts between each other's groups.

An interesting exercise is to draw a giant resources map on a long swath of butcher paper and plot the areas of resource allocation as islands. Draw the islands in scale relative to the number of resources they have. Then list out the types and numbers of resources (FTEs, dollars, etc.) for each island. At the top of the map, write down the organization's top three to five goals. Then discuss potential resource allocation shifts to meet those goals more effectively and efficiently. While you may spend a little time at the beginning in rearview mirror mode looking at the past allocation and results, move to windshield mode and invest the majority of your time there. Many teams invest far too much time looking in the rearview mirror, even though an automobile's rearview mirror is approximately 96 times smaller than the windshield for a reason.

The process of resource allocation can be thought of as a fire hose. If it's not proactively turned on, nothing new comes out and we're stuck in the status quo. If it's reactively turned on and left unattended, it can wildly spray resources in all directions, resulting in a wasteful mess. But if it's thoughtfully turned on and actively attended to by all leaders, you can powerfully direct resources to the focal areas and activities that will help you achieve your goals. And maybe then you can shift the culture from "Fire, aim, ready!" to "Ready, aim, fire . . . hose."

Reallocation of Resources

American historian Will Durant wrote, "We are what we repeatedly do." Perhaps no phrase is more hauntingly true in both beneficial and deleterious ways than this quotation. Olympians are world-class athletes because of the thousands of hours of physical and mental training they invest in each year. Actors and actresses starring in Broadway productions have made it there because they invest hundreds of hours each month practicing the craft of character development. On the flipside, those of us who could stand to lose a few pounds may invest more time binge-watching shows than exercising. And some managers may invest more time in meetings checking their smartphones or tablets than listening to colleagues, missing the insights that could have led to a shared understanding of the business.

To reach any new outcome we seek, we need to change how and where we invest our resources. Simple in concept, more challenging to do. In a business context, if you can strategically allocate—and just as important, reallocate—your resources to the right activities at the right levels, you'll give yourself the greatest chance to succeed. A study of 200 large organizations identified the number-one driver of revenue growth to be the reallocation of resources to the faster-growing parts of the business.[5] Unfortunately, most companies don't do it. In fact, research shows companies allocate 90% or more of their resources to the same activities in the same ways, year after year.[6]

Consider your group: How often do you reallocate resources—time, people, and budget—throughout the year from underperforming areas to ones with greater performance? If it's only once a year during the annual strategic planning process, you're not even coming close to maximizing your revenue potential. Studies show fewer than 33% of managers believe their organizations reallocate resources to other areas in a timely fashion so as to make a difference.

The reallocation of people is less common. Approximately 20% of managers indicate their companies are effective at moving people across the business to execute on strategies.[7] A whopping 80% of managers indicate their organizations do not move out of businesses that are declining or kill dead-end initiatives fast enough.[8] As Walmart CEO Doug McMillon said, "Once upon a time a company like ours might have made big strategic choices on an annual or quarterly cycle. Today strategy is daily. As a CEO, you need to have a framework in your mind, but strategic thinking is much more fluid. Like it or not, strategy is happening on a much faster cycle time."[9]

An exercise leadership teams find of great value involves a strategy conversation and working session around the reallocation of resources. Using a seven-step process, the team identifies resource pods, or focal areas that receive significant amounts of time, people, and budget. They then gauge their current allocation levels to the pods and discuss potential calibrated allocation levels, including both intended and unintended consequences of the potential actions. Visually graphing the outcomes of these steps can generate eye-opening, *aha* moments that create the urgency to change. In one such case, a leadership team realized they were investing no resources in understanding their competitor's strategies, which had led to an erosion of their market share as well as virtually no perceived product differentiation from the customer's perspective.

The strategy conversation around the reallocation of resources must be skillfully facilitated. We as human beings are inclined to prefer the status quo, especially when reallocating resources requires changes that may decrease a manager's head count, budget, or both. As Pieter Nota, former CEO of Philips Consumer Lifestyle, thoughtfully remarked, "It's hard to take resources away from one area and deploy them elsewhere, particularly with a strong team. Everyone tends to treat the past as an entitlement. But with the right trust between teams and a willingness to reward those who drive higher profits and sales growth, you can get significant top- and bottom-line improvements with resource reallocation."[10]

> **Off Course:** If you're not tracking your time for a typical week on a quarterly basis and assessing where it's spent, then you have no objective way to understand if your personal allocation of resources is aligned with your priorities. In this case, hope *is* your strategy.

While it can be challenging to reallocate resources, it's critical to long-term success. A study tracking companies' resource allocation trends during a 15-year time frame found that the companies reallocating the most resources across divisions saw shareholder returns 30% higher than the companies that reallocated the least.[11] In addition to being an important contributor to organizational success, reallocation is also a key factor in an individual's success. Research shows that chief executives who reallocated resources the most during their first three years were significantly more likely than CEOs who reallocated less frequently to still be in the role in years four through six.[12]

I once had an introductory conversation with the CEO of a midsized manufacturer. He was interested in developing a strategic plan because the company's sales had been stuck on a plateau for the past several years and the competitive landscape was becoming more crowded. The leadership team worked from an operating plan that captured the status of projects, internal systems, and processes along with a detailed budget, but he knew something was missing. He described the management team as being overly focused on tactics and not able to elevate their thinking out of the day-to-day. When I asked how much time he allocated during his senior leadership team meetings to this type of higher level, strategic thinking and discussion . . . crickets.

We talked about the amount of time, number of people, and financial investment that would be required for the company to embark on a strategic thinking and planning process along with the resulting strategic direction and plan that he identified as missing. He assessed those investments in strategy as "really high," so I asked, "High relative to what? Consider all the resources you're investing in tactics such as advertising, trade shows, marketing campaigns, and sales materials. Is that the same amount as the investment for strategy?"

"No," he replied, pausing for a few moments to make a mental calculation. "I guess the number of resources we allocate to the tactical stuff would be considerably more than the amount we allocate to strategy."

"Two or three times higher?" I asked.

"Actually, about 40 to 50 times higher," he answered.

If you're investing nearly all your resources in tactics, then you will have tactical managers running a tactical company. Organizations of all shapes and sizes get themselves involved in tactical arms' races, reacting to each and every tactic from the competition with versions of their own, leading to competitive convergence. Instead, they could be investing more of their time into strategy conversations about reallocating resources and developing the strategies that lead to competitive advantage. As entrepreneur Ramit Sethi said, "Tactics are great, but tactics become commoditized."[13]

If "we are what we repeatedly do," ask yourself what you really do. Do you like the answer? If not, review what you do and reallocate to what you want to be.

Discipline to Focus

"No is a positive word. No preserves. No is a vision. No diverts us from compromise and forces us from the middle ground. No stays away from maybe and is never drawn into negotiation. No demands more, And it waits for the right answer. There is no substitute. No settling. No has done its job. It has snuffed out mediocre and reminded us why there is no other choice."[14]

—Porsche

More. More information, more data, more content, more channels, more choices. In a world of more, it's important to master less. The path to less is not yes. To reduce more to less, we need the discipline to focus.

To focus is to intentionally channel your attention, effort, and resources toward a singular point. That point may be a person, project, activity, or goal, but it stands alone in your mind. At least for now. The moment your eyes, ears, hands, or thoughts wander to something else, it's gone.

Focus is a foundation of both organizational and individual success. When you think of successful companies, they typically begin by focusing in one area to become great: Google in search, Nvidia in graphics processing units, Amazon in online retailing, Nordstrom in service, and so on. As Kevin Plank, self-made billionaire and founder of sports equipment maker Under Armour, said, "Focus is one of the most important things to have in your business. For the first five years, as we grew our company from zero to $5 million, we made really one shirt. Another way to say it is that a company needs to become famous for something, to find that niche."[15]

The challenge is that in a world of more, it's easier to not focus. A survey of 350,000 people worldwide conducted by Franklin Covey found that people spend 40% of their time on things that are completely irrelevant to their goals and work.[16] This equates to wasting two out of five days of the work week, so in a 50-week working year, erasing any and all productivity in 100 of 250 days. *Ouch.*

Here are two reasons why we fail to focus along with tools and techniques to overcome them.

1. **Unclear on the core.** If focusing means we're directing attention toward a single point, we'd better make sure that it's the right point. The right point is an activity, area, offering, or initiative that will help you progress toward a predetermined goal. Are you and your team spending time on products or services that don't offer customers superior value relative to the competition? If so, why? What are the core competencies (areas of expertise) and capabilities (skill sets) that are most responsible for your success? Would everyone in your business agree on the same three to five? How much time is your team spending on these competencies and capabilities versus other less valuable aspects of the business?

A Bain & Company study of 8,000 companies found "the most common strategic root cause of stall-out is the premature abandonment of the core business, or the inability to say no to new opportunities that don't fit with a company's core mission." Once a company has stalled out, the research found that only 1 in 10 was able to regain their market position.[17] Therefore, it's critical that your team is not wasting time chasing the shiny objects outside of the core of the business without a solid innovation strategy in place. Apple CEO Tim Cook advises, "One traditional management philosophy that's taught in many business schools is diversification. Well, that's not us. You can only do so many things great, and you should cast aside everything else."[18]

To gain clarity on the core, consider the following exercise I refer to as Target Practice:

1. Draw a target with three circles and a bull's-eye in the center.
2. In the bull's-eye, write the product or service you're focused on that deserves to win in the market.
3. In the innermost ring, write the one customer group that finds the most value in this offering and is willing to pay for that value.
4. In the second ring, write the most important channel for reaching the most important customer.
5. In the third ring, write the most important competency (area of expertise) and capability (skill set) for creating and delivering value in this channel to this customer for this offering.
6. Below the target, identify the primary goal, corresponding objective, strategy, and tactics to successfully hit this target.

2. **Inability to make trade-offs.** In order to effectively allocate resources, trade-offs are required. Trade-offs are the ability to make judgments about competing alternatives with the intent of choosing one path and not the other paths that may appear equally promising. Trade-offs are a prerequisite of strategy. If you cannot identify the trade-offs inherent in your strategy, then you don't have one.

In order to make trade-offs, we need to make decisions. The Latin term for decision is *decidere*, which means "to cut off."[19] If you have trees on your property, you know that every few years you should cut off or prune the lower or dead branches in order to promote new growth in the tree. However, in business we have a harder time pruning—cutting things off from our attention, time, and other resources. A survey of 463 managers by McKinsey & Company asked if their senior leadership team cut off unsuccessful initiatives quickly enough, and 52% responded "no."[20]

When you agree to pursue a new opportunity that's not related to your goals or serve on a committee with little connection to your priorities, you've also agreed not to invest your time and talent in other potentially more valuable areas. By not making a trade-off, you've actually decided, even if you didn't consciously state the decision. In economics, it's referred to as the opportunity cost: the loss of potential gain from other alternatives when one alternative is chosen. Before agreeing to put your time, talent, or budget to something, consider the opportunity costs involved and then determine if it still makes sense.

Making Trade-offs

The inability to make trade-offs has serious repercussions throughout an organization, including overworked employees, poor morale, toothless strategies, and middle-of-the-roadkill offerings. Another key consequence is a lack of priorities, or stated differently, "everything is a priority." Research found that when it comes to employees' issues understanding and implementing corporate strategies, mid-level managers are four times more likely to point to too many priorities rather than unclear commu-nication.[21] John Chambers, former executive chairman and CEO of Cisco Systems said, "My biggest challenge is not growth but how well we prioritize."[22]

To improve your team's ability to make trade-offs, consider the fol-lowing techniques:

1. **Clarify priorities.** A survey of 5,000 managers and employees found that 24% of people blamed their inability to focus on bosses who set too many priorities. Morten Hansen, the professor from University of California, Berkeley, who led the research, concluded, "People who focused on a narrow scope of work, and said no to maintain that strategy, outperformed others who didn't. They placed an impressive 25 percentage points higher in the performance ranking."[23]

The next time your team gets together for a staff meeting, ask each person to write down what they believe are the organization's top three priorities. Read the cards aloud and see how many people had similar priorities listed for the organization. Then have them write down their top three priorities and see how many are aligned at the individual level. Once priorities have been whittled down and agreed upon, implement a Zero-Based Priority approach where no new priorities may be added without first eliminating an existing one.

2. **Say no.** If on a daily basis dozens of people asked you for money in varying amounts, from 50 cents to $50,000, you wouldn't say yes to all of them. If you did, you'd be bankrupt in a few days. We've heard the adage "Time is money." Now it's time to start acting that way. When people request your time for meetings, committees, or special projects, ask yourself if these requests are directly related to your goals or are valuable in helping others reach their goals. If the answer is no, then your response should be as well.

3. **Visualize the trade-offs.** A powerful technique for creating a short-list of priorities and not continually adding things to your team's already overflowing plate is to create a graph of trade-offs. When I facilitate the Prioritization Matrix exercise with teams, we first create a list of everything that's considered a priority. We then plot the priorities on a graph by evaluating each item on two criteria: Probability of Achievement, and Impact to the business using a numerical rating scale from 1 (low) to 10 (high) for each. Once priorities are plotted in this manner, it becomes clearer which should remain, and which are ripe for pruning. As Instagram co-founder Kevin Systrom said, "It's prioritizing that makes us efficient and makes us succeed."[24]

Focus saves us from the swamp of meaningless activity. Focus separates us from being middle-of-the-roadkill. Focus demands our full attention, and deserts us without discipline. Focus is our friend if we intentionally invite it into our day. Focus slaps more in the face, throws its arm around less, and responds to no. Focus . . . until it's gone.

Trail Blazes

Resources are at the core of any strategy.

Resources consist of tangible (e.g., real estate, equipment, financial), intangible (brand equity, positioning, intellectual property), and human resource assets (knowledge, time, talent).

Resources are considered relevant if they are not easily imitated, durable, able to capture value, and offer competitive superiority.

Three techniques to improve resource allocation:
1. Start with I
2. Prune to grow
3. See the system

When you allocate or reallocate resources in your business, you are typically either planting, growing, or pruning.

Companies allocate 90% or more of their resources to the same activities in the same ways, year after year.

Chief executives who reallocated resources the most during their first three years were significantly more likely than CEOs who reallocated less frequently to still be in the role in years four through six.

Two reasons people fail to focus:
1. Unclear on the core
2. Inability to make trade-offs

Three techniques to improve your ability to make trade-offs:
1. Clarify priorities
2. Say no
3. Visualize the trade-offs

CHAPTER 3

Decision Making

"The most difficult thing is the decision to act. The rest is merely tenacity. The fears are paper tigers. You can do anything you decide to do. You can act to change and control your life and the procedure. The process is its own reward."

—Amelia Earhart, aviator

History's greatest navigators, including notables such as Christopher Columbus, Ferdinand Magellan, Amelia Earhart, and Neil Armstrong, all faced critical decisions during their journeys. A decision is the act or process of making a judgment or stating a preference between several options. A study involving 17,000 CEOs found that of the CEOs who rated poorly on decision making, 94% had low scores because they were indecisive. Two-thirds of those CEOs who were fired over decision-making issues were let go because they did not make decisions quickly enough to keep pace with the business.[1] Stephen Gorman, former CEO of Greyhound, noted, "A bad decision was better than a lack of direction. Most decisions can be undone, but you have to learn to move with the right amount of speed."[2]

The definition of strategy begins with "the intelligent allocation of limited resources." The process of intelligent allocation requires decisions to be made. It is also worth remembering that companies don't make decisions—individuals do. Therefore, mastering the decision-making process is a vital skill of strong strategic leaders. Let's begin by breaking down decisions into their primary elements: Challenge, Goal, Options, Impact, Trade-offs, and Risk.

Challenge. Most decisions begin with a challenge to overcome. Not surprisingly, many poor decisions can be attributed to incorrectly assessing or framing the challenge being considered. The concept of "framing" was developed by Amos Tversky and Daniel Kahneman.[3] The way a challenge is stated frames the decision, and in turn determines the alternatives considered and the methods of evaluation. Consequently, posing the right challenge at the outset drives the remainder of the process.

The decision frame is partly influenced by the formulation of the challenge and partly influenced by the characteristics and habits of the decision-maker. It's important to understand the frames in which you operate (e.g., functional expertise, industry experience, etc.) and be aware of their effect on your decisions. Likewise, the better understanding you have of the decision frames of those involved in the situation, the more successful you'll be in interactions with them. One of the biggest obstacles to correctly framing a decision is the willingness to choose the most obvious frame, or the first that comes to mind. By not pushing yourself to creatively explore all of the other potential ways to frame a decision, you incur a greater risk of starting the process from the wrong point.

> **Rocket Burn:** Actively seek out different perspectives and frames in which to view decisions. While your experience and expertise can be great assets, they can also lay the tracks for a mental rut. Seeing a decision through different lenses can stimulate the widest array of options.

There are a number of ways to generate alternative frames to give yourself the best chance for correctly framing the problem.

- Describe the situation for others and ask them to articulate the challenge as they see it.
- Examine other situations you've faced and look for similar and dissimilar circumstances. What were the results of those decisions?
- Consider conducting a brainstorming exercise where you list all potential challenges. Follow proper brainstorming protocols and include anything and everything that comes up, no matter how unrelated it may seem at the time.

- Try and make analogies between this challenge and others. How would you articulate the challenge in the analogy?

Goal. Once the problem has been clearly stated, describe the goal or goals you wish to achieve through the decision-making process. The goal is the outcome you desire by making this decision. Goals provide a guide to the amount of time to spend on the decision. If the goals will result in significant impact, then the time spent on the decision-making process should be substantial.

Goals also provide a road map to the information required to make the decision. What data, numbers, or input will be necessary in order to make a decision that meets the goal? Finally, goals provide an unbiased and unemotional baseline for comparing alternatives. The extent that an alternative meets or does not meet the goal becomes the true measurement of validity for each alternative.

Options. A list of options is generated to form a comprehensive array of the available choices to the decision. Similar to the framing challenge, explore all potential alternatives using the same techniques. The most common error is bringing to the decision the "this is the way we've always done it" mindset that generates the same old options.

Utilizing the brainstorming technique encourages even the most outlandish alternatives at the outset, and one of those or their derivative may actually be the best option down the road. It's also important to challenge the constraints imposed on the alternative selection criteria. Take time to reevaluate the alleged constraints and see if any of them can be removed, opening the channel for new alternatives. Always work to create three to five options to review prior to deciding on how to move forward.

Impact. Impact is the result of the potential alternatives. Weighing both the positive and negative consequences allows the decision maker to understand the ramifications of the decision. A helpful exercise is to list all of the potential consequences under each alternative as either positive (+) or negative (−). This provides a visual display of the decision's impact and enables you to objectively review the potential outcomes.

Trade-offs. Every decision involves trade-offs. Trade-offs occur when activities are incompatible—more of one thing necessitates less of the other. Without trade-offs, strategy is not sustainable because any good idea would be quickly imitated. Trade-offs build sustainable advantage because they force competitors to allocate or remove resources in order to provide a comparative offering. By creating the need for choice, trade-offs purposefully limit a company's offering and prevent them from straddling positions. Companies that refuse to make trade-offs undermine their strategy and dilute the value of their existing activities.

Risk. If you deem a decision of considerable importance, there may be value in rating your risk profile as high, medium, or low. How much risk are you willing to accept in making this decision? Research in the field of decision making by Amos Tversky and Daniel Kahneman has shown that preferences between gains are risk averse and preferences between losses are risk-seeking.[4] Risk aversion occurs when a certain outcome is preferred to a gamble with an equal or greater (monetary) expectation. If the gamble with equal expectation is preferred, it is risk-seeking. Research shows that people are psychologically predisposed to risk aversion when facing a loss and will therefore select the option that reduces the potential for loss.

The threat of a loss has a greater impact on a decision than the possibility of an equivalent gain. The response to loss is more extreme than the response to gain.

Consequently, many strategy decisions place too much weight on the potential negative outcomes because psychologically, the displeasure associated with losing a sum of money or market share points is greater than the pleasure associated with gaining the same amount. This principle of human nature has a strong impact on strategy decisions and must be considered to avoid always acting in a risk-averse manner when the probability of success is actually greater.

Creating Decision Trees

A useful tool in the process of decision making is the decision tree. A decision tree (Figure 3.1) sequentially maps out the process involving a decision, resulting in a visual landscape of all the decision's elements.

Four steps in constructing a decision tree:

1. Identify the decision, challenge, or problem.

Example 1:

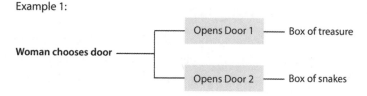

Figure 3.1 Decision Tree Construct.

2. Identify the major factors/issues (decisions and events) to be addressed in the analysis.
3. Identify alternatives for each of the factors/issues.
4. Construct a tree portraying all important alternative scenarios.

As you construct the decision tree, ensure the branches of the tree are mutually exclusive, meaning that if the actor (person making the choice) picks option 1, she can't also pick option 2. Ensure the branches are collectively exhaustive, meaning that the alternatives at each branch incorporate all possibilities; no other options (other decisions or events) are possible at that point in the sequence. Decision trees provide a useful framework for corralling all of the various factors involved in the decision-making process and laying them out in a simple and easy-to-understand format. The decision tree will also spark new avenues of consideration that move past anchoring information and represent truly innovative options.

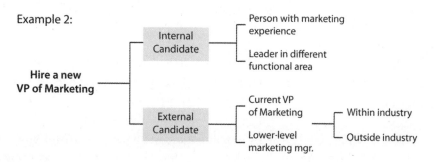

Figure 3.2 Decision Tree Example.

Avoiding Decision Traps

When it comes to enhancing the quality of decisions, it's important to be aware of potential decision-making traps in the realm of strategy development. Following are the most common flaws and techniques for overcoming them.

Absolute performance: forgetting that performance is always relative to the competition. Techniques to overcome absolute performance:

- Measure your progress against other organizations, offerings, and people.
- Create a system to monitor and record business intelligence (market, customers, competitors, and the company) and make it available to managers.
- When internal factors such as sales force or R&D are declared strengths, ask how they stack up against the best in the industry.

Anchors: giving initial information or impressions a disproportionate amount of weight. Techniques to overcome anchors:

- Create an open mind by actively considering the range of starting points available, not just the anchor point.
- View the issue from different frames (e.g., marketing manager should seek views of HR, sales, and operations managers).
- Identify anchors as soon as they appear and call them out mentally and physically (on paper/PC/flipchart) so everyone is aware of their presence.

Benchmarking: taking an incomplete view of what exactly is at the root of another firm's success. Techniques to overcome benchmarking issues:

- Identify what exactly is being benchmarked and what remains unknown.
- Describe the context in which the benchmarked practice is occurring and compare it to your situation.
- Identify the strategy ecosystem of the benchmarked practice and the relationships involved in the system.

Confirmation bias: seeking out data and information to support what one believes while discounting evidence to the contrary. Techniques to overcome confirmation bias:

- Record the evidence for each position in a ledger format to enhance an objective view.
- Acknowledge the underpinnings of your reason for taking a position and consider the opposite motivations.
- Bring in someone to present the other positions to provide a fresh perspective.

Forecasting: being overconfident, giving prominence to what is first recalled, and using an average when a range of numbers would be more precise. Techniques to overcome forecasting issues:

- Overconfidence: Use a range with the extremes as bookends to estimate a spectrum of values.
- Recollection: Identify the data or facts for the events to ground your thinking in an objective base.
- Averages: Use a range of numbers whenever possible versus a single figure.

Groupthink: the effect of a homogeneous group of people with little influence from outside sources and a high level of pressure to conform. Techniques to overcome groupthink:

- Assign one person in the group to play devil's advocate and take the opposite position of the majority.
- Utilize an external resource to ensure objectivity and divergent opinions.
- Bring in people from other functional areas (marketing, R&D, IT, HR) to offer fresh perspectives.

Halo effect: the habit of making specific conclusions based on a general overall impression. Techniques to overcome the halo effect:

- Carefully assess the sources of data being used to understand their level of bias.

- Visually diagram the system involved to help identify causes, effects, attributions, and unintended consequences.
- Understand the context in which the event or issue is unfolding prior to suggesting actions. Recall the three disciplines of being strategic: acumen (thinking), allocation (planning), and action (acting).

Sunk-cost effect: a bias toward making a choice that justifies a previous decision, even when that decision no longer appears valid. Techniques to overcome the sunk-cost effect:

- Use the blank-slate test: starting from today, what is the best use of resources moving forward, with no consideration given to past decisions?
- Ask someone detached from the situation to provide thoughts on the current decision and the best option moving forward.
- Determine the type of culture and environment in which decisions are made. Is it conducive to admitting mistakes and moving on, or does it motivate people to "stay the course at all costs" and foster the sunk-cost effect?

Following are best practices that are effective in advancing decision making across leadership teams, functional areas, or the company:

- Record on the meeting agenda the specific decisions to be made.
- Create a brief meeting summary that identifies decisions made and next steps.
- Communicate that the decisions made in the past that went through proper channels will not be revisited and reevaluated moving forward.
- Reduce swirl with decisions involving other teams by ensuring their decision maker is present and an active part of the process—not a last-minute drop-in.
- Cancel any decision-making meetings when the person with decision rights is not able to attend.

Determining Decision Rights

A foremost challenge in today's organizations is clarifying who owns which decisions. Perhaps nothing slows down progress in strategy development and kills momentum in strategy execution more than confusion on who ultimately makes a decision. With the proliferation of matrix-structured organizations, confusion on decision rights continues to be an internal barrier to greater success. A survey of 26,000 people by the consulting firm Booz Allen Hamilton showed that decision rights and information flow are the top organizational traits linked to successful strategy execution.[5]

One of the reasons it's crucial to have strategies in written form is that they provide a filter for what you should and shouldn't do. Leaders without clear strategies can be seen bouncing from one opportunity or fire drill to the next, because they don't have any guardrails in place. Strategy provides those guardrails on choices such as what offerings to provide, which customers to target, and the optimal configuration of resources. Additionally, research has shown that decision effectiveness and financial results are highly correlated at a 95% confidence level, leading to shareholder returns that were more than five percentage points higher than firms lacking effective decision-making processes.[6]

An insidious saboteur of decision rights is the need for consensus. Margaret Thatcher, former prime minister of Britain, provided a useful definition of consensus: "To me, consensus seems to be the process of abandoning all beliefs, principles, values, and policies in search of something in which no one believes, but to which no one objects."[7] One of the primary benefits of clarifying decision rights is that it eliminates the excruciatingly slow, laborious, and ineffectual slog to consensus. The "we're all in this together so let's all decide together" summer camp approach to decision making through consensus often cloaks a leader's inability and unwillingness to decide.

Using consensus as a target can inadvertently channel the group's thinking to the option that they believe will be most agreeable to others. Unfortunately, this is unlikely to be the optimal or most innovative course. Instead, it will be an alternative that's closer to what the group is already doing. The consensus target also does its best to avoid risk and any step toward the unknown, which is where breakthrough innovation resides. However, as Meg Whitman, former CEO of eBay and Hewlett Packard Enterprise, concludes, "The difference between a competent executive and a superstar often boils down to the willingness to decide and to move forward, even when the path is not crystal clear."[8]

Off Course: There's a big difference in decision making between a voice and a vote. Trying to reach consensus on every decision is a fool's errand. Give people a voice to gain their perspectives and insights and then make the decision.

While effective leaders seek the input of others to gain as much insight as possible on the decision at hand, they also make it clear that they are seeking their ideas and perspectives, not asking them to be a part of the decision-making process. Mike Lawrie, who drove an amazing turnaround at Computer Sciences Corporation (CSC) from a $4 billion loss to $21 billion in revenue while serving as chairman, president, and CEO of DXC Technology, shared this advice: "I think you draw a distinction between a consensual leadership style and a more mandated leadership style in the actual decision-making process itself. In a consensual process, it's much longer, it really requires a lot of deliberation, buy-in, cajoling, trade-offs, compromise. I use the word *compromise* because that often leads to regressing to the lowest common denominator, which often provides a mediocre response to what is a critical environmental situation."[9] Some will still try and make the case that if they don't gain consensus, then people won't support the decision and the execution will fail. This shouldn't be a reason to capitulate to consensus.

An important approach to overcoming this issue is the concept of "disagree and commit." Amazon founder Jeff Bezos explains the technique: "It's often the case that the more senior person should disagree and commit. I disagree and commit all the time. I'll debate something for an hour or a day or a week. And I'll say, 'You know what? I really disagree with this, but you have more ground truth than I do. We're going to do it your way. And I promise I will never tell you I told you so.'"[10] Don't allow the unwillingness to make decisions and unclear decision rights be cloaked by the need for consensus.

Consider your organization and the following questions:

1. Have we inventoried the most common decisions we face on a regular basis?
2. Is there a process in place to make these decisions effectively and efficiently?
3. Are people clear on their roles in the decision-making process?

4. Have decision rights for each decision been established with authority and ownership?
5. Are decision assessments and debriefs conducted following decisions to review outcomes and learnings?

In my work over the past two decades facilitating strategic thinking sessions for executive leadership teams, it's become evident how powerful and transformative it can be for executives to gain clear sight lines into the decisions they make and understanding of their accountability. As an organization grows, so too do the number of decisions. If these decisions are not inventoried and accounted for, they become like a tree that has never been pruned—poking out, intertwined, and choking off resources from the areas most in need.

Here are the steps you can take to inventory your team's decisions:

1. Create a list of the common decisions the team faces.
2. Identify at which level each decision is currently made.
3. List the decision maker.
4. Rate the importance of the decision as low, medium, or high.
5. Determine whether to keep or change the current decision rights.
6. Propose a modification for any changes in the decision rights.
7. Assign people related to the decision a role according to the phase they should be involved in.

An important consideration in the decision rights process is whether individual decisions have the quality of a revolving door or one-way door. This concept popularized by Amazon founder Jeff Bezos identifies decisions of a revolving-door nature as ones that can be readily entered into again and reversed if need be.[11] One-way-door decisions are those that cannot be reentered and therefore require more expertise. Decisions of the revolving-door nature are ripe for delegation to free up time for leaders to focus more energy on the one-way-door decisions. Consider your business: What are the one-way-door decisions your team is currently involved in? Have you inventoried these decisions and put the proper expertise, authority, and accountability in place?

Once the senior team has completed the exercise, it's helpful to cascade the process to the next levels of leadership so that efficiencies are gained throughout the organization. Look to consolidate decisions and in some cases eliminate them altogether if they can be rolled up elsewhere or replaced with a checklist. The decision rights process can be especially valuable to leaders assuming a new role, as it brings their new team together to work through who's deciding what and establishes accountability.

The act of decision making is woven into the fabric of strategy. When you see a business struggling and lacking strategic direction, it's often because leadership is afraid and reluctant to make real decisions. Real decisions require real trade-offs, and some leaders don't have the mental toughness to assume risk. But, as Meta CEO Mark Zuckerberg said, "In a world that is changing really quickly, the only strategy that is guaranteed to fail is not taking risks."[12]

Delegation: Lead at Your Level

How many people in your organization are wasting their time and talent performing tasks that they should be delegating? Research shows a startling 41% of activities managers are working on are actually items that could and should be performed by the people who report to them.[13] While it may feel good to roll up the sleeves and knock out these tasks, it's a disservice to the people who should be developing their capabilities by performing them. Lead at your level or get out of the way and let someone else do it.

To delegate means "to commit decisions, power and functions to another."[14] When working on delegation with executive leaders in strategic coaching engagements, we begin by identifying which types of tasks typically can be delegated. Here is a partial list of things to consider for delegation:

• Recurring decisions and actions that others can handle
• Priorities that you don't have time to handle but others can
• Tactical aspects of projects
• Meeting attendance

Meeting attendance is an obvious but often overlooked area of delegation. Consider the past month of meetings you attended: How many included yourself and one or more of your direct reports? Eliminate the duplicative nature of people from the same area attending meetings. Research shows that 20% of meeting participants shouldn't be there.[15] Should you?

As you delegate tasks and decisions to others, the following four elements should be present:

1. **Authority:** power and autonomy to make relevant decisions has been declared
2. **Capability:** person possesses or can acquire the knowledge, skill, and resources to get the job done
3. **Accountability:** responsibility for completing the task or making the decision has been clearly communicated and accepted
4. **Assessment:** taking time after completion of the task or decision to review the outcome

Too often, leaders become bottlenecks to their organization's activities and resources because of their failure to delegate. With the speed of events and communication in today's business environment, having to wait for several levels of approval or a leader with too much on their plate is a killer. An effective exercise to overcome this issue is to visually map out the tasks and decisions in your group and then determine who should be responsible for each.

Before you start deciding which of the activities and decisions to delegate, first consider the following: Are all of these activities and decisions still necessary? There's no sense in delegating items that shouldn't be there in the first place. Take a chainsaw to your day planner and cut out the tasks and corresponding decisions that aren't continuing to drive value and help you reach your goals.

The most common delegation trap is always to delegate to the same person. While it's comfortable to slide everything the way of your go-to person, it's also a recipe for burnout. Avoid the temptation of delegating the majority of decisions and tasks to the same person. This will ensure that they have the capacity and energy to assist with the truly important matters. It will also help you develop others to become the future go-to people and ensure they don't feel alienated by not having the opportunity to show what they can contribute.

Once you've successfully delegated decisions and tasks to a wider group of people, offer high-level guidance but do not micromanage how they complete the task. The power of diversity of thought is that others may have different approaches and techniques that you can learn from and add to your toolkit once you get to the assessment phase of the delegated task. Also, be on the lookout for people who have been delegated to, but continually seek to bring you back into the mix. Don't allow reverse delegation to occur.

Delegation Do's:

☐ Match skills and attitudes with task at hand.
☐ Be clear on the goal and objective; provide the "what," not the "how."
☐ Share the "why": reasons for delegating task to them (yours and theirs).
☐ Define authority as it relates to the delegated task; establish limits where appropriate as it relates to time, money, and so on.
☐ Confirm their understanding of the delegated task.
☐ Be prepared to discuss potential resources.
☐ Debrief following the completion of the task.

Delegation Don'ts:

☐ Delegate what should be eliminated.
☐ Always delegate to the most capable person—overloads and burns out best people and ignores and alienates the others.
☐ Micromanage the "how" of task completion.
☐ Allow reverse delegation: you end up completing the task.

To start: consider making a list of the top 20 regularly occurring decisions. Take the first decision and ask three questions: 1) Is this a reversible decision? 2) Does one of my direct reports have the capability to make this decision? 3) Can I hold that person accountable for making the decision? If the answer to these questions is yes, then delegate the decision. Continue down the list until you are only making decisions for which there is one shot to get it right and you alone possess the capabilities or accountability.

As you initially spread your delegation wings, it may be helpful to complete a Delegation Action Plan (Figure 3.3). This is a simple one-page

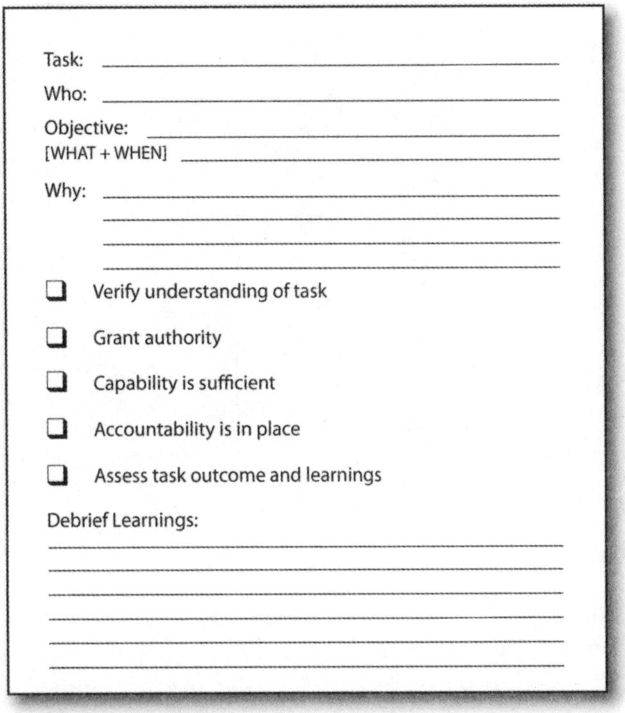

Task: _____

Who: _____

Objective: _____
[WHAT + WHEN] _____

Why: _____
_____
_____
_____

❑ Verify understanding of task

❑ Grant authority

❑ Capability is sufficient

❑ Accountability is in place

❑ Assess task outcome and learnings

Debrief Learnings:
_____
_____
_____
_____
_____

Figure 3.3 Delegation Action Plan.

overview to ensure that delegation goes as smoothly and successfully as possible. It includes a checklist of the key delegation criteria, items such as "capability is sufficient" and "accountability is in place," to provide a game plan for success.

Effective delegation enables leaders to invest more of their time thinking and planning for the business. A picture of the inability to delegate is the leader running on the activity treadmill, taking on more work than they need to, sweating every little task, and stinking up the place. Step off the activity treadmill, inventory tasks, decisions, and meetings, and create a delegation action plan to ensure an effective cool down. Lead at your level.

Trail Blazes

A decision is the act or process of making a judgment or stating a preference between several options.

The way a challenge is stated frames the decision, and in turn determines the alternatives considered and the methods of evaluation.

The primary elements of a decision to be considered are the challenge, goal, options, impact, trade-offs, and risk.

A decision tree sequentially maps out the process involving a decision, resulting in a visual landscape of all the decision's elements.

Eight Decision-Making Traps:
1. Absolute performance
2. Anchors
3. Benchmarking
4. Confirmation bias
5. Forecasting
6. Groupthink
7. Halo effect
8. Sunk-cost effect

A survey of 26,000 people showed that decision rights and information flow are the top organizational traits linked to successful strategy execution.

Seven steps to inventory decisions:
1. Create a list of the common decisions the team faces.
2. Identify at which level each decision is currently made.
3. List the decision-maker.
4. Rate the importance of the decision as low, medium, or high.
5. Determine whether to keep or change the current decision rights.
6. Propose a modification for any changes in the decision rights.
7. Assign people related to the decision a role according to the phase in which they should be involved.

Research shows a startling 41% of activities managers are working on are actually items that could and should be performed by the people who report to them.

To delegate means to commit decisions, power, and functions to another.

Four elements to support delegation:
1. Authority: power and autonomy to make relevant decisions has been declared.
2. Capability: person possesses or can acquire the knowledge, skill, and resources to get the job done.
3. Accountability: responsibility for completing the task or making the decision has been clearly communicated and accepted.
4. Assessment: taking time after completion of the task or decision to review the outcome.

CHAPTER 4

Competition

"Competition gives you a focus. Lots of times you need a mission, a bull's-eye that keeps you focused, and competition can do that."
—Anne Mulcahy, former CEO, Xerox

Behind every great achievement, behind every person who has accomplished something worthy, stands the spirit of competition. For those who cower in the comfort of complacency, waiting for others to give them something they haven't earned, competition is a stranger. The stranger invites them to rise up, which takes initiative and courage, two dwindling resources in the social media–laced haze of watching instead of doing. Competition extends a hand and invites you to meet your better self.

The ancient Greeks called it *aretas*—attaining excellence through competition. This Grecian virtue's endgame is not victory, although a common result, but rather the discovery of unseen reservoirs of effort that enhance performance. And this enhanced performance is boundless, occurring in the arts, music, athletics, business, science, medicine, engineering, and other areas and disciplines. Prolific American inventor Thomas Edison only turned his attention back to designing the phonograph because his rival Alexander Graham Bell was coming out with a similar product. Edison said, "I don't care so much for a fortune as I do for getting ahead of the other fellows."[1]

The term "compete" comes from the Latin *competere,* which means "to strive together," from the roots *com* (together) and *petere* (to seek).[2] Simply put, competition makes us try harder than we would without it.

As far back as 1898, Indiana University psychologist Norman Triplett's research demonstrated that bicyclists were faster when competing with other cyclists versus racing alone.[3] The conclusion that the element of competition increases performance greater than performance without competition has been confirmed in dozens of additional studies over the years in academics, athletics, arts, sciences, and other fields.

> **Rocket Burn:** Identify or create a competitor to increase your sense of urgency and effort.

The elite performers don't wait around for high-level competition to emerge. They intentionally seek it out or even create it. Competition can come in the form of a traditional rival, a new entry into your arena, colleagues, teammates, previous personal best performances, or the status quo. The key is to identify a competitive force that will trigger your higher level of performance and ride that wave to a higher plane. John Legere, former CEO and president of T-Mobile, said, "As we changed our business and rebuilt our network, we began pointing out the contrast with our rivals—loudly. Every good narrative has a villain, and we picked ours early on: AT&T. At Global Crossing, for instance, the enemy was bankruptcy."[4]

Assessing the Competition

Those who don't utilize the catalyst of competition or, worse yet, underestimate the competition, will face the consequences. Here are a few examples of successful business leaders who underestimated their competition and paid a price for doing so:

"This won't create another crisis for the Swiss watch industry. From the design point of view you cannot say it's a watch—more an iPhone for the wrist. People may travel with it, but it won't replace the watch you wear to a party."
—Jean-Claude Biver, former president of LVMH's watch business on the Apple Watch[5]

"I have never heard such rubbish. I accept that supermarkets are a thorn in our side, but not for the serious music . . . buyer and as for the other two (online retailers and downloadable music), I don't ever see them being a real threat; downloadable music is just a fad."
—Steve Knott, former managing director of
British music company HMV[6]

"If a company is not able to keep up with the changing needs of its customer, it will become irrelevant. There is a wonderful role for Netflix service in the marketplace, but it's very different from ours. I think we co-exist quite well with Netflix."
—Jim Keyes, former CEO, Blockbuster, four months
before filing for bankruptcy[7]

It appears that the more formidable a new competitor is, the level of underestimation and dismissal rises proportionately, as with these infamous examples from those crushed by Apple's iPhone:

"We've learned and struggled for a few years here figuring out how to make a decent phone . . . they are not going to just figure this out. They're not going to just walk in."
—Ed Colligan, former CEO, Palm[8]

"The iPhone is one more entrant into an already very busy space with lots of choice for consumers . . . but in terms of a sort of sea-change for BlackBerry, I would think that's overstating it."
—Jim Balsillie, former CEO, BlackBerry[9]

"No chance that the iPhone is going to get any significant market share."
—Steve Ballmer, former CEO, Microsoft[10]

Off Course: It's common to dismiss competitors as inferior. How often are you checking in with customers to gain their perspectives on competitive offerings?

As you are developing strategies to outperform your competitors in serving customers, it's critical to consider their potential responses. The following three questions may be of use:

1. What is the probability that the competition will react to this strategy?
2. If the competition does respond to this strategy, what are their three most likely options?
3. What, if any, would be our response to their counteraction?

Harvard Business School professor Michael Porter shares his insight on having an expansive view of the competition: "In essence, the job of the strategist is to understand and cope with competition. Often however, managers define competition too narrowly, as if it occurred only among today's direct competitors. Yet competition for profits goes beyond established industry rivals to include four other competitive forces as well: customers, suppliers, potential entrants, and substitute products."[11]

The ability to see competition in all shapes and sizes will also enable you to categorize competition as one of two types: symmetric competition or asymmetric competition. Symmetric competition occurs when the competition possesses similar competencies and capabilities to yours, resulting in comparable strategies. While many organizations start out with competencies and capabilities that generate differentiated value, over time those differences tend to fade. Success breeds imitation and competitive convergence ensues.

Asymmetric competition involves companies with competencies and capabilities and their configuration of resources that are different than yours. For example, symmetric competition can be seen in the ride-sharing market between Uber and Lyft, despite Uber's significantly greater market share, because their competencies and capabilities are more similar than different. Asymmetric competition is evident between Disney and Amazon in the content streaming market, because the competencies and capabilities between the two are more different than similar, even though they are now competing in a common arena.

Who will prevail in cases of asymmetric competition? Jim Barksdale, former CEO of Netscape Communications and their once dominant Netscape web browser, prophetically proclaimed, "In the fight between the bear and the alligator, the outcome is determined by the terrain.

Each animal presents a fearsome figure on its own turf. But the bear will flounder in a swamp, while the alligator surrenders many of its advantages when forced to fight on dry land. In a battle where the two are evenly matched, the victory will go to the one fighting on home terrain."[12]

Competitive Positioning

Once you've identified the players in your competitive landscape, their positioning starts to emerge. While there are many ways to describe one's position in a market, perhaps the two simplest are leader and challenger. For a market leader, two primary goals are to maintain current customers and minimize the rate of defection. These two goals can be accomplished by utilizing the strengths that advanced you to that leadership position and neutralizing competitors.

If you're in a challenger position, the goals are typically to take customers from your competitors and convert nonusers into customers. These goals can be accomplished by leveraging your strengths and exploiting the competition's weaknesses. A unique and underutilized approach for exploiting the competition's weaknesses has been described as judo strategy.

Judo is a modern Japanese martial art based on the principle of maximum efficiency with minimum effort. Judo's creator, Kano Jigoro, describes the core judo principle this way: "In short, resisting a more powerful opponent will result in your defeat, whilst adjusting to and evading your opponent's attack will cause him to lose his balance, his power will be reduced, and you will defeat him. This can apply whatever the relative values of power, thus making it possible for weaker opponents to beat significantly stronger ones."[13] Judo emphasizes the use of the opponent's strength and weight as a means to defeat them while conserving your energy and resources. It professes that technique can outperform sheer power.

Utilizing this principle in a competitive business arena involves three techniques:

1. **Movement:** Transition customers to value skill versus sheer size, attempt to look benign, and practice guerrilla warfare by avoiding head-to-head confrontation.

2. **Leverage:** Transform the leader's strengths into weaknesses (e.g., scale→inability to customize; national→lacks local knowledge and relationships).
3. **Balance:** Define the boundaries of the game by the places you can win and play your game—a different game—than the opponent's game.

When you first hear the words "Liquid Death," many unsavory things come to mind, but bottled water is likely not one of them. The global bottled water market size is estimated at $283 billion and is forecasted to grow at a compound annual growth rate of 6.7%.[14] It's dominated by large players, including National Beverage Corp.'s LaCroix, and PepsiCo Inc.'s Aquafina and Bubly to name a few. The large players have scale (they can be purchased nearly everywhere), size (plenty of money for traditional advertising), and branding that evokes a serious approach to life, health, and tranquility in pristine plastic bottles.

Liquid Death would not be able to successfully compete against their much larger competitors by taking the same approach. They have used nontraditional marketing skills versus competitors with much deeper pockets to begin carving a place for themselves in the market by turning the traditional player's strengths into points of stark contrast. Start with cans resembling those for beer or energy drinks, adorned with the color black and skull illustrations, instead of plastic bottles featuring soothing imagery. Mix in flavors such as Mango Chainsaw, Severed Lime, and Berry It Alive, coupled with their declarative slogans "Murdering Thirst," and "Death To Plastic," and their persona punches the norm in the face.

How about a YouTube video entitled, "The Blind Taze Test," where two men who posted comments on the internet that Liquid Death was the worst water they have ever tasted were challenged to a taste test. If after the blind taste test of an assortment of the leading bottled waters they chose Liquid Death as the worst, they would receive $1,000. However, if they selected another brand, they would get electrocuted with a 50,000-volt taser. As the video shows, they were indeed electrocuted.

Liquid Death has released an album entitled *Greatest Hates,* which comprises product review comments with hits such as "I Thought This Was Alcohol," and "Your Product Is Dumb." Liquid Death has transformed the traditional competitors' strengths of scale, size, and conservative traditional marketing into weaknesses in the eyes of their target market. As Steve Nilsen, Vice President of Lifestyle Marketing, said, "No one has done anything interesting with the branding and the messaging of water. We're going to be the bee in the bonnet."[15]

When a new competitor enters a market, or when an established competitor makes a new move, it's common for a leader to immediately react to their competitor's move with a move of their own. These knee-jerk reactions often derail their current strategy, cause disruptive internal fire drills, and put them in a worse position than they were before. Sometimes the best response to a competitive move is . . . no response at all. Case in point: Square.

Jim McKelvey and Jack Dorsey launched Square in 2009 as a merchant-services and mobile-payment platform. They provided merchants with a small white square credit card reader that charged customers 2.75%. Then in 2014 Amazon decided to crash their party by creating a competitive product called Register with eerily similar software, a black rectangle design, and a fee of 1.95%—30% lower than Square's—with live customer support. Cue the funeral bagpipes.

Wait—not so fast.

Square's Jim McKelvey conceded that Register worked better than Square, due to Square's smaller square shape, which wobbled a bit when people ran the credit card through it. While McKelvey tested a wider reader, it failed the "cool" test. Square was small and unique, it commanded attention, and people had to practice using it.

A common response would be to react to all of these issues—change the shape to a rectangle, lower the price, and quickly add live customer support. After all, it's Amazon for God's sake! Square did none of these. McKelvey describes his thought process: "By the middle of 2014, we had made literally thousands of decisions about what our company would be. We'd made them with our customers and employees in mind. Making each decision had forced us to make other decisions, so everything was interrelated. We couldn't change one thing and not affect the others. The only way we could respond to Amazon was to change something we were doing, but everything we were doing was done for a good reason. So, we did nothing."[16] One year later, Amazon exited the market.

Off Course: Overreacting to every competitor move distracts from focusing resources on providing superior value to customers. Understand and assess competitor activity, but don't overreact to everything they do.

In Square's case, they didn't try to battle Amazon on scale or price. They allowed their cool little card reader to stand on its own, and they let the brand and their relationships with small businesses determine who would win in their defined arena. Upon their exit, Amazon amazingly sent their Register customers the now classic white Square card readers, demonstrating once again how they truly live their vision "to be the earth's most customer-centric company."

Learning to Differentiate

"When you've got only single-digit market share and you're competing with the big boys, you either differentiate or die."[17]

—Michael Dell, founder, Dell Technologies

The words of Michael Dell may seem alarmingly harsh. After all, there are plenty of examples of products and services that aren't much different from their competition that are still around. The question is, for how long? A study of 25,000 companies during the past 40 years found the companies that focused on differentiation were in the top 10% in return on assets.[18] As Peter Thiel, co-founder of PayPal, wrote, "All happy companies are different. All failed companies are the same. If you want to create and capture lasting value, don't build an undifferentiated business."[19]

Differentiation for competitive advantage in business has its roots in science. In 1934, Moscow University professor G. F. Gause published the results of a landmark study. He placed small animals in an enclosure with an ample amount of food. If the animals were of the same genus and a different species, they could live together peaceably. However, if the animals were of the same genus and the same species, they were not able to coexist. This led to the principle of competitive exclusion, which states that no two species can coexist that make their living in the identical way.[20] If we stay in the animal kingdom and think of two male lions in the same small territory, it makes sense. After a while, one of the male lions will no longer be around because they're trying to do the same thing in the same way.

Rocket Burn: Differentiate . . . or die.

Observe the companies that are struggling today and it's a good bet one of the reasons is their failure to heed the principle of competitive exclusion. They are stuck doing the same things in the same ways as their competition. Think of prominent companies that went into bankruptcy and their close competitors: Circuit City and Best Buy; Borders and Barnes & Noble; Sports Authority and Dick's Sporting Goods. When a company continually fails to differentiate their offerings from competitors, sooner or later they're going to be someone's lunch.

This failure to differentiate is often due to a propensity for operational effectiveness. Operational effectiveness is the wolf in strategy's clothing. The majority of companies in nearly all industries are constantly fighting battles of operational effectiveness: trying to do the same activities in the same tactical ways as others. When companies fall into this trap and rely on doing the same things in the same ways as their competitors (e.g., taxis and limousines), differentiated entrants come into the marketplace and begin to take their business (e.g., Uber, Lyft). Authors Michael Raynor and Mumatz Ahmed share insights from their study of 25,000 companies: "The more you compete on price, and the less differentiated you are on non-price dimensions, the less likely it is that you'll achieve exceptional outcomes. More compelling still, when an exceptional company abandons 'better' for 'cheaper,' its performance often suffers."[21]

A study of nearly 5,000 global executives found that the top business challenge for their organizations during the next few years was achieving competitive differentiation.[22] Differentiation has been shown to be three times as strong and clear in top market performers versus the bottom set of performers.[23] Narayana Murthy, founder of Infosys says, "At the end of the day, for us to succeed in the marketplace, we have to create sustainable differentiation—and sustainable differentiation comes from the power of the human mind. I believe that asking the right question is the first step."[24]

Off Course: Doing the same things in the same ways as the competition, only trying to do them better, is not strategy—it's operational effectiveness. If your competitive strategy does not contain elements of differentiation, then it's not a strategy at all.

We often seek to be better than our competitors, but being different in ways they value is truly what's important. It's much easier to convince someone that your product, service, company, team, or favorite food is different than others by simply pointing out how those differences are manifested and relevant to their interests. However, tell someone you're better and they'll immediately think of reasons you're not necessarily better. Difference invites an inquisitive look while better insinuates superiority. Is blueberry pie *better* than banana cream pie? Depends on whom you ask. We can be like kids on the playground and get into the "my pie's better than your pie" argument, but it solves nothing. Different is objective. While it's nearly impossible to convince someone blueberry pie is better than banana cream pie, you can easily convince someone it's different: it contains blueberries, which have antioxidants, which makes it a healthy choice and perhaps contributes to our longevity.

A key challenge then is to shift mindsets from a focus on "How are we better?" to "How are we different in ways customers value?" Research from Harvard University shows that 80% of adults believe the task of "thinking differently" is exhausting and uncomfortable.[25] Some managers believe that because of the industry in which they reside or the regulatory environment, there simply aren't any places left to differentiate. However, the appropriate use of strategic thinking tools and techniques can begin to uncover hidden sources of differentiation as well as ideas for future innovation.

The auto industry serves as one example where competitive convergence has been the norm. Enter Tesla. It shot to the top of *Forbes* magazine's World's Most Innovative Companies list due in large part to its differentiated approach and offerings. Starting at the high end of the automobile market, it introduced the Roadster, the first electric sports car, and then the Model S, an electric luxury sedan. They currently produce the top two bestselling electric cars in the U.S. according to Automotive News in the Tesla Model 3 coming in at number two and the Tesla Model Y compact SUV coming in at number one.

Tesla has used a different approach than other automakers to gain traction in the market. They bypassed the traditional automotive dealerships and have created 222 Tesla dealerships in the form of galleries and stores and sell directly to customers via the internet and non-U.S.-based stores. Traditional automakers outsource around 80% of components to suppliers, whereas Tesla's *vertical integration*, including component production, is roughly 80%. While their electric car competitors use single-purpose, large battery cells, almost half of all Tesla cars are equipped with prismatic lithium iron phosphate batteries and they have started their own battery production. They also built all the software used to run the cars from scratch, instead of the customary outsourcing.

Tesla also benefits from CEO Elon Musk's other venture, SpaceX, an American aerospace manufacturer. Tesla has borrowed from SpaceX's techniques of extensive use of aluminum for the Model S body and chassis, in addition to casting and drawing designed to produce the bodies of the SpaceX's Falcon rocket and Dragon capsules. Tesla's differentiated approach and offerings have resulted in both financial success (U.S. leader in sales of electric vehicles) and customer delight (number one in *Consumer Reports'* Annual Owner Satisfaction Survey). As Michael Porter, professor at Harvard Business School, said, "There is no best auto company. There is no best car. You're really competing to be unique."[26]

Do you think your offerings are unique? More important, do your customers think they are unique? According to research, the answer is, "probably not." One study showed 80% of executives believed their offering was highly differentiated, but only 8% of their customers agreed with them![27]

It's important to remember that the differentiation starts in the allocation of resources. It's often the configuration of resources in different activities or different ways that is the genesis of product or service differentiation, which leads to innovation. Research shows that companies tend to allocate 90% or more of their resources to the same places, year in and year out. But during the 15-year study, the firms that reallocated the most resources—more than 50% of capital on average across divisions—achieved 30% higher shareholder returns than those firms that reallocated least.[28] Allowing a status quo mindset to limit your reallocation of resources is one of the greatest threats to your company's profitable growth.

Take a moment and answer these ten questions related to differentiation:

1. What are the activities we perform that are truly different from the competition?
2. What are the similar activities we perform in different ways than the competition?
3. How is our business model different from the competition?
4. What resources do we have that are different from the competition?
5. How do our core competencies differ from those of our competitors?
6. How do customers describe the differences between the competition and us?
7. How does our culture differ from our closest competitor?
8. Are there any real differences between our people and our competitor's people?
9. How does our professional development differ from that of competitors?
10. What is the primary differentiated value our offering provides to customers?

Rocket Burn: Good strategy demands differentiation, which means trade-offs: choosing one path and not the other. Companies trying to be all things to all people are the easiest to beat. The mark of a great company is that their differentiation creates trade-offs that competitors cannot or will not meet.

Understanding Competitive Advantage

For all the debate and consternation over what competitive advantage in business really is, we can look to nature and our friend the good ol' wood frog. How's this for competitive advantage: the wood frog positions itself in the damp woodlands of North American mountains. When the brutal winter comes, it actually changes into another form of life, packing its cells with glucose (a natural antifreeze) and freezing its own fluid into crystals small enough not to damage itself. Fifteen hours after the first ice crystal forms, the wood frog is completely frozen, including its blood. It stays in suspended animation for the duration of the winter—with no heartbeat, no blood flow, and no breathing—which is normally the definition of death.

When spring arrives, the wood frog's heart is shocked back to life. Sparks from the static built up by the electrically charged chemicals are forced out by the stretching fibers of the heart muscle, reconnecting the wood frog with life. The wood frog is then free to enjoy the competitive advantage of his domain. Achieving competitive advantage is really quite simple—as simple as being brought back from the dead.

Fortunately in the business arena, understanding what constitutes competitive advantage and the methods of achieving it are not quite as drastic. A study of more than 2,000 global executives found that 47% do not believe their organization's strategies embodied the creation of advantage versus competitors.[29] Instead, they described their strategies as focusing on operational effectiveness and emulating undifferentiated best practices, which we know aren't technically strategies at all. Too often, people are wasting their time and talent working on things that don't contribute to competitive advantage. Consider your team: How much time and effort is being spent on activities that are not supporting the development of competitive advantage? When asked what the key was to return the LEGO Group to brand and financial success, former CEO Jørgen Vig Knudstorp said, "Only do the things where we had unique advantage."[30]

Competitive advantage can be described as an offering of superior value based on differences in capabilities and activities. These three elements—capabilities, activities, and offerings—form the foundation of competitive advantage. Capabilities consist of the assets or resources of a business. Activities are what you do with those resources to create value. And offerings are the manifestation of the capabilities and activities in the form of value received by customers.

Capabilities can be classified as one of two types: distinctive or reproducible. As the descriptors acknowledge, distinctive capabilities are those that cannot be emulated by competitors or can only be emulated with extreme difficulty. In the end, distinctive capabilities allow an organization to do things for less money than its rivals or do something that rivals simply cannot do. Reproducible capabilities are those that can be successfully replicated by competitors. A fundamental component of competitive advantage is to have distinctive capabilities. Distinctive capabilities come in a variety of forms, including intellectual property, marketing expertise leading to strong brands, effective leadership, and organizational culture, to name a few.

Most initial searches for competitive advantage begin with the offerings themselves, examining products for differentiating attributes such as efficacy, safety, ease of use, convenience, and so on. However, true competitive advantage takes root at the deeper levels of capabilities and activities. Examine your capabilities by listing them in one of two columns: distinctive or reproducible. This provides a clearer understanding of the competitive advantage dynamic for your business.

Rather than looking at broader functional areas such as R&D or marketing, it's more helpful to consider activities as the fundamental components of competitive advantage. Activities are the basic elements of competitive advantage because they are where capabilities merge with resource allocation to transform into the things that impact customers. The activities you choose to invest in—or just as importantly not invest in—determine your strategic focus. The challenge that most people face in trying to determine their competitive advantage is that they look at the entire organization or product as a whole. It's not until we break down the organization or product into its individual activities that we get a clearer view of competitive advantage.

The weapons we ultimately brandish in our competitive battles come in the form of offerings (products, services, experiences, etc.). Author Kevin Coyne offers three steps in which competitive advantage can emerge:

1. Customers perceive a consistent difference between offerings and that difference occurs in an attribute that impacts the buying decision.
2. The difference in the offering stems from a distinctive capability and unique activities.
3. Both the offering difference and the distinctive capabilities/activities last over time.[31]

After we've taken an in-depth look at our capabilities, activities, and offerings, and determined which end of competitive advantage that we're on, the question arises—"Is this competitive advantage sustainable?" The sustainability factor results from gaps in capabilities which trigger gaps in activities and lead to gaps in offerings. Sustainable competitive advantage can be worked toward if there is a continuous honing of distinct capabilities, the creation of new ones that drive differentiated activities, and anticipation of the changing market dynamics. While it's been debated whether sustainable competitive advantage can be achieved over long periods of time, what's not debatable is the importance of striving to provide unique value to customers through differentiated capabilities and activities.

If, after going through this process, we determine that we do not have competitive advantage, former Harvard Business School professor Bruce Chew provides options to help achieve it:

- Change the offerings by reconfiguring capabilities and activities to generate new outputs (e.g., Marvel Comics transforming original comic book characters and stories into action films, video games, LEGO sets, etc.).
- Create new capabilities through the development or acquisition of unique assets or resources (e.g., Oakland Athletics baseball team in the early 2000s development of a sophisticated sabermetric approach to scouting and assessing players).
- Change the target customer's perception of value by influencing the relevance of certain decision-making criteria (e.g., Chipotle's emphasis on quality ingredients in pioneering the concept of the fast-casual restaurant).
- Change the game by migrating value into new areas where competition has been static (e.g., Tesla's high-end design of electric vehicles).[32]

Too few leaders dedicate themselves to creating competitive advantage. The next time you're debating on whether to take the risk of making a sizable resource allocation to create distinct capabilities and a unique system of activities that can generate superior value, remember our friend the wood frog. After all, it's not like we're killing ourselves to do so.

Trail Blazes

The term "compete" comes from the Latin *competere,* which means "to strive together," from the roots *com* (together) and *petere* (to seek).

Competition can come in the form of a traditional rival, a new entry into your arena, colleagues, teammates, previous personal best performances, or the status quo. The key is to identify a competitive force that will trigger your higher level of performance and ride that wave to a higher plane.

Symmetric competition occurs when the competition possesses similar competencies and capabilities to yours, resulting in comparable strategies.

Asymmetric competition involves companies with competencies and capabilities and their configuration of resources that are different than yours.

The primary goals of a market leader are to maintain current customers and minimize the rate of defection. These two goals can be accomplished by utilizing the strengths that advanced them to the leadership position and neutralizing competitors.

The primary goals of a challenger are to take customers from competitors and convert nonusers into customers.

The principle of competitive exclusion states that no two species can coexist that make their living in the identical way.

Operational effectiveness is the wolf in strategy's clothing: doing the same activities in the same ways as others.

Competitive advantage can be described as an offering of superior value based on differences in capabilities and activities. These three elements—capabilities, activities, and offerings—form the foundation of competitive advantage.

Capabilities consist of the assets or resources of a business. Activities are what you do with those resources to create value. Offerings are the manifestation of the capabilities and activities in the form of value received by customers.

The emergence of competitive advantage comes through three steps:
1. Customers perceive a consistent difference between offerings and that difference occurs in an attribute that impacts the buying decision.
2. The difference in the offering stems from a distinctive capability and unique activities.
3. Both the offering difference and the distinctive capabilities/activities last over time.

Four ways to alter competitive advantage:
1. Change the offerings by reconfiguring capabilities and activities to generate new outputs.
2. Create new capabilities through the development or acquisition of unique assets or resources.
3. Change the target customer's perception of value by influencing the relevance of certain decision-making criteria.
4. Change the game by migrating value into new areas where competition has been static.

PART II

Leadership Fitness

"To each there comes in their lifetime a special moment when they are figuratively tapped on the shoulder and offered the chance to do a very special thing, unique to them and fitted to their talents. What a tragedy if that moment finds them unprepared or unqualified for that which could have been their finest hour."

—Winston Churchill, former prime minister
of the United Kingdom

As the tale goes, a troop of Hungarian soldiers were on military maneuvers in the Alps when they became lost. It snowed for two days. They were cold and hungry, and as day three approached, they were resigned to the fact that they would not make it out alive. Then, on the brink of death, one of the soldiers found a map buried deep in his pack. The detachment got their bearings, pulled themselves up, and followed the map out of the Alps to safety. When they returned to camp, the commanding officer asked how they finally found their way back. The soldier pulled out the map and laid it on the table. The commanding officer discovered, to his astonishment, that it was not a map of the Alps, but a map of the Pyrenees, an entirely different mountain range.

We may not always have the right map to help us navigate, but we can always bring with us the right mindset and skills to get us from here to there.

CHAPTER 5

Leadership

"Business leadership, business acumen, and business strategy development—these three areas of expertise are considered non-negotiable: they are essential for success in any C-Suite position."
—Omar Ishrak, former CEO, Medtronic

When you think back on the seasons of your life, from childhood through your teenage years to college and then your working career, who were the best leaders you've experienced? Perhaps a math teacher, scout leader, basketball coach, English professor, or your first manager. What makes them memorable? Can you recall something they said to you, maybe even in passing, that changed your life?

A leader can change the trajectory of our lives. Leaders challenge us to dig deep and bring forth our best efforts on a daily basis. Leaders clear a path through the jungle of the urgent, irrelevant, and unimportant so we can focus on the few tasks and decisions that matter. Leaders speak the truth, act with empathy, and put our needs ahead of theirs. How many real leaders do you know?

Leadership can be defined as setting direction and serving others to achieve goals. The best leaders practice the concept of servant leadership by ensuring their people are equipped with the knowledge, skills, and tools to effectively perform their functions. Inherently, a leader must articulate a destination, a vision, and goals that concentrate the team's resources into progress and achievement. The importance of leadership is clear: a study of two million managers found that the most important factor in how people rate their place of work is how their leaders behave.[1]

> **Rocket Burn:** Leadership involves the ability to set direction and serve others to achieve goals. How are you developing capabilities to forge direction and serve others?

To help leaders excel in these areas, we can break these three responsibilities into skills that can be practiced and honed over time. The skills comprising the ability to set strategic direction include situational awareness, problem solving, decision making, resource allocation, developing goals, and thinking strategically. An important byproduct of the ability to set strategic direction is the confidence it instills in the team. Research by Kouzes and Posner has shown that a team is 40% more committed to executing strategies when their leader has demonstrated the ability to set clear direction.[2]

In addition to setting clear direction, it must be communicated effectively. Reed Hastings, CEO of Netflix, has charted the company's strategic direction from DVD mail delivery to streaming and now content creation. His direction has been so keen that his vision to split the mail-delivery DVD business from the streaming business initially lost them subscribers because it surged ahead of the appropriate communication and execution. Undaunted by short-term challenges such as a plunging stock price, Hastings said, "Companies rarely die from moving too fast, and they frequently die from moving too slow."[3]

Situational Awareness

Situational awareness is an underappreciated and underdeveloped skill. Great leaders are continuously aware of and assessing their situations to more effectively allocate resources and make course corrections in their strategic direction when appropriate. As former World Chess Champion Garry Kasparov said, "The key is the ability to correctly assess and evaluate a situation. By becoming more aware of all the elements, all the factors in play, we train ourselves to think strategically, or as we say in chess, positionally."[4]

Imagine the scene: you're sitting in a physician's exam room. The doctor enters the room, looks you over, writes a prescription, and instructs her nurse to call it into your preferred pharmacy. As she's about to leave the room, you muster up the courage to say, "But you didn't ask me any questions or take any tests before you gave me this prescription." The doctor responds, "Yes, but I'm in a hurry and these pills worked for my last patient so I'm confident they'll work for you, too."

In medicine, this would be referred to as prescription without diagnosis, which equals malpractice. We'd never accept a remedy without a thorough examination of our medical condition. However, in business, we commit this sin all the time. We're constantly prescribing new activities, strategies, and tactics without first diagnosing our business condition.

> **Off Course:** Prescribing a course of action or set of tactics without first diagnosing your situation is business malpractice.

A key component of being strategic is an awareness and understanding of the current situation, or business context. Context is defined as "the set of circumstances or facts that surround a particular event, situation, etc."[5] How often have you seen a business following a strategy that worked in the past but has no chance of working now because the context is different? As academicians Anthony Mayo and Nitin Nohria wrote, "The central lesson we can take from business history is that context matters. The ability to understand the zeitgeist and pursue the unique opportunities it presents for each company is what separates the truly great from the merely competent."[6]

To think, plan, and act strategically requires a continual awareness of both the internal and external environments in which you operate and an understanding of what the patterns, trends, and events in each mean. The internal environment is comprised of your organization's culture, processes, systems, service, and other elements involved in performing your function. The external environment consists of the marketplace, customers, competitive landscape, government policies, and other factors outside of your control.

If we know how important the readily available information and data in our internal and external environments is to our business, then why don't we invest more time taking notice of and using it to our advantage? Donald Sull, senior lecturer at the MIT Sloan School of Management, explains, "You might think that this first step—observing the relevant data—is the easy one. However, studies of air traffic controllers have found that up to 70% of mistakes result from a failure to observe key variables that signaled a change in the situation, even though this information was available."[7]

A key to successfully navigating your business is having a trigger to cause you to take note of and record the changes in your business situation. Where do you currently record the key factors influencing the context of your business? For many leaders, the answer is that all of these factors are constantly floating around in their head, taking up valuable mind space. The key is to find a single repository where you can record these factors to free up your thinking and have them in a single spot to review. By recording the factors in your internal and external environments, you can much more easily take note of what's changing in your business and then respond accordingly.

Radar is a method of detecting objects and determining their positions, velocities, or other characteristics using high-frequency radio waves reflected from their surfaces. In a similar fashion, the Contextual Radar can provide a visual snapshot of the key factors in the four primary areas of your business: market, customers, competitors, and company. Market represents the patterns and trends that are influencing the business. Customers are those you serve and can be both internal (other functional areas, field sales, etc.) and external (clients, board of directors, etc.). Competitors represent the activities and offerings of other viable ways of meeting customer's needs. Company includes initiatives, issues, and events within the organization, from global headquarters, business units, functional areas, and geographic teams.

The Contextual Radar is populated with the items you deem important or potentially influential in your business situation. These items and their potential combinations provide the foundation of the thinking that will eventually create strategies and solutions. Figure 5.1 is an example of the Contextual Radar.

The Contextual Radar has proven to be an excellent catalyst for strategy conversations within teams and across functional areas. It is typically one of the first exercises I use when I facilitate strategic thinking workshops with executive leadership teams because it enables individuals to think deeply about the business and then share their key insights.

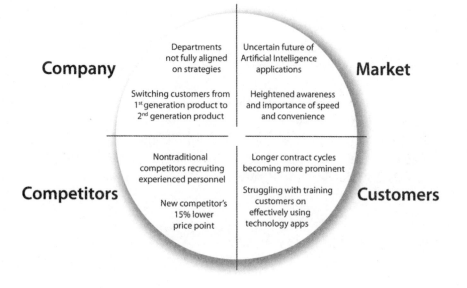

Figure 5.1 Contextual Radar.

The framework also provides a guide for the conversation and categories for insights that are identified.

Additionally, if you are performing a SWOT Analysis (strengths, weaknesses, opportunities, and threats) as part of your planning, the Contextual Radar is a productive exercise to do prior to the SWOT Analysis. This is because it generates thinking and conversation around the four areas covered in the SWOT Analysis. I've also worked with leaders who have used the Contextual Radar with their customers, both visually with the radar screen and verbally by asking customers about their perspectives on each of the four areas.

Finally, there's significant value in updating your Contextual Radar on a regular basis—weekly, monthly, or quarterly—because this enables you to recognize patterns and trends over time more quickly than others who aren't documenting the changes in their business. A study of electronic warfare technicians who varied in experience level from six months to seven years was conducted to assess their decision-making ability. Researchers Randel, Pugh, and Reed concluded with this statement: "The results showed that the experts placed a greater emphasis on the situation analysis (context) while the majority of novices emphasized deciding on the course of action."[8]

It's easy to be swept up in the tide of daily activity, bobbing up and down in a sea of fire drills, texts, and emails trying to stay afloat. The problem with this common approach is that it doesn't allow you time to observe, understand, and leverage the truly important factors that comprise your situation. Do you and your team have productive and efficient conversations about your business situation and then use those insights to fuel your strategies? If not, start with this simple question: "What's on your radar?" If the response is "What radar?" then you might want a life preserver.

Emotional Intelligence

The second element of leadership is serving others. The skills comprising the ability to effectively serve others include empathy, listening, asking thoughtful questions, determining needs versus wants, turbocharging high performance, and managing underperformance. At the root of many of these skills is emotional intelligence. Emotional intelligence is defined by authors Bradberry and Greaves as "the ability to recognize and understand emotions, and your skill in using this awareness to manage yourself and your relationships with others."[9] A study by PwC found, for the first time in nearly 20 years, more CEOs were fired for poor behavior rather than poor financial performance.[10] Serving others effectively requires emotional intelligence, and with it the ability to enable others to grow.

Off Course: In recent years, more CEOs were fired for poor emotional intelligence than poor financial performance.

The two focal areas of emotional intelligence consist of personal and social competence and are realized by what you see and what you do. Following is a checklist you can use to enhance your emotional intelligence in real-time situations such as meetings to develop this competency:

☐ Self-Awareness: What are my emotions?
☐ Self-Management: How do I need to adjust my behavior?

☐ Social Awareness: What are others' emotions?
☐ Relationship Management: How can I adapt to and influence the conversation to maintain and grow this relationship?[11]

At the core of emotional intelligence is the ability to listen. With the proliferation of multitasking, listening is becoming a rare quality. Many people are listening at about 50% of their capacity due to a lack of discipline and being easily distracted by their phones. A leader is defined in part by their ability to serve others and the most effective way to serve others is listening to them to fully understand their needs, wants, and expectations.

One technique for enhancing listening in this era of increased virtual meetings is to record the audio and video of the interaction (receive permission first) and assess how well you listened to the other person. A key gauge of this video analysis is how effectively you use questions to stimulate thinking and sharing from others. You can also use AI software to transcribe the conversation, which then provides you with a breakdown of the percentage of time each party was talking, and consequently the amount of time the other party was listening.

Another tool is the 5S Listening checklist, which you can keep on a physical note card or on your mobile phone. Prior to one-to-one interactions or meetings, review the checklist to prep for the session. Following the meeting, review and check off each area that you successfully executed.

☐ Stop: I monotask this conversation.
☐ Still: I quiet my mind and stay in the moment.
☐ Story: I discover their thoughts and emotions through the stories they tell.
☐ Suspend: I do not judge, I simply process.
☐ Summarize: I repeat back what I heard to confirm it.

The third and final element of leadership is the achievement of goals. The skills comprising the ability to achieve goals include planning, communication, energy management, and execution. Goals represent desired ends or targets to be reached. They are supported by objectives, which are more specific, quantifiable, and time-based. Together, goals and objectives answer the first question of any quality plan: What are you trying to achieve?

Establishing goals that are challenging, energizing, and realistic provides focus for a team's resource allocation. Meg Whitman, former CEO of eBay and HP Enterprise, explains her approach using the lens of a parent: "Do you hold up a real stretch goal, with the secret hope that the challenge will motivate the child to achieve far more than he or she otherwise would have, even if the goal isn't met? Or do you nudge along, focusing on each incremental effort—each additional hour of practice the child puts in and talk positively but vaguely of where that will lead? Personally, I am a fan of the stretch goal."[12]

A primary pitfall to avoid is creating a laundry list of too many goals. Research by the firm FranklinCovey on thousands of teams found that the number of goals you set matters. Teams with 2 or 3 goals are likely to achieve 2 or 3 of them. Teams with 4 to 10 goals typically achieve 1 or 2 of them and usually the easiest, least important of the bunch. Teams with 11 or more goals aren't likely to achieve any of them. When you do set goals in writing, you're nearly 40% more likely to achieve them than those who don't record them. And if those goals are written, shared with others, and updated on their progress, the accomplishment rate skyrockets to 77%.[13]

Leadership Philosophy

A powerful force in the navigation of your business is a crystallized leadership philosophy. A leadership philosophy is represented by the values, identity, legacy, and principles that serve to form the foundation of a leader's qualities, characteristics, and behaviors. The process of developing a leadership philosophy begins with a look back.

1. **Values.** Begin by describing three to five key leadership moments from your life in detail from areas such as school, sports, work, hobbies, or the like. Then assess these examples and identify any common themes that emerge. Reference these themes as you then jot down a list of your potential leadership values, those traits that best represent your strong beliefs with regards to setting direction, serving others, and achieving goals. From the initial list, select three to five values that most accurately represent you. Examples of leadership values include courage, helpfulness, ingenuity, optimism, and wisdom.

2. **Identity.** An identity statement acts as a leadership anchor when times are tumultuous to remind us of who we are and what we do in setting direction and serving others. To articulate your identity statement, begin by describing how you use your values and strengths to serve others in your chosen field. Examples of identity statements include "I am relentless in the pursuit of finding good in others and helping them become the best version of themselves through training and development," or "I serve others in a leadership role with empathetic honesty, and active listening to discover obstacles in their path and how to most effectively help people overcome them." Create your leadership identity statement by stating in the current tense how you use your values and strengths and the resulting accomplishment.

3. **Legacy.** In my experience, few leaders have taken the time to think about what they'd like to leave behind and be remembered for from their years of service. A legacy is defined as "a gift handed down." What gift would you like to hand down before you pass the leadership baton? Here is an example of a legacy statement for Amelia Earhart: "She inspired all as an aviation pioneer and blazed an educational and career path for women in aeronautical engineering."

   Review your work on the leadership values and identity statements and ask yourself what gifts you can leave others based on these characteristics and activities. Then encapsulate it in a one-sentence legacy statement.

4. **Principles.** Leadership principles are specific guidance on the appropriate actions for one who sets direction and serves others to achieve goals. Values form the foundation of an organization's culture by shaping the behaviors of the collective whole. Leadership principles build on values by illuminating the actions that guide those who lead others toward their vision and goals. Following is a sample of leadership principles:

   - Lead at our level and don't do our direct reports' work.
   - Agree or disagree but then commit to the chosen course of action.
   - Build trust by doing what we say we're going to do.
   - Clarify decision rights to eliminate the escalation of issues.
   - Give people our full attention when engaged in meetings.

Begin the process by identifying the leadership actions and behaviors you've exhibited and observed in the past that contributed to clear direction and effective interaction with others in the achievement of goals. Then ask yourself what leadership actions and behaviors you believe are important in setting direction. Consider areas such as decision making, problem solving, allocating resources, setting goals, making trade-offs, and prioritization.

Follow that with your insights on the leadership actions and behaviors you believe are important in the service of others. Consider areas such as turbocharging high performance, managing underperformance, communication, situational awareness, empathy, and emotional intelligence.

Finally, identify what you believe to be the leadership actions and behaviors instrumental in the collective achievement of goals. Review all of your work and transfer the key concepts, actions, and behaviors to a short list for consideration. Use this thinking to then articulate your three to seven leadership principles.

In business, it's common to equate someone's job title with their leadership status. However, when we pull back the curtain on the concept of leadership and define it as "setting direction and serving others to achieve goals," many so-called leaders simply are not. Setting direction and serving others are manifested in one's actions. If you want to be a leader, act like one. As the late professor of management Peter Drucker noted, "Only three things happen naturally in organizations: friction, confusion, and underperformance. Everything else requires leadership."[14]

Trail Blazes

Leadership can be defined as setting direction and serving others to achieve goals.

Context is defined as "the circumstances in which an event occurs; a setting."

The Contextual Radar can provide a visual snapshot of the key factors in the four primary areas of your business: market, customers, competitors, and company.

The skills comprising the ability to effectively serve others include empathy, listening, asking thoughtful questions, determining needs versus wants, turbocharging high performance, and managing underperformance.

Emotional intelligence is defined as "the ability to recognize and understand emotions, and your skill in using this awareness to manage yourself and your relationships with others."

Emotional intelligence comprises four skills:
1. Self-Awareness
2. Self-Management
3. Social Awareness
4. Relationship Management

5S Listening Checklist:
1. Stop: I monotask this conversation.
2. Still: I quiet my mind and stay in the moment.
3. Story: I discover their thoughts and emotions through the stories they tell.
4. Suspend: I do not judge, I simply process.
5. Summarize: I repeat back what I heard to confirm it.

Leadership philosophy is composed of one's values, identity, legacy, and principles.

CHAPTER 6

Personal Performance

"My opponent did not understand preparation. He had little idea of the weeks, sometimes months that I spend in lonely isolation preparing my case. What he saw, without knowing it, was a lawyer who had been freed by acquiring a fund of eloquently prepared facts."

—Gerry Spence, trial lawyer who has never lost a criminal case

When we see the greatest performers in any domain, whether art, business, engineering, law, medicine, music, sports, or teaching, what we're seeing is the product of preparation. It's easy to watch two-time Olympic Gold Medal skier Mikaela Shiffrin race down a mountain and think how lucky she is to be so talented. It's also dead wrong. Mikaela Shiffrin's high-school roommate, Bug Pech, had this to say about the all-time winningest women's World Cup skier: "She had the work ethic of Tom Brady when she was 13."[1]

As former NBA All-Star and sharpshooter Ray Allen said, "When people say God blessed me with a beautiful jump shot, it really pisses me off. I tell those people, 'Don't undermine the work I've put in every day.' Not some days. Every day. Ask anyone who has been on a team with me who shoots the most. The answer is me."[2]

Studies conducted by Florida State professor Anders Ericsson on violin players demonstrated the power of preparation. He observed that the general music education students had practiced on the violin an average of 3,240 hours by their 18th birthday, the better violin students had practiced an average of 5,301 hours, and the best violin students had practiced an average of 7,410 hours. He concluded, "These were clearly major differences in practice time."[3]

Amazon founder Jeff Bezos popularized the practice of banning PowerPoint presentations from meetings in favor of six-page memos. He believes that the time required to prepare a cogent description of a new product, service, or other topic of importance is a valuable step in helping the team clarify their thinking. He says, "Often, when a memo isn't great, it's not the writer's inability to recognize the high standard, but instead a wrong expectation on scope: they mistakenly believe a high-standards, six-page memo can be written in one or two days or even a few hours, when really it might take a week or more!"[4]

Consider your current role and responsibilities. Now think about the knowledge and skills that go into performing your role and responsibilities on a daily basis. How much time are you investing in preparing to perform these activities at a high level? Here are a few examples from exceptional performers, for comparison's sake:

- Tom Brady, seven-time Super Bowl champion quarterback, watched 17 hours of football video per week.
- Chief Justice of the United States Supreme Court John Roberts Jr., when preparing for an oral argument, would write down several hundred questions on notecards, shuffle them, and test himself.
- Boxing champion Manny Pacquiao did 2,000 sit-ups every day.
- In his autobiography *Open*, tennis champion Andre Agassi wrote, "My father says that if I hit 2,500 tennis balls each day, I'll hit 17,500 balls each week, and at the end of one year I'll have hit nearly one million balls. He believes in math. Numbers, he says, don't lie. A child who hits one million balls each year will be unbeatable."[5]

If the business arena is your forum of competition, would you describe yourself as unbeatable at your work? Your level of performance and results are directly proportional to your level of preparation. Want better results? Increase your preparation. Where do your years of experience factor in? They don't. It's common in society to equate experience with excellence. However, studies show that experience alone doesn't mean much. Research on several types of medical doctors revealed that mammographers actually become less accurate in their diagnoses as their experience increases.[6] Neurosurgeons who have been operating for 15 years are typically no more skilled than their peers who have been operating for just a few years unless they have increased their preparation through deliberate practice of the primary skills of the procedures.[7]

Rocket Burn: Elite performance requires elite preparation. How are you preparing differently than others to excel in your work?

Three Principles of Preparation

Here are three principles of preparation to help guide your efforts at dramatically increasing your performance and results:

1. **Purpose.** It's impossible to properly prepare for something that you don't care about. Finding one's purpose is a critical component of sustained success. Earlier in this section, we explored techniques for crafting your leadership philosophy in the form of values, identity, legacy, and principles. These elements all form your purpose as a leader and should be referenced on a daily basis to refresh on why you do what you do. Clarifying your purpose at this high level enables you to determine what activities and tasks will aid your preparation and which ones to filter out.

In my strategic coaching work with executive leaders, we'll analyze their calendar and attempt to tie a purpose to each item. Any items that are not tied to a purpose are then eliminated. As you think about your calendar and the items that consume the most time, ask yourself how much preparation you're investing in each area. The rule of thumb is that the activities and tasks you're investing the most time in each day should also be the ones you're investing the most time preparing for beforehand.

Three areas that warrant closer consideration on your level of preparation are the day ahead, meetings, and strategy sessions. When you arrive at your desk in the morning, do you have a plan for the day? Have you allocated chunks of time to your most important priorities? Or are you operating like a bumper car at the carnival, bouncing from one thing to the next with no rhyme or reason? Don't be a carny . . . be strategic.

An effective technique for preparing for your day is to do so the afternoon before. Finish your day by identifying the priorities and activities for the following day so your mornings don't begin with a mindless scrolling of emails. Get something important done early.

Here's an interesting exercise: review your calendar from last week and total up the number of hours you spent in meetings. Then consider how many hours you spent preparing for those meetings. The most effective leaders use a 1:1 ratio—one hour of preparation for every one hour of meeting time. I know what some folks are thinking: Are you out of your mind? I don't have one hour to prepare for each hour of meeting time! If you don't have that 1:1 ratio available, then I'd suggest one of two potential causes:

1. You're wasting your time attending too many unimportant meetings.
2. Some of these meetings shouldn't even be meetings—look for other formats to communicate the information.

Strategy sessions shouldn't resemble an impromptu group psychotherapy session where conversations ramble down rabbit holes and you don't address the competitively relevant competencies, capabilities, and activities that drive your competitive advantage. Any strategy session should be preceded by thoughtful prework in the form of a Strategy Survey that acts as a catalyst to help people wrestle with business-defining questions that form the foundation of the workshop. A strategic leader understands that framing the session with key questions and challenges is the source of highly productive strategy conversations.

2. **Plan.** Developing a plan for your preparation is often overlooked in the flurry of activity we find ourselves in on a daily basis. As noted earlier, all good plans answer two questions: 1) What are you trying to achieve? 2) How will you achieve it? While some leaders have plans for their business, far fewer have plans for their preparation.

Michael Phelps, the U.S. swimmer who is the most successful Olympian of all time with a total of 28 medals, developed a plan for preparation early in his career that enabled him to excel like no one in history had before. Beginning when he was 14 years old, Phelps practiced seven days a week, up to six hours a day in the pool, every single day of the year, including holidays such as Thanksgiving and Christmas. The plan calculated that by practicing on Sundays, he would have 52 more days of training than his competition each and every year.[8] As Mike Krzyzewski, former NCAA Championship basketball coach for Duke University, said, "The most important lesson of leadership I've learned is that in order to get better, you change limits."[9]

In developing your plan to prepare to improve in key skill sets in your role, look to do things differently than others. After all, excellence is defined as "deviation from the norm." If we're doing the same normal things in the same normal ways as everyone else, we're not going to separate our performance from others. We can go back to the swimming pool for an example. U.S. Olympic gold medal swimmer Michael Andrew trained in the exact opposite manner as his competitors. He practiced by swimming shorter distances at higher-intensity levels instead of swimming longer distances at lower-intensity levels. His differentiated plan has support in neuroscience research, which has shown the efficacy of the myelination of neuro-networks through repeated behaviors—in this case, taking the longer race distance and chunking it into shorter stretches performed at higher speeds.[10]

Tim Grover, personal trainer for a number of National Basketball Association greats, including Michael Jordan and Kobe Bryant, reinforces the importance of preparing differently: "When I was training Michael Jordan, we set up a schedule that had him training on game days. This was unheard of at the time. People said: He'll be fatigued, he'll be less athletic. He played three to four games a week, plus travel days, plus practice, plus rest days. When was he supposed to train? 82 extra workouts more than competitors. Mike did not want to be like anyone else. Which led us to training on game days."[11]

A helpful exercise is to create a preparation chart with the following column headers: Topic/Activity, Goal, Objective, Strategy, and Tactics. The GOST Framework developed to help leaders set strategic direction with plans for their business is equally applicable in the context of preparation. As it relates to your area of preparation, the goal is generally what you want to achieve, the objective is specifically what you want to achieve, the strategy is how generally you'll achieve your goal, and the tactics are how specifically you'll achieve your goal. A good place to start may be your professional development plan and determining the GOST Framework for your preparation of enhancing your competencies and capabilities.

3. **Prevention.** The primary reason we prepare for anything is to increase our probability of success and reduce our chance of failure. But wait! Isn't one of today's most popular mantras "Fail fast"? Why would we want to prevent failure when a lot of people are advocating for it? Because "failing fast" as a consistent route to success is a myth. Professor Bradley Staats provides insight on failure in the medical field: "Our analysis of ten years' worth of data across seventy surgeons revealed not only that on average, they learned more from others' failure than from their own, but also that an individual's own failure led to worse future performance."[12]

> **Off Course:** The advice to "Fail fast and fail often" does not produce greater success in the future. In fact, research shows failure typically leads to poorer performance and worse results. Instead, ramp up your level of preparation.

Research with 8,400 startup firms was conducted to determine if the new companies started by entrepreneurs that had failed in their previous venture performed better than first-time entrepreneurs. The results showed that they had worse results in their second venture. The experienced entrepreneurs that had failed were more likely to go bankrupt than first-time entrepreneurs.[13] Here's what some of the most successful leaders in recent business say about the importance of preparation as a means of preventing failure:

"I think failure is massively overrated. Most businesses fail for more than one reason. So, when a business fails, you often don't learn anything at all because the failure was overdetermined. I think people actually do not learn very much from failure."
—Peter Thiel, self-made billionaire[14]

"My goal is not to fail fast. My goal is to succeed over the long run. They are not the same thing."
—Marc Andreesen, co-founder of Netscape and partner in venture capital firm Andreesen Horowitz[15]

"What is the worst advice you see or hear given in your trade? 'Fail fast!'"

—Jack Dorsey, self-made billionaire, CEO of Square and former CEO of Twitter[16]

Pull back the curtain on the greatest contributors and performers in any field and you'll see thousands of hours of preparation. But peer inside the home offices and video meetings of many businesspeople and you'll see waves of activity with little to no preparation in sight. The best performers have the best preparation. So decide what knowledge, skills, and activities are key to your success and turbocharge your preparation. As Abraham Lincoln said, "If I had eight hours to chop down a tree, I'd spend the first six sharpening my axe."

Energy Management

An essential element in preparing to perform at a high level as a leader is energy management. Energy management consists of your approach to rest, nutrition, exercise, mindfulness, and spirit. In the past, "burning the candle at both ends" and measuring someone's contribution to the business by quantity of hours clocked instead of the quality of the work was commonplace. Today, there are still a few holdouts for this approach, but many more understand the significant consequences, most notably in the condition of burnout. Even Amazon founder Jeff Bezos, known for his outsized work ethic, realized when his thinking, decision making, and performance were optimal: "By 5 pm I'm like, 'I can't think about that today. Let's try this again tomorrow at ten.' I need eight hours of sleep. I think better. I have more energy. My mood is better."[17]

Bezos's need for eight hours of sleep for high performance is supported by research demonstrating the importance of a good night's rest. Sleep has been shown to fuel the functioning of a wide range of biological processes, including emotional well-being, memory and learning, the immune system, hormonal balance, and the removal of toxins from the brain. In addition to the biological benefits of sleep, it has also been shown to improve performance in a variety of people, from athletes to fighter pilots.

A number of studies by physician Cheri Mah, a researcher out of Stanford's Sleep Disorder Clinic and Research Laboratory, showed that with more sleep, college athletes—including swimmers, tennis players, soccer players, and basketball players— performed better. In one of Mah's studies, a cohort of players on Stanford's men's basketball team were required to sleep at least ten hours per night. The results of 10-plus hours of sleep included a nearly 10% increase in free-throw percentages and a 9.2% increase in made three-point field goals.[18]

Professional sports teams have taken the research seriously as well. When the Golden State Warriors professional basketball team built their Chase Center facility, they included individual sleep pods to give players a place to nap. Neurologist W. Christopher Winter, MD, whose research found that jetlag and the corresponding loss of sleep was related to Major League Baseball teams losing games, concludes, "The research that's coming out now is unequivocal. People who sleep more and sleep better perform better, both in the short and the long term."[19]

The National Sleep Foundation recommends between seven and nine hours of sleep on average per night. For one week, track what time you typically go to bed and the time you wake up in the morning and calculate the number of hours of sleep you're getting. Going to bed and waking up at approximately the same time each day is also recommended to provide the best opportunity for a good night's sleep.

Mindfulness has emerged as another area to restore and refresh one's mental and spiritual approach to both professional and personal life. One of the most common techniques for achieving mindfulness is meditation. The technique of meditation transitions us from a participant in our thoughts to an observer. As an observer, we realize we are not our thoughts and can therefore determine how we experience them. In stressful situations, the ability to observe and not absorb the emotion of the moment enables one to see the situation clearly and act intentionally instead of the more typical knee-jerk reaction that lacks coherent thought. This behavior can be shaped through the practice of meditation.

Several types of meditation include phrase-based, where a word or few words are the focal point; guided meditation, where one is led through the process through verbal instruction by another; and breathing-based, where the center of attention becomes one's breath in a rhythmic pattern, such as box breathing, the 4x4x4x4 formula: inhale for four seconds, hold for four seconds, exhale for four seconds, and hold for four seconds, repeating this pattern for a designated period of time.

A large trove of research extols the benefits of meditation. University of North Carolina researchers found that after even a few days of meditation, participants experienced significant improvement in creativity, mental agility, attention span, and memory. The researchers concluded: "Simply stated, the profound improvements we found after just four days of meditation training are really surprising."[20] High performers in business and sports often cite meditation as a core part of their daily routine.

SalesForce CEO Mark Benioff described his experience: "A meditation practice has really paid off for me as CEO. Because I had that before I even started the company, it's paid off for decades where I'm cultivating my beginner's mind. I'm trying to encourage my executives and my company to do the same thing."[21] During the University of Michigan's journey to the NCAA college football playoff's Final Four in starting quarterback J.J. McCarthy's sophomore season, he said that meditation enabled him to become "completely there, completely present . . . I wake up, I'll meditate for 30 minutes. And then, as everyone sees, out by the field goal post, meditate for 10 more minutes, just as that quick tune-up to really make sure that I'm completely present in the moment."[22]

Nutrition and exercise are two additional components of energy management. Having a protein-based breakfast along with smaller meals/snacks throughout the day has strong support from national nutrition experts as a way to keep energy levels up. A good rule of thumb is to eat just enough to fuel you through the next two to three hours until you eat again. Hydrating by drinking water throughout the day is also suggested because it normalizes your temperature, protects sensitive tissues, and cushions joints. According to the Mayo Clinic, "The U.S. National Academies of Sciences, Engineering, and Medicine determined that an adequate daily fluid intake is 15.5 cups (3.7 liters) of fluids a day for men and 11.5 cups (2.7 liters) of fluids a day for women."[23] As with sleep, it's helpful to keep a log for a week to track what you're eating and drinking, when, and the quantities, and adjust from there.

Exercise is described as movement that makes your muscles work and requires your body to burn calories. The benefits of exercise are many and include increased energy levels, reduction in the risk of chronic diseases (e.g., Type 2 diabetes, heart disease, hypertension, high cholesterol, etc.), stimulation of hormone production that enhances the growth of brain cells, improved sleep quality, and improving mood due to the production of endorphins. The CDC recommends that adults engage in 150 minutes of moderate-intensity physical activity per week along with two days of muscle strengthening. As an executive's schedule becomes busier, one of the first things that gets bumped off the calendar to make more room for work is exercise. However, due to the overwhelmingly positive benefits from both a physical and mental perspective, it's important to embed exercise in your regular schedule and keep it there.

Executive Presence

As a leader rises to higher levels within an organization, how they project themselves to both internal and external stakeholders increases in importance as well. The persona a leader projects to others through their appearance, communication, and behavior can be described as executive presence. The following seven factors contribute to the aggregate of executive presence possessed by a leader:

1. **Authenticity:** Leveraging one's unique strengths and exhibiting vulnerability through communications to demonstrate sincerity in the development of trust
2. **Composure:** The ability to control one's state of mind and project that poise to others, especially in situations filled with urgency, confusion, or volatile emotion
3. **Empathy:** Identifying with the thoughts, perspectives, and emotions of others and communicating that understanding to them
4. **Concision:** Expressing written or verbal communication with brevity of form yet comprehensiveness in scope
5. **Energy:** Display of an appropriate level of enthusiasm, emotion, and excitement when interacting with others
6. **Honesty:** Respecting others' time and perspectives by giving them candid input and feedback in a nonjudgmental manner to move things forward, versus the proverbial "beating around the bush"
7. **Self-Efficacy:** Demonstrating confidence and assurance through clear and concise communication based on a foundation of competence and expertise

These seven factors can be modified and enhanced since they are driven by mindset and behavior. The first step is to baseline your current projection of each of these qualities through self-awareness and the feedback of others whom you interact with, both professionally and personally, on a regular basis. Keep a chart with the factors and make notes throughout the day on which you've excelled at and which need development. Use trigger questions to help transform these traits into habits. For example, "On a scale of 1–10 with 1 being low and 10 being high, what was my energy level in the executive leadership team meeting? Did I display empathy in the one-to-one meeting with my direct report? What was the level of self-efficacy I projected during the all-employee town hall meeting?"

As noted earlier, during the past few years, more CEOs have been fired for issues related to emotional intelligence such as ethical lapses and poor moral decisions than financial performance. Combined with preparation and emotional intelligence, the factors involved in energy management and executive presence will go a long way in determining a leader's success.

Trail Blazes

Your level of performance and results are directly proportional to your level of preparation.

Three principles of preparation:
1. Purpose
2. Plan
3. Prevention

The advice to "Fail fast and fail often" as a means to greater future success is a myth. Research shows consistent failure fosters poor performance in the future.

Energy management consists of your approach to rest, nutrition, exercise, and spirit.

Sleep experts recommend between seven and nine hours of sleep on average per night.

Exercise is described as movement that makes your muscles work and requires your body to burn calories. The benefits of exercise are many and include increased energy levels, reduction in the risk of chronic diseases, stimulation of hormone production that enhances the growth of brain cells, improved sleep quality, and improving mood due to the production of endorphins.

The persona a leader projects to others through their appearance, communication, and behavior can be described as executive presence.

Seven factors that contribute to executive presence:
1. Authenticity
2. Composure
3. Empathy
4. Concision
5. Energy
6. Honesty
7. Self-efficacy

CHAPTER 7

Mental Toughness

"The physical aspect of the sport can only take you so far. In the Olympic Games, everyone is talented. Everyone trains hard. Everyone does the work. What separates the gold medalists from the silver medalists is simply the mental game."
—Shannon Miller, U.S. Olympic gymnastics gold medalist

Does your mind at work feel like a business pinata, minus the candy falling out? Does it feel like time to stop the swirling in different directions, streaming of interruptions, and constant pummeling of time-wasting activities? What would it be like to eliminate that "treading-water" feeling and replace lingering doubt with confident direction? Strengthen your mind, and you gain greater control of your time, talent, and performance.

The journey requires mental toughness. Psychologist Daniel Gucciardi describes mental toughness as "the psychological capacity to drive toward a goal, particularly in response to challenging circumstances. High levels of mental toughness enable individuals to achieve and sustain high levels of performance because they can optimally direct energy toward their personal goals, maximize congruency between their behavior and valued goals and efficiently adapt their thoughts and actions when confronted with stressors."[1]

We know this to be absolutely true as it relates to sports. Find the best players in their athletic arena and a large contributor to their success is their mental game. As former tennis pro and author of the book *Winning Ugly*, Brad Gilbert writes, "The difference in the world #1 and the world #3 is usually mental."[2] NBA legend and all-time scoring leader LeBron James said, "I believe when your mind is at its strongest, when the physical fades away, you can still be at your best because you're just head over heels over a lot of people on the mental side. And for me to be able to train my mind as much as I train my body, I think that's why I'm able to do the things I'm doing right now."[3]

Seven Saboteurs of the Mind

It's now common for high school athletes to be doing some form of mental training to complement their physical game. However, in business, the mental side of the game is typically bankrupt. There are seven saboteurs to the mental side of our business performance:

1. **Anchors away:** allowing another's comment to anchor us to an erroneous or mistaken starting point. Counter: Think through and process the opinion, information, or data that others are planting as the conversation starting line and redraw the line by sharing your view.
2. **Power outage:** giving away our autonomy, choice, or power to another. We often perceive others have "power" over us, but that ignores the fact there are always options. As Ralph Waldo Emerson wrote, "Nothing external to you has any power over you." High-performing organizations create an environment where people with insights, not just job titles, drive initiatives.
3. **Judge Dread:** prematurely passing judgment on an event, person, or result as good or bad, when it's not necessarily either. Our proclivity for snap judgments reduces our options and boxes up events and people. Keep a gavel on your desk and each time you find yourself passing judgment too quickly, bang it on the block as a reminder.
4. **Embracing noise:** spending too much time worrying about the uncontrollable elements in a situation. For situations you're evaluating, create two columns, labeled "Controllables" and "Uncontrollables," and list the factors that fall into each. Focus on the controllables. This is especially valuable in team meetings when it's easy for a group to get off track by belaboring things they cannot possibly influence.
5. **Time traveling:** continually replaying past events or worrying about future events that may never occur. When you find your mind

rewinding or fast forwarding in time, use a trigger word to bring your focus back to the present situation. As Lao Tzu, the father of Taoism, wrote, "If you are depressed, you are living in the past. If you are anxious, you are living in the future. If you are at peace, you are living in the present."

6. **Energy vampires:** putting ourselves within reach of habitually negative people. We all battle that little voice inside us that raises doubt and instigates negative self-talk. That battle is challenging enough without also having to ward off the negative energy from people who constantly criticize, condemn, and complain. Find a way to disconnect from these energy vampires.

7. **Brain ruts:** creating artificial constraints for ourselves. Our past experiences—both successes and failures—have created mental ruts in which our lives run. Intentionally steer your mind out of those ruts through exposure to new people, events, experiences, and resources (e.g., books, blogs, magazines) that represent higher and different plateaus that can alter your view.

Mental Training Techniques

The following techniques are proven ways to enhance your mental approach to the business:

1. **Assert yourself.** Mentally resilient leaders tend to be less passive and more assertive than their counterparts. *Assertive* is defined as "confidently aggressive or self-assured; positive, bold." Research out of the University of Chicago studied the profiles and performance of 313 CEOs and characterized them in one of two ways: 1) lambs—those CEOs who operate primarily using soft skills, are slower in making decisions, and rely heavily on the input of others for consensus; 2) cheetahs—those CEOs who move quickly, act aggressively, and hold others accountable to high standards. The study found the "lambs" were successful in creating significant value for their investors 57% of the time while the "cheetahs" were successful 100% of the time.[4]

Assertive executives are driven by strong set of principles and don't kowtow to the latest whims and vagaries espoused by politicians and other nonexperts in a variety of fields. They've thoughtfully considered and recorded their leadership philosophy, built on their values and purpose, and use them to navigate with pace in turbulent times. Marketing guru Seth Godin said, "Most people spend their time on defense, in reactive mode, in playing with the cards they got instead of moving to a different table with different cards."[5]

Creating a list of affirmations can be a powerful way to maintain an assertive, performance-enhancing approach to your work. Why is there potential value in using affirmations, or performance-based self-talk? According to the National Science Foundation, the average individual has anywhere between 10,000 and 60,000 thoughts per day, 95% of which are repetitive and 80% of which are negative.[6] Without a determined effort and technique to transition your thoughts from negative to positive, the tsunami of unproductive thoughts will wash away many good ideas and intentions. A list of five to seven affirmations (e.g., I am an empathic listener, I am a servant leader, etc.) read each morning and following lunch can focus your mind on the key drivers of performance and instill genuine confidence. Former heavyweight boxing champion Muhammad Ali said, "It's the repetition of affirmations that leads to belief. And once that belief becomes a deep conviction, things begin to happen."

2. **Create a competitor.** The fastest I've ever moved was a decade ago when I was chased by two wild dogs in a rural field during a long run. Heart pounding, sweat flying—I felt like Usain Bolt. Why? I was competing, in this case for what seemed like my survival. Research dating back to 1897 shows conclusively that competition catalyzes latent reserves of extra effort. In the first study ever published in the field of sports psychology, Norman Triplett's research on bicycle riders' speeds showed that riders paced by a competitor rode 34 seconds faster per mile than solo riders.[7]

These findings have been replicated in a number of other academic and social settings. Dallas Stars professional hockey player Tyler Seguin observed, "When I'm at the hardest point in a workout, I picture my strongest competitors doing the exact same workout but flying through it with no fatigue. My competitive drive kicks in and that inspires me to work as hard as I imagine those guys are working."[8] To ignite your efforts and fuel mental toughness, consider a competitor in your field and envision their initiatives to outperform you. Then let your competitive drive take over and channel it into your work.

3. **Pump some insights.** A physical workout can build muscle, improve cardiovascular health, increase energy, and generate other powerful benefits. However, it takes discipline, commitment, and a plan to improve your physical fitness. The same is true for your mind, and the exciting news is that by incorporating a regular mental workout into your routine, you'll be in rare air.

In my strategic coaching engagements with executives, we often develop a customized mental workout that helps them maintain a high level of resilience. The mental workout strengthens their leadership muscles by giving them a framework to ride the waves of challenges that continuously roll through their calendars. The mental workout I've created can be completed in five minutes and features the following core steps:

1. **Performance statements:** three to five keys to optimal performance (e.g., "I bring my undivided attention to meetings and do not multitask while others are talking.")
2. **Visualization:** recalling positive recent events in detail, including the sights and sounds, and imagining upcoming events and the way you'd like them to play out (e.g., replaying a one-to-one meeting with a direct report where you shared difficult feedback in an honest, direct, and caring manner)
3. **Personal statements:** one to three phrases that encapsulate your best self at work (e.g., "I am a good listener and ask thoughtful questions without judging others in order to best meet their needs.")

Rocket Burn: Scientific data in numerous disciplines shows that visualizing an activity can help improve your performance even without physically performing that activity.

If you want to be an Olympic-caliber executive, invest time training your mind to be more resilient and generate insights. What you'll need to watch out for is the activity whirlpool and status quo quicksand that pull the passive back to the mediocre middle.

Assertive executives tend to be anomalies in that they spend more time seeking gains than avoiding risk. As Sofia Viranyi and Virginia Morell commented in the journal *Scientific American,* "You can leave a piece of meat on the table and tell one of our dogs 'No!' and he will not take it. But the wolves ignore you. They'll look you in the eye and grab the meat."[9]

Be the wolf. Grab the meat.

Nonjudgmental Observation

"There is nothing either good or bad but thinking makes it so."
—William Shakespeare

Good night's sleep. Bad dream. Good weather. Bad storms. Good meal. Bad service.

Our lives are peppered with the good and the bad. But they don't have to be. In fact, they shouldn't be. Constantly assigning things with the designation as "good" or "bad" wastes both time and energy, preventing us from evolving more quickly. A key ingredient in the mental training to become an effective leader is the ability to observe events, people, and situations without passing judgment.

For those of you with children who have participated in sports, you've most likely encountered at least one of those maniacal coaches whose primary technique is yelling at players, sometimes with rhetorical questions, such as "What are you doing!?" Contrast that with UCLA's 10-time NCAA basketball championship coach John Wooden. He was studied during practices for his comments to players, and the researchers recorded and coded more than 2,000 discrete acts of teaching. Of these, only 6.9% were compliments and 6.6% were expressions of displeasure. The vast majority, 75%, were pure information: simple directions on how to play basketball.[10] Coach Wooden didn't waste time with good and bad. He objectively told the players what he wanted them to do and had them immediately do it. What if we took that approach in business?

Two areas tend to garner most of our good/bad assessments at work: people and process. Can you recall one full week where you didn't rate the actions, performance, or style of a boss, colleague, customer, supplier, or vendor as good or bad? Or a week where a strategy, meeting, decision, or other process wasn't labeled as positive or negative? Probably not.

The norm of instantly judging—assigning a rating of good or bad to things—significantly limits our ability to improve our people, processes, and business performance. It's a habit so intricately ingrained in our lives that it's a constant work in progress to overcome. And precisely because most executives won't have the discipline or commitment to overcome the act of immediate judgment is the reason it can give you a huge advantage in your career.

Off Course: Labeling people and events as either positive or negative holds us back from improvement and solidifies opinions that may not be valid over time. Stop labeling and start seeing objectively without judgment.

Tennis provides an illuminating laboratory to see the effects of immediate judgment. Anna hits her forehand into the net on set point, shouts at herself, "What are you doing!?" and then slams the extra ball into the back wall and trudges back to her serve-receive position for the next point. As her opponent bounces the ball in preparation for her serve, Anna is no closer to winning the next point because she has just wasted precious time and mental energy on something that has already happened and has absolutely no impact on the next point. By wasting that time on categorizing her shot as bad, she lost the time to mentally make the modification on her swing and didn't recalibrate her strategy for winning the game.

In business, this same process plays out each time we deem something good or bad: "What a waste of time that meeting was." "He is always unprepared for these business reviews." "That was an amazing presentation." None of these statements helps our colleagues or ourselves get better or leads to improved business performance.

Practicing nonjudgmental observation doesn't mean that we ignore what's happening. It means we observe people, situations, processes, and events as they are without categorizing them as positive or negative. This level of objective observation enables us to immediately assess and make modifications where appropriate, moving us closer to an improved condition. Not judging things as good or bad also prevents people and processes from being labeled, and needlessly condemning them to a category for one issue, when there may be many other things to consider.

For instance, labeling someone as "too tactical" would be better described with objective detail to help them improve. Transforming "too tactical" into one of the following descriptions provides the objective detail needed to help them shed that image and think, act, and plan strategically:

- He is reactive and wasting too much time on fire drills.
- She doesn't have a strategic plan driving her activities.
- He doesn't understand the difference between strategy and tactics.

Breaking the Judgment Habit

These statements all point us in a direction that can help them improve, and just as important, don't needlessly label someone as "tactical," which becomes quite difficult to shed. I've developed a simple formula for helping executives move out of the judgment mindset and behavior:

Awareness—Insight—Evolution

Awareness. Perhaps the biggest challenge in moving to nonjudgmental observation is awakening ourselves to the moments that we're judging people or things as good or bad. This is because judging has often become a habit. Researchers from MIT have broken a habit down into three phases:[11]

1. Cue (trigger)
2. Routine (behavior)
3. Reward (result)

An example of a judging behavior would be the following:

1. Cue: Monthly update meeting on new CRM system
2. Routine: Following the meeting, complaining to colleagues that the CRM update meeting is a waste of time

3. Reward: Feelings of satisfaction and superiority ("We lead much more productive and efficient meetings in our group.")

How we might change this habit of judgment:

1. Cue: Monthly update meeting on new CRM system
2. Routine: Two weeks prior to meeting, having a conversation with the meeting chair to review different formats for the session to make it more interactive, different timing (one or two times per month), or different delivery vehicles (eliminating the meeting and converting it to a video)
3. Reward: Feeling of satisfaction from improving the use of everyone's time, including your own

Insight. Once we're objectively aware of the situation, the next step is to analyze or break down the event to determine the root cause. From this analysis, we can then determine the insight—learning that leads to new value—which acts as the catalyst for the changes we need to make.

Evolution. After we've determined the learning, we now chart the path from where we are to where we want to go. This can often take the form of describing the key factors that represent the difference between the current state and the ideal future state. Here we can imagine UCLA Coach Wooden and ask, "What brief instruction can I provide to guide this process of development, for myself or others?"

There's a strange satisfaction that comes from labeling people, processes, or other items as good or bad. In some senses it feels like we've made a decision and gives us permission to stop thinking about the issue. Ultimately, though, we haven't improved the situation. Practicing non-judgmental observation requires awareness, insight, and evolution. It can dramatically improve your effectiveness as a leader, and the productivity and performance of your business. The question is: Are you ready to drop the gavel?

Trail Blazes

Mental toughness is described as "the psychological capacity to drive toward a goal, particularly in response to challenging circumstances."

Seven saboteurs to the mental side of our business performance:
1. Anchors away: allowing a comment to anchor us to an erroneous or mistaken starting point
2. Power outage: giving away our autonomy, choice, or power to another
3. Judge Dread: prematurely passing judgment on an event, person, or result as good or bad, when it's not necessarily either
4. Embracing noise: focusing on the uncontrollable elements in a situation
5. Time traveling: continually replaying past events or worrying about future events that may never occur
6. Energy vampires: putting ourselves within reach of habitually negative people
7. Brain ruts: creating artificial constraints for ourselves

Three techniques for enhancing your mental approach to the business:
1. Assert yourself: mentally resilient leaders tend to be less passive and more assertive than their counterparts.
2. Create a competitor: to ignite your efforts and fuel mental toughness, consider a competitor in your field and envision their initiatives to outperform you and use that to fuel your drive.
3. Pump some insights: incorporate a regular mental workout into your routine.

A mental workout consists of performance statements, visualization, and personal statements.

A key ingredient in the mental training to become an effective leader is the ability to observe events, people, and situations without passing judgment.

To move out of the continuous judgment loop, use this formula: Awareness—Insight—Evolution.

CHAPTER 8

Time and Calendar

"Think about your time very strategically, because it is part of your strategy. You can't let it be a reactive process that bubbles up from the bottom. You have to manage it from the top down, and you can't delegate it."

—Tom Gentile, president and CEO, Spirit AeroSystems

One of the most common refrains heard in the workplace is "I don't have enough time."

Sure you do. Unless you're operating in the fifth dimension of the Twilight Zone, we all have 24 hours per day to use as we see fit. How much of that time do you acquiesce to others and their agendas and how much of that time do you use to drive achievement of your initiatives?

Think of the 1,440 minutes in the day as marbles in a glass jar. It's your jar when you wake up. You, or your executive assistant, opens the jar and determines how many marbles to take out and to whom they get distributed. If you are constantly operating with a "don't have enough time" mindset, perhaps it's time to collect the marbles, close the jar, and rethink your approach.

If you can't effectively use your time and calendar to lead yourself to achieve your goals, it will severely diminish your capacity to lead others. Are you running your calendar or is your calendar running you? Professor Heike Bruch summarized her research on the ability of leaders to match their calendar with their priorities: "Our findings on managerial behavior should frighten you: Fully 90 percent of managers squander their time in all sorts of ineffective activities. In other words, a mere 10 percent of managers spend their time in a committed, purposeful, and reflective manner."[1]

Eliminating Time Traps

There are several traps to avoid when it comes to using time productively: multitasking, interruptions, and meetings. The crack cocaine of the business world is multitasking. Both flood the brain with dopamine, provide a brief high, and kill your productivity. The primary pipe for multitasking is your smartphone. Studies show people check their smartphones, on average, once every 10 minutes, or roughly 96 times a day.[2] This constant shuffling back and forth between tasks has become the norm and is assumed by many to be a hallmark of highly productive people. It's not.

Professor Clifford Nass's studies from Stanford University suggest that managers who continually shift between multiple tasks do not manage those tasks as well as those who focus on one thing at a time. His data show that when people switch between tasks, they take up to 30% longer to complete them and make twice as many errors as those who don't switch.[3] While multitasking may make you feel more productive, it's actually hurting your overall performance much more than you imagine. Professor Nass concluded, "High multitaskers are suckers for irrelevancy. Multitaskers were just lousy at everything."[4]

When it comes to consuming media, Americans have doubled their time investment from approximately 40 hours per week 20 years ago to 80 hours per week today. Dr. Carl Marci, a psychiatrist at Massachusetts General Hospital, offers his explanation: "How do people spend the equivalent of two full-time jobs a week consuming media? It isn't possible unless they're doing two things at once."[5] Often, multitasking happens in the presence of others, specifically in meetings. At Ford, when Alan Mulally was CEO and people were checking their phones during his meetings, he would halt the meeting, look at them and say, "What are you doing? We're making decisions here."[6]

People throughout the organization will take their cues from the actions and behaviors of the executive leadership team. If senior leaders are punctual and begin meetings on time, their direct reports tend to adopt a similar approach and a positive domino effect occurs throughout the organization. If senior leaders are checking their phones and texting during meetings, their direct reports interpret inattention during meetings as acceptable and behave in a similar fashion. This creates a negative domino effect, careening through other levels of leadership and, inadvertently, senior leaders have dramatically decreased their organization's productivity and ability to achieve their goals.

> **Off Course:** People who multitask make twice as many errors as those who don't and take 30% longer to complete tasks.

There are a host of clever ways to curtail phone checking during meetings, including paying a fee into a money jar or doing pushups if caught. The tactic of no phones out during meetings may be the simplest and most effective. Another way to increase the sense of urgency to eliminate multitasking during meetings is to calculate the cost of the meeting by multiplying the number of attendees by their hourly pay rate and then multiplying that number by .3 or 30%, which is what researchers estimate we lose due to multitasking ineffectiveness. Ask the habitual multitaskers to take that amount from their budgets and allocate it to the rest of the group. Then watch the phones disappear.

While you may not have the ability to control everyone else's proclivity for multitasking, to dramatically improve your productivity, focus on monotasking. Here are some tips for maintaining a monotasking approach to your work:

Three Ways to Monotask

1. **Block time.** If you intentionally carve out time in your calendar to work on significant initiatives, projects, and decisions, it creates a greater sense of purpose and enables you to get more done. Ensure that you and your assistant protect those time slots and don't allow others to book over them. If people are constantly calling urgent meetings to deal with fire drills, it's a strong indicator of a lack of purposeful planning. It's also a sign of a culture that doesn't respect people's work if they are continually being put in a position of having to drop what they're doing to attend to others' needs that may not even align with their goals and priorities. Ryan Breslow, self-made

billionaire and co-founder of Bolt, says, "I live a monk lifestyle. It's amazing what you can get done if you remove distractions. . . . There's too much work theater, where people go through the motions to appear busy."[7]

2. **Manage transitions.** A subtle source of diminishing productivity is what I refer to as multitopic disorder. Multitopic disorder is characterized by random movement throughout the day between different topics and formats, resulting in an accelerated depletion of attention, energy, and bandwidth. This haphazard approach to one's day results in a high number of mental transitions required to understand context and content, as well as to make decisions. To spotlight exactly how problematic this can be, a study of software engineers working on five projects simultaneously found that a startling "75% of their time was lost to switching mentally between projects—leaving only 5% work attention per project amid the fog of attention residue."[8]

As with many situations, it's helpful to first do an audit of the number of transitions you're currently making in a typical day and week. As you audit the number of transitions, be sure to include checking your mobile phone for texts and emails as these consume mental calories and add to your total number of transitions. Research has shown that workers who use computers during the day change windows or check email or other programs nearly 37 times an hour.[9] Once the audit is complete, you can use the technique of batching to reduce the number of transitions, which will dramatically improve your attention and energy levels.

3. **Batch your work.** A technique popular with some of the most productive leaders in the world, including Elon Musk and Jack Dorsey, is batching. Batching is the act of processing similar items together and can save significant energy and bandwidth by dramatically reducing the number of transitions you have during your day between different areas, topics, activities, and tasks. In the case of Musk and Dorsey, who were leading two large organizations at the same time (Musk with Tesla and SpaceX; Dorsey with Twitter and Square), they would batch their time in larger chunks such as half-days and full days in their respective companies and areas within those companies. Here is how Jack Dorsey described his approach years ago: "I theme my days.

On Monday, at both companies, I focus on management and running the company. Tuesday is focused on product. Wednesday is focused on marketing and communications and growth. Thursday is focused on developers and partnerships. Friday is focused on the company and culture and recruiting. Saturday I take off. Sunday is reflection, feedback, strategy and getting ready for the week."[10]

Prior to batching your work, it's valuable to identify where you are currently investing your time. For one week, you or your assistant can record where you're spending your time in 30-minute increments. Categorize the time investments and calculate the total amount of time spent in each. It's helpful and enlightening to then visualize the summary by graphing your time investment, with the areas or categories of time on the horizontal x-axis and hours invested on the vertical y-axis. Figure 8.1 provides an example where categories might include email, one-to-one meetings, planning, and so on.

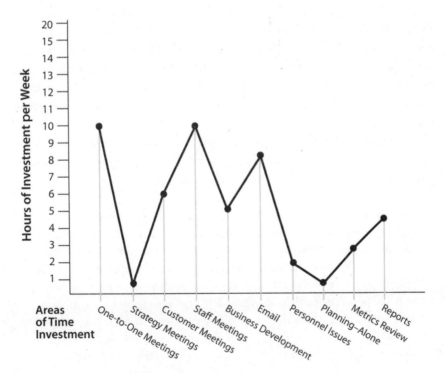

Figure 8.1 Time Investment Graph.

> **Rocket Burn:** Highly productive leaders analyze their work and then batch similar activities to attend to on specified days and times. Start with email—identify how many times a day it's necessary to review and then schedule those reviews in your calendar. And no peeking at email between those designated times!

To begin the process of batching your work, identify the groups of tasks and areas of the business that you are working on during the week. Consider batching areas of the business for certain days. For example, talent issues on Monday afternoon, operations issues on Tuesday morning, board member relationship building on Wednesday mornings, and one-to-ones with direct reports on Thursdays.

Another example is batching email review and processing at three intervals per day (e.g., 9:00 a.m., 1:00 p.m., and 4:30 p.m.). Many of you may have fallen out of your chair at the thought of only checking email three times per day, believing, "I couldn't possibly do that. I need to be highly responsive to my team." Here's a newsflash for some: your team would prefer it if you weren't checking and sending email every 15 minutes so that they could get significant work done and not be continually chasing fire drills. And for nearly everyone out there: you're not a trauma surgeon—there isn't a patient waiting on a table somewhere for you to save their life by checking your email every few minutes.

In addition to monotasking as a proven method for improving productivity, here are several other techniques to consider implementing in your approach to mastering time and calendar:

Scoring. An effective tool to enhance your performance is scoring. We can fall into ruts where we're continuing to perform activities that are no longer adding value or helping us achieve our goals. Scoring puts tasks and activities under a microscope for closer examination to determine their real worth. A simple scale such as 0 – 3 [0 = no value, 1 = low value, 2 = moderate value, 3 = high value] can be an effective way to evaluate meetings and other regularly occurring items on your schedule. For each meeting, interaction, activity, or task during the day that lasts greater than 15 minutes, score it on a scale of 0–3. At the end of the week, review the scoring and take the following actions based on the scores:

0 = Eliminate or delegate these activities.

1 = Determine how to increase their value; if their value cannot be raised, eliminate or delegate them.

2 = Determine how to increase their value; if their value cannot be raised any further, spend less time on them or delegate them to someone else.

3 = Look to invest the same amount or perhaps more time in these areas.

Minimizing Interruptions. As the mountains of research on multitasking's harm have shown, it's crucial that a leader intentionally guards their time and channels larger chunks of it to monotask the activities creating the greatest value. While a key aspect of a leader's role is to serve others, that doesn't equate with allowing interruptions at any and all times of the day. The Pollyannaish idea of a leader being available to their team 24/7 smashes into the reality that interruptions severely handicap a leader's productivity on their own priorities. Research shows that on average, people are interrupted four times per hour, and nearly half the time they do not resume the previous activity or task. When they do resume the task, it's nearly 30 minutes before they get back to their original work.

In addition to regularly scheduled meetings with others, consider establishing precise methods of communication based on the needs of those you lead. One technique is to apply time frames to the various communication vehicles available. For example, text messages are restricted to information or actions that must be known or acted upon within 24 hours, emails within 72 hours, and staff meetings within one week. If you're in a situation where you have a newer team or team members who require more frequent interaction, you can create an additional interaction time period on a daily or weekly basis similar to the "office hours" concept used by university professors. The insight here is to create solutions that marry up with the context of your business and ensure that you are protecting your time against interruptions that will delay your progress.

Optimizing Email

While a few organizations have taken drastic measures to reduce the burden of email by either eliminating it altogether or creating and enforcing strict protocols, research shows that a majority of leaders still spend at least 30% of their time on email, approximately 2.4 hours per day. Perhaps the most startling data on email is the fact that 70% of all emails are opened within 6 seconds of their receipt due in large part to the fact that 84% of people keep their email viewable on their computer backgrounds all of the time.[11]

Following are techniques for consideration to improve productivity with email:

- Have your executive assistant be the initial filter of your email. Establish times for them to review your email throughout the day so you know when to expect new items.
- Identify criteria for emails they send to others that you would like to be copied on.
- Determine the email folders that make sense for ease of filing and reviewing.
- Divide email into congruent (those that align with your priorities), or incongruent (those that do not align with your priorities). Filter the incongruent and have standard replies that can be sent for those in the future.
- Create an action or to-do folder where your assistant can file emails that require your immediate attention with a response or action.
- Establish another channel of communication outside of email for highly urgent issues that come through email (e.g., text, voice).
- Write several standard replies to reoccurring emails (industry event invitations, vendor sales pitches, etc.).
- Determine if your assistant will handle personal emails from family and friends. If not, establish a rule that all personal emails are simply forwarded to you.
- Have one project/task list that your assistant owns that includes everything they are working on, including tasks from emails; consider color coding (e.g., red text is new information on the list).

Trail Blazes

If you can't effectively use your time and calendar to lead yourself to achieve your goals, it will severely diminish your capacity to lead others.

There are several traps to avoid when it comes to using time productively: multitasking, interruptions, and meetings.

When people multitask, they take up to 30% longer to complete tasks and make twice as many errors as those who don't switch between activities.

Three techniques to maintain a monotasking approach to work:
1. Block time in your calendar.
2. Manage the transitions from different topics.
3. Batch your work into chunks of similar activities.

Scoring tasks and meetings from 0 (no value) to 3 (high value) can shine a light on things to eliminate, improve, or delegate.

Take steps to minimize interruptions during periods of the day where you're working on bigger-picture projects that require deeper thinking.

Use recommended techniques such as executive assistant filtering and the creation of standard replies to reduce the amount of time spent on email.

PART III

Organization Fitness

"When we create organizations, we're doing it to give people focus. We're essentially giving them a license to be myopic. We're saying: This is your problem. Define your mission and create your strategy and align your resources to solve that problem. And you have the divine right to ignore all of the other stuff that doesn't align with that."
—Mark Okerstrom, former CEO, Expedia

When navigating a new trail in a wooded area, it's common to view a tree at the path's juncture from one angle and quickly move on. While it is more time consuming, it's helpful to walk around the tree in a full circle, observing it from multiple sides. This single tree can take on distinctly different appearances from various vantage points as well as different times of the day or night. Seeing a landmark from new angles can help us discover insights about its orientation and use it to find our way back.

CHAPTER 9

Organizational Foundation

"Nature uses only the longest threads to weave her patterns, so that each small piece of her fabric reveals the organization of the entire tapestry."
—Richard Feynman, American theoretical physicist

The earliest forms of navigation took place on land and sea and enabled people to move on, over, or through an intended course. Inherently, navigation is shaped by flow. Flow is to move along or circulate. Anything that inhibits flow in turn inhibits navigation, which prevents the movement from here to there.

The recurring patterns in nature, including neural networks, trees, lightning bolts, circulatory systems, and tributaries, all follow the constructal law of organization, which states, "For a flow system to persist in time it must evolve in such a way that it provides easier access to its currents."[1] From the maple tree on your front lawn to the organizational structure of your company, all structures evolve to facilitate the movement of the things that flow through them. As Adrian Bejan, professor of mechanical engineering at Duke University and author of the constructal law, writes, "Life is movement, and all movement is physics. It's about moving stuff from here to there. The constructal law observes the natural tendency of everything to evolve freely to keep moving. When the movement stops, whether it's a human being or a dried riverbed, it is 'dead,' according to thermodynamics."[2]

Organizational Structures

Thinking of your business through the lens of the constructal law can be instructive. Is your organization, division, function, and team structured in a way that facilitates the free flow of conversations, ideas, input, and strategies, or is it a dry riverbed? Here is a brief overview of the most common types of organizational structures:

Hierarchical: A pyramid shape in which decisions and assignments are typically made top down by leaders to their direct reports and other employees.

Functional: Employees are grouped according to their competencies and capabilities as represented by functional areas that are independently managed and led from the top down.

Horizontal: A flat shape with minimal layers between the executive leadership team and other employees providing a decentralized approach to decision making and responsibilities.

Divisional: Separate entities that operate independently of other divisions within the parent company and control their own resources along with their own functional teams. Typically divisions are separated based on geography, product, or markets.

Matrix: Characterized by dual or multiple chains of command (responsibilities and accountabilities), typically along product, client, project, geographic, or functional lines.

Network: Based on grouping employees, vendors, satellite locations, and other players by common relationships.

Team: Grouping of employees with varying competencies and capabilities for continual collaboration around clients, problem solving, or projects.

Rocket Burn: One of your responsibilities as a leader is to assess the organization and determine if there are any barriers or impediments to the optimal flow of activities, insights, processes, or resources.

When we organize our company, group, or team, we're doing so to provide clarity to all involved on where decisions are made, where accountability resides, where collaboration is beneficial, and where capabilities create value. When there is a universal understanding of these four foundational components, an organization can benefit from and promote the movement and flow of insights and solutions across the business.

Purpose

For any parent who has stepped on one of their children's plastic LEGO bricks as they made their way to bed at night, I too have felt your pain. Having just noted the importance of organization, seeing piles of LEGO bricks strewn across the basement floor, basking in their randomness, also took some getting used to. After a few years, I noticed the instruction manuals disappear, and instead of prefabricated boxed sets being built by my son Luke, new creations of his own design began to take shape. Then, when he was 15 years old, he designed and built the world's first life-sized, fully functioning pinball machine made entirely of LEGO (https://www.youtube.com/watch?v=H_KaJtnIAoQ), winning the prized Red Brick first place award for Best Replica out of more than 1,000 adult exhibitors at the Brickworld Convention. Six months later, he constructed a six-foot-tall fully functioning arcade style claw machine entirely out of LEGO and the headline in *Mental Floss* magazine read, "LEGO Genius Built a Fully Functioning Claw Machine with More Than 13,000 Bricks."[3] The LEGO Group's purpose is described as "Inspire and Develop the Builders of Tomorrow." Millions of parents around the world, including myself, can attest to the power of this purpose.

Mission

In business, there are three types of purpose that can inspire the members of an organization to consistently give their best effort. A mission statement expresses the current purpose, or why you exist. A vision statement captures the future purpose, what you aspire to be. And values are the guiding purpose, the core beliefs that influence people's thinking and actions. When taken together and developed by capturing the organization's unique characteristics, they can help shape strategy, make decisions, and anchor activity in key focal areas.

The mission statement expresses the "why?"—why does your organization exist? Examples of mission statements:

Starbucks: To inspire and nurture the human spirit—one person, one cup and one neighborhood at a time.

American Red Cross: To prevent and alleviate human suffering in the face of emergencies by mobilizing the power of volunteers and the generosity of donors.

Forbes: To convene, curate, and cover the most influential leaders and entrepreneurs who are driving change, transforming business, and making a significant impact on the world.

Tesla: To accelerate the world's transition to sustainable energy.

LinkedIn: Connect the world's professionals to make them more productive and successful.

Cirque du Soleil: Invoke the imagination, provoke the senses, and evoke the emotions of people around the world.

Under Armour: Make all athletes better through passion, design, and the relentless pursuit of innovation.

LEGO: Inspire and develop the builders of tomorrow. Our ultimate purpose is to inspire and develop children to think creatively, reason systematically and release their potential to shape their own future—experiencing the endless human possibility.

Consider the following questions as you develop or reevaluate your mission statement:

1. What function is performed?
2. How is the function performed?
3. For whom is the function performed?
4. Why is the function performed?
5. What tone will convey the company's uniqueness?

Satya Nadella, CEO of Microsoft, wrote in a memo to employees, "I believe that we can do magical things when we come together with a shared mission, clear strategy, and a culture that brings out the best in us individually and collectively."[4]

Vision

The vision statement paints a picture of the organization's desired future—what it seeks to become in the future, 10–20 years and beyond. Here are some examples of vision statements:

Avon: Our vision is to be the company that best understands and satisfies the product, service and self-fulfillment needs of women globally.

Southwest Airlines: To be the world's most loved, most efficient, and most profitable airline.

Amazon: Our vision is to be Earth's most customer-centric company; to build a place where people can come to find and discover anything they might want to buy online.

Hertz: We will be the first-choice brand for vehicle and equipment rental/leasing and total mobility solutions.

Nordstrom: To serve our customers better, to always be relevant in their lives, and to form lifelong relationships.

Warby Parker: We believe that buying glasses should be easy and fun. It should leave you happy and good-looking, with money in your pocket. We also believe that everyone has the right to see.

Ikea: To create a better everyday life for many people.

Netflix: Becoming the best global entertainment distribution service.

Consider the following questions as you develop or reevaluate your vision statement:

1. Does it paint a picture of the desired future?
2. Will it create a burning ambition?
3. Is it distinct from long-term goals?
4. Does it allow for creativity and flexibility?
5. Can people imagine the realistic pursuit of it?

As Jeff Bezos, founder of Amazon, said, "We are stubborn on vision. We are flexible on details."[5]

Values

Values are the three to five strongest and most differentiating beliefs guiding the thoughts and actions of an organization's people. These beliefs are manifested in the predominant behaviors that define the organization's culture. Here are examples of values statements:

MD Anderson Cancer Center: Caring; Integrity; Discovery; Safety; Stewardship.

Target: More for your money; The best shopping experiences; A healthy, happy, and valued team; A brighter future; Ethical business practices.

Build-A-Bear: Reach; Learn; Di-bear-sity; Colla-bear-ate; Give; Cele-bear-ate.

Headspace: Selfless drive; Courageous heart; Curious mind.

CoverMyMeds: Be Yourself; Do the Right Thing; Embrace Challenges; Results Matter; Be Selfless.

Lululemon: Personal responsibility; Entrepreneurship; Honesty; Courage; Connection; Fun; Inclusion.

Zoom Communications: Care: for Community, Customers, Company, Teammates, Selves.

Intuit: Integrity without Compromise; Customer Obsession; Stronger Together; We Care and Give Back; Courage.

Consider the following questions as you develop or reevaluate your values statement:

1. What ideals and principles do we believe in deeply?
2. What traits are essential in delivering on our mission and reaching our vision?
3. What characteristics make us unique?
4. What are the behaviors we'd like to see spring from these values?
5. How would we describe our best selves in the service of our customers?

Danny Meyer, founder of Union Square Hospitality Group, said: "It's the job of any business owner to be clear about the company's nonne-gotiable core values. They're the riverbanks that help guide us as we refine and improve on performance and excellence. A lack of riverbanks creates estuaries and cloudy waters that are confusing to navigate. I want a crystal-clear, swiftly flowing stream."[6]

As you assess, create, and hone your mission, vision, and values statements, be aware of and avoid the following three Purpose Pitfalls:

1. CC: A carbon copy in email is often unnecessary or a CYA move, and in purpose statements, it's even worse because it means your mission, vision, or values look the same as everyone else's in the market. If you can replace your organization's name with a competitor and the statement still holds true, use the guiding questions to dig a deeper divide of differentiation.
2. Bogus: As the character Jeff Spicoli from the 1980s movie *Fast Times at Ridgemont High* explained to his high school history teacher, "So what Jefferson was saying was 'Hey! You know, we left this England place because it was bogus. So if we don't get some cool rules ourselves, pronto, we'll just be bogus too.'" Same goes for purpose statements. If it's not true to who you really are or who you're investing resources to become, then don't include it. Innovation, I'm looking at you!
3. Blah: As in *blah, blah, blah* . . . too many well-intentioned purpose statements become rambling manifestos that include each and every idea that the committee surfaced in the 90-minute brainstorming session. Typically, concision is power and shorter is more memorable.

Culture

Culture can be defined as a system of shared behaviors based on core values. Just as strategy is more about how your people utilize their resources (time, talent, budget) on a regular basis than what's written in the PowerPoint deck, culture is more about how your team behaves each day than the values framed on the walls of HQ. Values are the traits that guide the thoughts and actions of a group. Behaviors are the observable activities of your people. Has your leadership team clearly defined the values and behaviors that form the foundation of your culture?

To be described as "strategic" is to possess insight that leads to advantage. Therefore, a strategic culture is a system of shared behaviors that cultivates learnings, leading to new value. Here are three techniques to shape a strategic culture:

1. **Remove the poison.** Sometimes the biggest boost to culture is not through addition but rather subtraction. Poison is defined as "a substance with an inherent property that destroys life or impairs health." FamilyDoctor.org suggests, "The best way to prevent poisoning is to avoid contact with the harmful substance. . . . The first step is to remove the poison if you can." When it comes to an organization's culture, poison can come in three forms: negativity, bullying, and blame. Even in large organizations, it only takes one person to poison the culture.

> **Off Course:** In his book, *Championship Behaviors*, former U.S. Olympic Men's Volleyball gold-medal-winning coach Hugh McCutcheon cites the Rule of 1.5 as it relates to dealing with chronically dysfunctional people: "You should have no more than one-and-a-half people who are not culturally aligned on your team at any given time. The first rule of behavior is that you get what you tolerate. You should only tolerate dysfunction until you can teach that person to become functional, or until you can replace them."[7]

Negativity manifests itself in attitudes such as killing the energy in a room instead of creating it, focusing on problems instead of proposing solutions, and shutting down others and their ideas instead of inviting and exploring new options. Bullying is defined by the Workplace Bullying Institute as "a pattern of repeated mistreatment, abusive conduct or work sabotage that humiliates, intimidates, or harms the target and interferes with the ability to work." Blaming is the continual refusal to accept responsibility and accountability for outcomes of situations and faulting others for not delivering the expected results.

A leader who manages a person who repeatedly exhibits one or more of these three forms of poison—negativity, bullying, and blaming—should only be asking one question: Why am I allowing my best people—the high performers who represent our ideal values—to ingest this poison each and every day? It's common to rationalize the company should keep the poison pill—they're a high performer/producer, they're just having a bad week/month/year, they've been a long-time, loyal supporter—and all this rationale taken together just forms a higher mound of manure. A leader who tolerates and makes excuses for a person who carries these poisons eventually loses credibility in the eyes of their followers and before long will also lose their best people, who ironically represented the ideal behaviors of the culture. Remove the poison . . . now.

2. **Upgrade the team.** In the arts, business, and sports, it's common to hear people equate their culture to that of a family. In these cases, they're referring to positive family characteristics such as caring, loyalty, and unconditional support. Even if Uncle Tony quits his job, sleeps all day, and constantly borrows beer money, he's still in the clan. Reed Hastings, CEO of Netflix, prefers a different analogy: "If we are going to be a championship team, then we want the best performer in every position. The old notion is that an employee has to do something wrong or be inadequate to lose their job. But in a pro, or Olympic, sports team, the players understand the coach's role is to upgrade—if necessary—to move from good to great."[8]

Hastings's notion of constantly looking to upgrade is a dramatically different approach than most organizations take to managing their talent. Let's start with tolerating consistent underperformance. First, we need to determine the root cause of underperformance and assess whether the person has received the appropriate amount of preparation, training, and tools to succeed in their role. If the answer is no, then those steps need to be taken to provide them with the proper development. Once those areas have been adequately addressed, the responsibility shifts to the underperformer.

In multiple studies, groups with one underperformer did worse than other teams by a whopping 30–40%. Worse yet, the behavior of the one underperforming individual was adopted by other group members despite the fact they were only together for about one hour. A researcher commented, "Eerily surprising was how the others on the team would start to take on the [underperforming] person's characteristics."[9] Underperformance by one person leads to underperformance by many.

Executives working through succession planning can use a Talent Scorecard to assess their key employees on a monthly basis. The Talent Scorecard is a real-time gauge to determine performance in areas such as technical capability, people leadership, and executive skills. This helps leaders have a constant pulse on performance and offers them a way to influence changes in a highly responsive fashion. In high–performance organizations, leaders are always looking at options for improving the team's ability to achieve its goals. This coupled with a "two–deep approach" to key positions asserts that the leader and their HR partners always have two other personnel options for key roles—one internal and one external—that can take performance to a higher level. As Stella & Dot Jewelry's founder Jessica Herrin said, "Shaping your culture is more than half done when you hire your team."[10]

3. **Set the thermostat.** One of the universal truths of a leadership team offsite meeting is that the temperature of the meeting room is never quite right for everyone.

"Is it cold in here or is it just me?"

"Yes, it is cold. I'm putting on my jacket."

Five minutes later, a person on the other side of the room says, "Is it warm in here or is it just me?" The temperature tango continues.

One of the keys to a strategic culture is setting the thermostat. Unlike the thermometer that reacts to the temperature around it, the thermostat establishes and maintains a desired temperature. Does your culture feel more like a reactionary thermometer—fire drills and flavor-of-the-month initiatives—or a carefully calibrated thermostat?

The development of a Strategic Culture Map is an effective way to begin shaping your culture without using a command-and-control approach that is sure to backfire. The process to develop a Strategic Culture Map includes charting the three-year GOST Framework (goals, objectives, strategies, tactics), overlaying the values and behaviors critical to achieving the GOST Framework, and creating the environment that nurtures the desired behaviors. The result is a one-page process visual that captures and communicates the directional elements and guiding principles of the strategic culture that all leaders can use to reinforce the desired values and behaviors.

For instance, your GOST Framework may include building a new ecosystem platform to connect your customers with third-party suppliers. The construction of this new ecosystem platform will require the key behaviors of enhanced collaboration and consultative inquiry. The environment to nurture these new behaviors may feature a change to the incentive compensation plan to focus on effort and willingness to collaborate and the dismantling of the IT department to move IT resources directly to the business partners. The key is to use the Strategic Culture Map as a real-time repository for new insights about what's working and what needs to be enhanced relative to your system of shared behaviors.

The adage "Hope is not a strategy" should be followed with "and culture shouldn't be left to chance." Founders of successful companies drive a distinct culture in the early years that is fundamental to their growth. However, like a rose garden overrun with weeds, a culture left unattended can become choked with inconsistent values and negative behaviors. Shaping a strategic culture starts with a clear understanding of what you're trying to achieve, and it's realized through the right behaviors. Are you the thermostat or the thermometer? You're getting warmer. . . .

Internal Obstacles

When we think about competition, in sports we point to the team on the opposing bench. In politics, we point to the group with the opposing policy views. In business, we point to the company with the opposing products or services. But what if your most dangerous business competitor wasn't across town, online, or a global behemoth? What if it was you?

Research by Bain & Company on the factors that cause companies to miss their financial goals found that 90% of the time, the primary causes were internal. Surveys with more than 400 executives across 56 companies found that 94% of executives in large companies identified internal issues as the key barrier to profitable growth.[11] Let's review five internal competitors and techniques for overcoming them.

1. **Complexity.** As an organization grows, layers of process, systems, products, services, and people grow to support it. However, if the growth in these areas isn't approached in a thoughtful way, the organization begins to look like the tree that never gets pruned. The unmanaged complexity becomes the root cause of slowing down the decision-making processes, wasting resources on projects that aren't adding real value and fogging up the strategic direction. If you've missed opportunities because of slow decision making, or are not

crystal clear on the company's mission, vision, goals, objectives, and strategies, complexity may be clouding your view.

2. **Silos.** While silos have proven to be helpful in containing and protecting valued materials such as grain or coal, in business they can fracture a company's success by cutting off people and their ideas from one another. Silos can be just as prevalent in small companies with dozens of people as they are in global enterprises with tens of thousands of people. Silos can be intentionally constructed to protect budgets and power bases or unintentionally developed as groups operate without a keen awareness of what their colleagues in other functional areas are doing. If you don't understand how your work meshes with the work of your colleagues in other departments or levels, then silos may be rising.

3. **No priorities.** One of the great sources of frustration in business is working for a leader where everything—and consequently nothing— is a priority. Working on too many initiatives or tasks without clear priorities submerges people's will to the point where they are frantically trying to keep their heads above water. A leader who does not establish clear priorities for their team isn't a leader at all—they're an order taker at a fast-food drive-through window. Instagram co-founder Kevin Systrom said, "Most companies that serve half a billion people have thousands of people. We're still in the hundreds, so we have to focus. It's prioritizing that makes us efficient and makes us succeed."[12] If you can't identify the businesse's top-three priorities, when another nonprioritized request comes in, ask if they'd like fries with that.

4. **Risk aversion.** Human nature demonstrates that we have an affinity for the status quo. While change may be good and even necessary in certain circumstances, it takes effort and discipline to escape the pull of the safe or familiar route. If the aversion to risk and doing things differently is left unchecked, it can cause us to miss taking advantage of some game-changing opportunities. When Amazon founder Jeff Bezos was asked, "What would you say has been the nature of your biggest strategic mistakes?" he replied, "I think most big errors are errors of omission rather than errors of commission. They are the ones that companies never get held to account for—the times when they were in a position to notice something and act on it, had the

skills and competencies or could have acquired them, and yet failed to do so."[13] If you continually allow promising new opportunities to go by because they all seem too risky, then a culture of risk aversion is being cemented.

5. **Fire drills.** Fire drills are events where urgent but unimportant matters receive an undue number of resources—attention, time, people, and budget—to resolve them. While they may seem like exciting and adrenaline-inducing activities, they should not be confused with real work. In some companies, managers who react and respond to fire drills quickly are viewed as go-getters, when in fact the only thing they should be getting is your coffee. As Henry David Thoreau wrote, "It's not enough to be busy, so are the ants. The question is, what are we busy about?" If you work in an environment where urgent but unimportant events receive immediate resources, you're going to need a bigger hose.

To help eliminate these internal competitors, consider using the following techniques:

Strategy conversations. If your meetings and videoconferences continually devolve into reactionary fire drills and the same discussions about the same tactics, it's time to add a little structure. I've found the most effective managers are the ones who dedicate separate meetings or blocks of time to strategy, operations, budgets, and tactical activities. Fail to keep these separate and the discussion will lunge to tactics in the first five minutes. Make these strategy conversations productive by ensuring each in-person or video meeting meets three criteria: intent (goals for the interaction), decisions (items to move forward), and insights (identifying the key learnings).

Decision rights. A simple method of eliminating several internal competitors is to assign decision rights for specific initiatives, projects, events, or processes (see steps in Chapter 3). Too often, opportunities are missed and complexity results in confusion because it's not clear who owns the decision. There are a host of frameworks, including RACI (Responsible, Accountable, Consulted, Informed) and RAPID (Recommend, Agree, Perform, Input, Decide), that help clarify the various roles that ensure decisions are being made and acted upon.

I've found that visually mapping the events or processes that are causing bottlenecks and then overlaying the different roles, including who has decision rights, is a powerful tool for change.

Trade-offs. It's one thing to know that great strategy is as much about what you choose *not* to do as it is about what you choose to do. It's another to have the courage to make those trade-offs. Strategy inherently involves risk because by making a trade-off, you are intentionally saying no to certain internal and even external customers to focus your value. Develop your priorities by focusing on those items that are most essential to helping you achieve your goals and strategies. Then prune the extraneous activities and tasks that are not instrumental in helping you achieve your goals.

It's comfortable to make an external competitor the bad guy, the one keeping us from turning a profit or being successful. In some cases, the external competitor is changing the value equation in the market, and they are a legitimate obstacle to overcome. But in many cases, the real issues are staring us in the face on a daily basis because they are internal. Look in the mirror. What do you see? Friend or foe?

Trail Blazes

The constructal law of organization states: "For a flow system to persist in time it must evolve in such a way that it provides easier access to its currents."

Seven types of organizational structures:
1. Hierarchical: A pyramid shape in which decisions and assignments are typically made top down by leaders to their direct reports and other employees.
2. Functional: Employees are grouped according to their competencies and capabilities as represented by functional areas that are independently managed and led from the top down.
3. Horizontal: A flat shape with minimal layers between the executive leadership team and other employees, providing a decentralized approach to decision making and responsibilities.
4. Divisional: Separate entities that operate independently of other divisions within the parent company and control their own resources along with their own functional teams. Typically divisions are separated based on geography, product, or markets.

5. Matrix: Characterized by dual or multiple chains of command (responsibilities and accountabilities), typically along product, client, project, geographic, or functional lines.
6. Network: Based on grouping employees, vendors, satellite locations, and other players by common relationships.
7. Team: Grouping of employees with varying competencies and capabilities for continual collaboration around clients, problem solving, or projects.

A mission statement expresses the current purpose, or why you exist. A vision statement captures the future purpose, what you aspire to be. And values are the guiding purpose, the core beliefs that influence people's thinking and actions.

Culture can be described as a system of shared behaviors based on core values.

Three techniques to shape a strategic culture:
1. Remove the poison
2. Upgrade the team
3. Set the thermostat

Five internal competitors to overcome:
1. Complexity
2. Silos
3. No priorities
4. Risk aversion
5. Fire drills

Three techniques to overcome internal dysfunction:
1. Strategy conversations
2. Decision rights
3. Trade-offs

CHAPTER 10

Business Model

"The holy grail of strategic thinking is, how do you come up with a business model that differentiates you, creates value for your customers and puts you in a unique position in your industry?"
—Sam Palmisano, former CEO, IBM

At the core of a company is the business model. While the business model receives the white-hot spotlight of attention during a company's startup phase as it's raising capital and generating the first drops of revenue, it is typically ignored once the organization is launched. Attention turns to products, sales, and budgets, with little ongoing regard for the core of the company. Does your team find itself battling competitors primarily on product specifications and pricing? If so, then you have a tremendous opportunity to separate yourself from the pack through business model innovation.

Research has shown companies that continue to develop and innovate their business models outperform industry peers by 7% in total return to shareholders over a three-year period.[1] While cool new products garner the lion's share of publicity in business publications, it's the innovation of business models that transforms industries. As *Fortune* magazine senior editor Geoff Colvin writes, "Business-model innovation is the new essential competency. It's hard. It will separate tomorrow's winners from the losers."[2]

A business model is how your group creates, delivers, and captures value. For instance, a professional services firm in the area of marketing can create value through the development of a proprietary brand design process; a creative staff, including writers, graphic designers, and web developers; and an account management team steeped in business acumen that translates into winning competitive strategies for their clients. They might deliver value through the production of digital media campaigns, ecommerce websites, and AR/VR customer experiences developed on their clients' behalf. They can capture value through a project fee, retainer, or hourly billing rate, and potentially winning industry creative achievement awards.

Evolving Your Business Model

Here are three techniques to consider as you assess ways to enhance your business model:

1. **Swim downstream.** Most organizations focus their efforts on the upstream, or the Create phase of the business model. These efforts take the form of new product development and product line extensions—the "what" people buy. However, it can prove extremely profitable to invest time exploring downstream, or the Deliver phase of the business model. Downstream activities focus primarily on interaction with the customer—how offerings are purchased, delivered, used, saved, or discarded. Whether it's purchasing a LEGO set from an airport vending machine, ordering a Wolfgang Puck fennel sausage pizza from a self-service kiosk, or Tesla introducing showroom stores and operating all of its own service centers, it's worthwhile to check the temperature of the water downstream. It can also be more profitable. Think how often we are willing to pay a higher price for the same product delivered in a different way or location, as in that piping hot cup of coffee at the rustic Colorado ski lodge as opposed to the bag of ground coffee from the local supermarket.

> **Rocket Burn:** A maniacal focus on improving product features can obfuscate the path to greater innovation that can be found by focusing on the "how" instead of the "what." Move your thinking from the "what" (product) to where, when, and how your offerings are experienced by customers.

A tool I developed to help you think through options for creative ways of moving from the upstream to the downstream is the Downstream Growth Grid. Column one identifies the three phases of the business model: Create, Deliver, and Capture. Create value is *what* you are offering to customers and is represented in the Upstream. Deliver value is the Downstream *how* value is accessed—where the offering is purchased, delivered, and used and encapsulates the user's experience with it. Capture value represents the revenue generating options (how much) in the Downstream.

Using bottled water as an example in Table 10.1, the Upstream Create (what) would include the sourcing, production, bottling, and packaging. The Downstream Deliver area (how) would include distribution through grocers, warehouse clubs, convenience stores, vending machines, and concession stands. The Downstream Capture (how much) would be the revenue generated from sales in different forums, such as

Table 10.1   Downstream Growth Grid.

UPSTREAM (What)	Business Model	Bottled Water
	Create Value (Offering)	Sourcing, production, bottling, packaging
DOWNSTREAM (How)	**Deliver Value** (Access point, use, storage, disposal, service, network, experience, reliability, knowledge, reputation)	Large scale distribution: grocers, warehouse clubs, convenience stores, vending machines, concession stands
DOWNSTREAM (How Much)	**Capture Value** (Revenue streams: subscription, usage, licensing, leasing, renting, advertising, broker, sponsorships)	Walmart: $.01/Fl.Oz. Amazon: $.13/Fl.Oz. Concession Stand: $.31/Fl.Oz.

Walmart at \$.01/fl. oz., Amazon at \$.13/fl. oz., and \$.31/fl. oz. at a professional sports team's concession stand. Consider how your team delivers value to your customers. How might you change the delivery method or access points of your offering through technology, place, and experience to add greater value and capture more revenue?

2. **Change your capture.** One of the primary mental ruts business leaders fall into revolves around how they capture value in the form of sales and profits. Manufacturers tend to just sell things, brokers tend to just collect brokers fees, and subscription services tend to just issue subscriptions. This singular-path mindset can significantly stunt growth because it ignores the host of other options for generating revenue. However, old dogs can learn new tricks, as evidenced by one of the oldest businesses around, Procter & Gamble.

   Founded in 1837, this consumer goods company has recently shaken up how they capture value. In addition to their traditional product sales and their more recent foray into product subscriptions, Procter & Gamble introduced Tide Cleaners. These stand-up retail locations offer customers dry cleaning, shirt laundry, wash-and-fold laundry, household items cleaning, wedding dress cleaning, and even shoe cleaning and repair. Users can download an app to drop off and pick up their laundry at a conveniently located locker or visit a Tide Cleaners store.

   In addition to their community locations, they are also popping up on college campuses. including the University of Alabama, Baylor University, and Texas Christian University, to name a few. Consider how your team has historically captured value relative to the other potential options: sales, subscriptions, advertising, brokerage fees, rental fees, licensing, and so on. What other value capture channels could you employ for your offerings?

3. **Deviate from the norm.** One of the most productive exercises in the strategic thinking workshops I lead involves a methodical process for deviating from the norm. Excellence can be described as "deviation from the norm." In order to excel, you can't simply do the same normal things in the same normal ways as everyone else—you must deviate from the normal course of action.

GymGuyz deviated from the norm in the personal training industry to become one of the fastest-growing franchise brands in the U.S., serving more than 700 cities, along with locations in Canada and the United Kingdom. Their motto is: "We bring the workout to you." GymGuyz stocks vans with 365 pieces of workout equipment and then delivers the workout to the location of your choosing, whether that's a park, a pool, or a parking lot. GymGuyz offers a good example of deviating from the norm—instead of going to the gym—they bring the gym to you.

Consider how your team creates, delivers, and captures value. In what ways might you deviate from the norm in these business model phases to create greater differentiated value? When we look at the business model through this lens of create-deliver-capture, it's clear to see how this framework can be used by business units, functional areas, and intact teams to generate ways to enhance value to both external and internal customers.

Creating a Value Proposition

An important component of increasing the value you bring to customers through your business model is the value proposition. The value proposition describes the rationale behind why customers would choose your offering over others. While the creation of a clear value proposition would appear to be a given for the leaders of any organization, research shows it's not. As authors Robert Kaplan and David Norton write, "In our research, we have found that although a clear definition of the value proposition is the single most important step in developing a strategy, approximately three-quarters of executive teams do not have consensus about this basic information."[3]

The value proposition can be broken down into four pieces:

1. Who: customer to be served
2. What: need to be met or job to be done
3. How: unique approach to satisfy need or fulfill job
4. Benefit: customer's advantage of using the offering

The value proposition begins with a specific customer segment and their unmet need, or job to be done, and explains how they uniquely provide their offerings along with the resulting benefits. Value propositions can be developed at both the offering and organizational levels. The following is a hypothetical example of a value proposition at the offering level for the Apple iPhone:

> The Apple iPhone serves affluent customers with premium designed communication and computing devices through a unique, secure ecosystem of interconnected services including iCloud, the App Store, and iTunes resulting in a high-quality, reliable, safe, and hassle-free user experience.

From this example, we see the elements of the value proposition clearly identified:

1. Who: affluent customers
2. What: premium, high-end designed communication and computing device
3. How: unique secure ecosystem of interconnected services including iCloud, the App Store, and iTunes
4. Benefit: high-quality, reliable, safe, and hassle-free user experience

The next example is at the organizational level and features Amazon Marketplace, the consumer website:

> Amazon serves consumers and sellers who are looking to purchase and sell products through an easy-to-use online platform featuring the ability to search and compare competitive offerings from the largest selection of products in the world resulting in a fast, cost-effective, and convenient shopping experience.

After reviewing each of these examples, it becomes readily apparent why Amazon and Apple have become the dominant players in their respective markets. Their market dominance is in direct proportion to the extraordinary value they have created and delivered, which is captured and represented in their profits.

If your team is struggling to find differentiation in your value proposition, imagine how your customers feel. If you have a clear value proposition, each member of your organization should be able to answer this question: What is the primary differentiated value our offering provides to customers?

Mapping a Value Chain

A useful tool for analyzing the strategically relevant activities that make up your business model is the value chain. Originally conceived by Harvard Business School professor Michael Porter, he describes his rationale as such: "I developed the notion that competitive strategy is manifested in the discrete activities a company performs in competing in a particular business. Activities such as order processing, process design, repair and sales force operations, are narrower than functions (e.g., marketing and production) . . . my conclusion is that activities were actually the causal, first order unit of analysis where the choices needed to be made and where the advantages arose."[4]

A value chain visually depicts the configuration of key activities used to create, deliver, and capture value. Value chains can be developed at the industry level and the firm level. They typically consist of primary activities or player activities and the secondary activities that contribute to each primary activity. Examining an industry or business at the activity level focuses a lens on areas of differentiation and costs, the two key contributing factors in a customer's perception of value. Figure 10.1 is an example of a value chain constructed by player activities for the rather complex healthcare industry.

Due to its complexity, there are a number of ways to approach the representation of the primary and secondary activities in the healthcare industry. In this example, the primary activities are represented by the key players or roles and the secondary activities represent the functions these players perform in the creation, access, and delivery of healthcare. Note that there are a number of tertiary activities that could have been added, but the intent was to present a reasonable representation of the healthcare industry and offer a starting point for analysis and discussion.

If you're a member of the healthcare industry, it can be beneficial to explore the following questions:

1. What is the unique value we currently provide within the chain?
2. How do we see the value chain evolving in the next three years?
3. What opportunities could we create to change our role or activities within the chain to create greater value in the future?

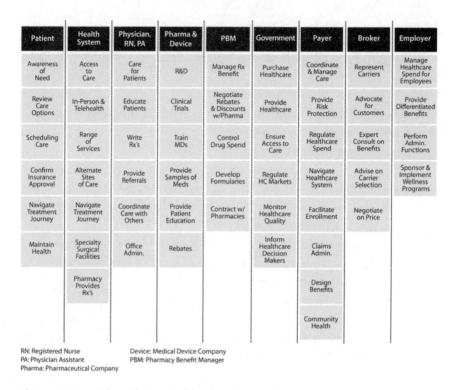

Patient	Health System	Physician, RN, PA	Pharma & Device	PBM	Government	Payer	Broker	Employer
Awareness of Need	Access to Care	Care for Patients	R&D	Manage Rx Benefit	Purchase Healthcare	Coordinate & Manage Care	Represent Carriers	Manage Healthcare Spend for Employees
Review Care Options	In-Person & Telehealth	Educate Patients	Clinical Trials	Negotiate Rebates & Discounts w/Pharma	Provide Healthcare	Provide Risk Protection	Advocate for Customers	Provide Differentiated Benefits
Scheduling Care	Range of Services	Write Rx's	Train MDs	Control Drug Spend	Ensure Access to Care	Regulate Healthcare Spend	Expert Consult on Benefits	Perform Admin. Functions
Confirm Insurance Approval	Alternate Sites of Care	Provide Referrals	Provide Samples of Meds	Develop Formularies	Regulate HC Markets	Navigate Healthcare System	Advise on Carrier Selection	Sponsor & Implement Wellness Programs
Navigate Treatment Journey	Navigate Treatment Journey	Coordinate Care with Others	Provide Patient Education	Contract w/ Pharmacies	Monitor Healthcare Quality	Facilitate Enrollment	Negotiate on Price	
Maintain Health	Specialty Surgical Facilities	Office Admin.	Rebates		Inform Healthcare Decision Makers	Claims Admin.		
	Pharmacy Provides Rx's					Design Benefits		
						Community Health		

RN: Registered Nurse
PA: Physician Assistant
Pharma: Pharmaceutical Company

Device: Medical Device Company
PBM: Pharmacy Benefit Manager

Figure 10.1   Value Chain: Healthcare Industry.

Examining an industry value chain can be helpful in thinking through where the profit pools currently exist and where you believe value may migrate over the next few years. This in turn can inform you as to what competencies, capabilities, and activities should be developed and implemented to capture the greatest share of this value in the future.

Using a similar process, a value chain can be constructed for your company as well as competitor organizations within your industry to assess and compare the key contributing activities to differentiation and cost. Figure 10.2 offers a hypothetical value chain for Uber.

In this example, we've hypothesized that Uber's primary activities include inbound logistics, operations, marketing and sales, and service. The secondary activities under each can then be scrutinized for current levels of differentiation and cost as well as projected levels of future value relative to the competition.

Once we've broken things down to the individual activity level, we can assess the activities and, equally as important, the linkages between

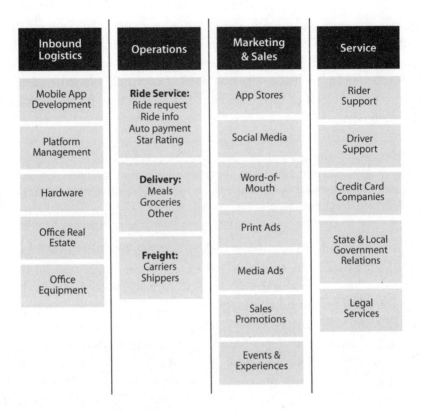

Inbound Logistics	Operations	Marketing & Sales	Service
Mobile App Development	**Ride Service:** Ride request Ride info Auto payment Star Rating	App Stores	Rider Support
Platform Management		Social Media	Driver Support
Hardware	**Delivery:** Meals Groceries Other	Word-of-Mouth	Credit Card Companies
Office Real Estate		Print Ads	State & Local Government Relations
Office Equipment	**Freight:** Carriers Shippers	Media Ads	
		Sales Promotions	Legal Services
		Events & Experiences	

Figure 10.2   Value Chain: Uber.

the activities. The linkages between activities can lead to competitive advantage through both optimization (combining activities across functions to become more efficient or effective) and coordination (providing a seamless offering to customers).

Designing the Future State

"Friends congratulate me after a quarterly earnings announcement and say, 'Great quarter!' I say, 'Thanks, but that quarter was baked three years ago.'"

—Jeff Bezos, founder, Amazon

Are you working on a quarter that will happen three years from now? How about three weeks from now? Three days? If you're like the majority of leaders, the answer is no. In fact, 63% of leaders surveyed said they do not have a plan with a time horizon greater than one year, and half of leaders don't have a formal plan for this year![5] You wouldn't trust a pilot without a flight plan, and you wouldn't trust a physician without a treatment plan for your affliction. Why then would we trust a leader who isn't capable of or disciplined enough to set a plan for the future of their business?

> **Off Course:** Being so consumed with the current business so as not to spend any time thinking about the future of the business is derelict in one's duty as a leader. Future thinking can be inspiring and potentially generate new ideas on enhancing the current state of the business as well.

The best leaders I've worked with have a plan for their current business, and also dedicate time to thinking about the future state of their business—how they would like to be positioned for the next three to five years. While your initial thought may be your team is too consumed working on their current business to spend time discussing the future, I've found that it can be a highly energizing experience. Frans van Houten, CEO of Philips, describes his approach to this balance: "We talk about the need to both perform and transform. If you only transform but don't perform, you have no here and now. If you only perform but don't transform, you have no future. Therefore, in our scorecards we measure both. In our reviews we talk about both. And the targets I give to all my executives . . . always include some transform objectives."[6]

Shifting people's thinking to the future—new opportunities and areas for growth—moves them to a different mind space that's exciting and motivational. Following is a process guided by six key questions for helping leadership teams think through the future state of their business and prepare accordingly.

1. **Where are we today?** An underrated and untapped activity is to have your executive team talk about the current state of the business: what's working, what's not, and why. You'd be amazed at the different assumptions and perspectives on what's happening and why that result from discussing the current context of the business. The Contextual Radar, referenced earlier in the Leadership section, is a powerful tool to assist executive teams in creating a picture of the "As Is" state of

their business. The Contextual Radar facilitates conversation around what the individual leaders of the executive team are seeing with the market, customers, competitors, and company.

2. **What challenges should we solve?** Research on creativity and innovation indicates that to maximize productivity, it's helpful to establish parameters for the pursuit of new value. In this step, we use a simple formula driven by three questions to identify the most relevant customer pain points or challenges and then generate a range of potential solutions:

   1. Why do I have to . . .?
   2. What if we . . .?
   3. How could we combine . . .?

For example, the company Mirror created a business worth $500 million they sold to Lululemon by following this formula and answering the three questions specific to their customers' pain points:

1. Why do I have to go to a gym to exercise with an instructor?
2. What if we brought the gym to your home?
3. How could we combine the professional instruction of a gym with the convenience of an in-home workout?

They created "the nearly invisible home gym" housed in a sleek 52-by-21-inch reflective screen with a companion app offering expert instruction from certified trainers. The Mirror's advanced camera technology and customized playlists enables users to compete for points or connect with friends to exercise and track results.

3. **What can we do differently?** In watching the development and introduction of new products and services across many markets, it's astonishing how often new offerings converge with the competition. Competitive convergence occurs when we fail to create any meaningful and relevant differentiation from the competition. To excel, or achieve excellence, means "to deviate from the norm." Doing the same normal things in the same normal ways as the competition is a formula for failure, leaving your offerings to battle it out on price.

In this step, we think about current market norms and identify deviation from those norms in ways that customers might value. For instance, the norm in the auto industry has included two primary options for regular use of an automobile: buy or lease. Volvo was one of the first companies to deviate from this norm by offering an all-inclusive automobile subscription service characterized by no down payment, one flat monthly fee, no end-of-lease fee, and the inclusion of insurance. Volvo also provided ease of use with online or mobile app signup, fast delivery within a few weeks, and the ability to upgrade to a new car after twelve months.

4. **How can we do things differently?** Former Apple CEO Steve Jobs said, "Creativity is just connecting things." One of the great untapped sources of growth and innovation in your business is the reconfiguration of your current offerings into new sources of customer value. To facilitate this conversation, I developed a framework called the Strategy Spectrum to visually lay out an offering's current components, alongside some new ones, and then mixing and matching combinations. To build a Strategy Spectrum, use a chart with the top row consisting of the Five Ws (what: offerings; who: customers; where: point of offerings; when: timing of offerings; why: intent of offerings); and how (use of offerings). Then below each of these headers add current factors and then some potentially new ones. Play around with different combinations across the columns to stimulate newly configured products, services, and experiences.

5. **What new value can we provide?** A huge source of frustration for sales reps and account managers within organizations is having to continually visit with customers without having any new offerings or information to share with them. To innovate is to create new value for customers, and many organizations fail to innovate because they refuse to get off the activity treadmill and dedicate time to creating new value for customers. There are a number of innovative thinking exercises you can use to stimulate your thinking around generating new value, including the Value Mining Matrix, Domain Jumping, Strategy Spectrum, and Business Model Innovation, to name just a few. These models and detailed examples can be found in the book *Elevate: The Three Disciplines of Advanced Strategic Thinking.*[7]

6. **How should our business evolve?** This final step of the Future State Process coalesces the insights from the previous questions into a focused area of customer need. This need is then used to seed the future business model by identifying how the business will create, deliver, and capture value in three to five years. As you shape the future business model, outlining the potential scenarios in that time frame along with contingency plans can be a useful exercise. To construct three to five scenarios, begin with asking the "What if . . .?" question to generate a range. Be sure to include an option or two that may be highly unlikely but could create significant disruption if it did occur. Give each scenario a concise, memorable name, identify the causal factors, consequences, and rate the impact. The final step is to complete a GOST Framework for each scenario. Figure 10.3 is a hypothetical example for a pharmaceutical company.

A survey of more than 4,000 CEOs found that nearly 40% believe their company will no longer be in business in ten years if it continues on its current path.[8] Seeing the future path requires think-time and

Issue/Topic: **Product X at Hospital Z**

		Scenario 1	Scenario 2	Scenario 3	Scenario 4
Scenarios	**What if...?**	Product taken off of Hospital Z formulary	Product moved from Tier 2 to Tier 3	Product moved from Tier 2 to Tier 1	Access to Hospital Z contacts restricted
	Name	The Apocalypse	"Man down"	Fuel the Flame	Lock Down
	Causal factors (How & Why)	-KOL departure -Pharmacy director gains greater power; cost containment -Hospital acquired	-Competitor successful creating change -Support of department chair weakens -Pharmacy uses price to lower tier	-Sales force pull-thru -MSLs gain KOLs to support earlier use -HEOR data moves Medical Director to execute change	-Policy change -Government pressure -Hospital acquired -Too many reps -Improve productivity
	Impact [+/-; 1-10]	-10	-6	+7	-5
Contingency Plans	**Goal**	Increase access to product X at Hospital Z	Increase product X tier placement	Increase product X pull-thru of Rx's	Increase access to key contacts
	Objective	Gain formulary reinstatement to Tier 1 or 2 by year end	Obtain and submit five support letters by end of Q3	Achieve 35% increase in new Rx's by end of Q2	Create 3+ new contact channels to key personnel
	Strategy	Leverage KOL relationship to forge additional support	Grass roots drive to create urgent sense of loss	Use cross-functional SWAT team to leverage Tier move awareness	Use non-face-to-face channels to reestablish communication
	Tactics	-KOL mtg. with key personnel -Identify value drivers of key personnel -Develop value plan	-Identify MD champion -Collect five letters of support -MD champion makes case for Tier change	-Tier 1 mktg. campaign -Double # calls on top 50 MDs at Hospital Z -Develop NP/PA conversion guidelines	-Create network map -Overlay philanthropic access points to map -Create new medical resource position

Figure 10.3 Scenarios and Contingency Plans Example.

conversations focused on the evolution of the business. It's easy to become addicted to the adrenaline-inducing fire drills and flurry of activity that happens on a daily basis. It's easy to fixate on today's issues, this week's finish line, and this quarter's numbers. But if you're a senior leader, easy is not good enough. Pick your head up, stare into the distance, and squint to see it. Is it starting to come into focus? Yes, there it is . . . your future. Do you like what you see?

Trail Blazes

A business model is how your group creates, delivers, and captures value.

Three techniques to enhance your business model:
1. Swim downstream
2. Change your capture
3. Deviate from the norm

The value proposition can be broken down into four pieces:
1. Who: Customer to be served
2. What: Need to be met or job to be done
3. How: Unique approach to satisfy need or fulfill job
4. Benefit: Customer's advantage of using the offering

A value chain visually depicts the configuration of key activities that make up your business. Value chains can be developed at the industry level and the firm level and typically consist of primary activities (four to seven) and then the secondary activities that contribute to each primary activity.

Six questions to guide your thinking about the future of the business:
1. Where are we today?
2. What challenges should we solve?
3. What can we do differently?
4. How can we do things differently?
5. What new value can we provide?
6. How should our business evolve?

CHAPTER 11

Talent and Succession

"My main job was developing talent. I was a gardener providing water and other nourishment to our top 750 people. Of course, I had to pull out some weeds, too."

—Jack Welch, former CEO, GE

U nless you are an organization of one, your success will depend on the people around you. The ability to assess, develop, and manage talent can make or break a leader's tenure. Shantanu Narayan, CEO of Adobe, describes his approach to talent management this way: "Every year I try and say: What are one or two big areas where it feels like I can have an impact and I can influence where the organization should be headed both in terms of learning from the talent that exists within the company and outside the company? And then, having the ability to use that to change priorities. I think way too often people do what they're good at, rather than perhaps where the company wants them to make an impact."[1]

The kaleidoscope of personalities and perceptions viewed through the subjectivity of the human lens make talent challenging to harness. However, there are tools and frameworks you can employ to shed a spotlight on the "who" of your business. Developing an evergreen awareness of how your key people are performing on their priorities is of paramount importance.

Talent Scorecard

A tool I designed called the Talent Scorecard is a simple yet effective means of assessing the people around you in leadership roles. There are three focal areas to consider:

1. **Technical capability:** The knowledge and skills to complete the tasks of their responsibilities
2. **People leadership:** Clarification of roles, exhibiting emotional intelligence, creating accountability, and providing the right level of support in achieving the group's goals
3. **Executive skills:** The ability to set direction, execute strategies, and effectively collaborate to deliver on initiatives

For each area, use a scale of 1–3, where 3 = excellent, 2 = satisfactory, and 1 = insufficient. Once you've totaled and then averaged the score, indicate which path they are currently on in terms of your attention: coach on, coach up, or coach out. Table 11.1 provides an example. Complete the concise Talent Scorecard for your direct reports every two to four weeks and then provide them with the appropriate feedback. It's also helpful to identify three people they interact with on a regular basis and gain their input on a monthly or quarterly basis to augment the assessment.

Rocket Burn: Use the Talent Scorecard or a modified version to keep a pulse on your key contributors. Being surprised by feedback from colleagues on your direct reports is a sign that more frequent monitoring of key behaviors is warranted.

The great leaders, teachers, and coaches are skilled at correcting their people, students, and athletes, and then providing them with an immediate opportunity to practice the activity again to improve on it. As noted earlier, legendary college basketball coach John Wooden was studied in the 1970s to better understand his highly successful practice habits. The researchers recorded and coded more than 2,000 discrete acts of teaching during his practices and found that the majority were just short bits of objective instruction, not scathing criticism, sarcastic remarks, or long-winded monologues. One of Wooden's former players, Swen Nater,

Table 11.1 Talent Scorecard.

Key Personnel	Technical Capability	People Leadership	Executive Skills	Total Score	Average Score	Coach On, Up or Out
Jane	2	3	1	6	2	On
Alex	3	1	1	5	1.67	Up
Martin	1	2	1	4	1.33	Out

described his process of talent development: "It was the information I received, during the correction, that I needed most. Having received it, I could then make the adjustments and changes needed. It was the information that promoted change."[2]

The key to implementing this concept to coach on or coach up is to focus on specific behaviors. Instead of telling a direct report, "You need to be less tactical and more strategic," share with them feedback on the behavioral change you're seeking. In this example, provide input such as "Instead of reacting to future customer comments by immediately calling an urgent meeting involving six other people asking them to change our strategy to meet the customer's demands, develop a checklist to analyze the situation first. The checklist might include the following: actual customer comment; customer value to the company; company's strategic approach to this customer segment; range of standard solutions for this customer." The sequence we're seeking here is to observe the person's initial performance in the situation, provide feedback on the specific behavioral change, have the person perform the activity again using the feedback—ideally, multiple times—and then reflect and discuss.

Five Talent Traps

Here are the most common talent traps I've observed during the past 20 years of coaching executives and their leadership teams:

1. **Rationalizing bad:** If a direct report is continually scoring below 2 on the Talent Scorecard and they've been given the appropriate

knowledge, tools, and training consistently over time to perform at a higher level, then coach out. Not in six months. Now.

2. **I didn't know:** Establishing leadership principles and performance goals are effective ways to ensure the team has a clear understanding of the guard rails for their actions and outcomes. It's your responsibility as a leader to help the team establish what flies and what doesn't—in writing—so that there aren't continual misunderstandings about what's acceptable and what's not from a behavioral and performance perspective.

3. **N of 1:** Nothing derails the productivity and efficiency of teams faster than making one-off exceptions on a regular basis to use resources and perform activities outside the normal scope of the team's strategy for internal or external customers. The biggie here is people chumming the water with the CEO's name as the wild card that trumps any semblance of strategic direction and trade-offs that have already been agreed upon. Have each team member complete a one-page strategic roadmap for their area of the business and then share those roadmaps with one another on a monthly basis to ensure there's understanding and alignment of priorities. Use the strategic road maps as Kevlar vests when others are asking people to do things outside of their priorities.

4. **Fine wine:** A business is only as good as the people who lead it. If a business improves, it's generally because the people have improved. When a business is stagnant or declines, it's often because the thinking and actions of leaders have not improved. Unlike fine wine, leaders do not naturally get better with age. Identify the two to three critical competencies (areas of expertise) and capabilities (skill sets) for each role and work with the leader in that role to develop a practice plan for improvement. Have them provide a written update of specific developmental progress on a monthly basis.

5. **Stone-cold impression:** Mom always told us to make a good first impression. She didn't say you only have seven seconds. That's the amount of time research suggests it takes for you to form an impression of someone you meet. However, as a leader, it's wise to revisit that impression on a regular basis. If you set the first impression in stone and it's not favorable, then the person has been latently banished to your company's netherworld with no way out. Instead of locking yourself into a first impression, ask yourself: Based on our last six months of interaction, what's my next impression?

Succession Planning

"If we get the right people on the bus, the right people in the right seats, and the wrong people off the bus, then we'll figure out how to take it someplace great." Sage advice from the pages of the book *Good to Great*.[3] But what happens if there's a bomb aboard that bus that will detonate if its speed drops below 50 mph? Well, now we've crossed over genres into the 1994 Keanu Reeves and Sandra Bullock movie *Speed,* but it's still worth considering:Who should be on the next bus in case there's a sequel?

Mike Lawrie, highly accomplished technology leader and founder of the Lawrie Group, said, "Some people get off the bus voluntarily, others, you need to open the emergency door and throw them out.You have to have the right people around you because. . .you need to have people that share that vision. In a consensus model, not everyone agrees, which can lead to a lot of passive-aggressive behavior, and on a turnaround or at a start-up situation that can be endemic to success."[4]

A good place to begin in determining the right people in the right roles is with role assessments. Identify the role by name and then add the following categories of information: knowledge, skills, responsibilities, metrics for success, and "other" for additional topics germane to the role. It's helpful to describe those areas today and then in a separate column project what you envision will be important to the role in those areas in three years.This will ensure that as you evaluate your current leaders and potential successors, you're using criteria that will maintain their relevance.

After delineating the various roles, take time to compare roles relative to one another in terms of value to the organization. As with most areas of the business, roles too can proliferate and, if not pruned on a periodic basis, lead to bloat. A technique to appropriately trim roles and, more important, identify the ones critical to organizational success, is the Difference Maker Role assessment (Table 11.2).

Begin by listing the roles in your group and rate each role on a scale of 1–5, with 5 = most important to the business's success and 1 = least important.Then rate the individual's performance who currently inhabits the role, using a traditional school grading scale of A to F. Following the role and individual's ratings, articulate the options moving forward (e.g., role elimination, individual promotion, etc.) and then outline next steps.

Table 11.2   Difference Maker Roles.

Role	Role Importance	Individual Performance	Options	Next Steps
New Business Development	4	C	Transition Ava into role; hire from competitor	Review position with Ava; HR to work with recruiter
IT Business Partner	3	D	New training; Review outsourcing options	Identify external sources and pilot project in area
Product Innovation	5	A	Assess bench strength for succession; add responsibilities	Add more resources to build team faster

It's essential that the roles evaluated as the most important in the Difference Maker exercise are filled with the highest-rated performers. Too often, this critical connection is not verified and puts the organization in a much more precarious position than it needs to be. Difference maker roles need to be filled by difference makers.

Once you've determined the roles and the competencies and capabilities required to successfully fill them, you can assess the person in the role or multiple candidates for the role. To provide a complete picture, it's recommended that you develop both a qualitative and quantitative assessment. The qualitative assessment would include competencies (areas of expertise), capabilities (skills and activities), relevant experiences, performance results, gaps, areas for development, and overall fit.

The quantitative candidate comparison involves identifying the primary success factors for the role, typically 5 to 10. The success factors should be customized to the role and may include items such as industry expertise, setting strategic direction, emotional intelligence, decision making, executive presence, and so on. These factors can be inputted into an Excel spreadsheet and weighted with the following scale: 3 = highly important; 2 = moderately important; 1 = important. After each factor is weighted, the person is then rated on a scale of 0–3, with

Table 11.3   Quantitative Candidate Comparison.

		Jane		Alex		Martin	
Success Factors For Role	Weight	Rating	Score	Rating	Score	Rating	Score
Executive presence	2	2	4	3	6	1	2
Strategic planning	3	3	9	2	6	2	6
Problem solving	1	2	2	2	2	3	3
Decision making	3	1	3	3	9	2	6
Innovative thinking	2	3	6	1	2	3	6
Total			**24**		**25**		**23**

3 = excellent; 2 = above average; 1 = average; and 0 = below average. For each factor, the weight times rating equals the score. Individual factor scores can then be totaled for a cumulative score. The total score can be used for one person to compare with their scores at future dates or it can be used in comparison with other candidates for the role. Table 11.3 provides an example of a quantitative assessment for several candidates being reviewed for promotion.

Off Course: The most common evaluation criterion for assessing new hires and potential promotions is industry experience. Eighty years of data shows that experience is only the fifth best predictor of job success. Stop using experience as a key criterion and focus on recent behaviors relevant to the role.[5]

The final step is to create a recommendations plan. The plan includes the roles, specific recommendations for each role, rationale behind the recommendations, target date for changes, and next steps. It's easy to fall back on years of experience as the de facto criterion for selecting and promoting people. However, research across domains shows that evidence does not support the idea that people with more experience will perform at a higher level or be more effective at the job than those with less experience. In fact, the research shows that rather than experience, past behavior is the best predictor of success.[6]

Just because someone has experience in a role doesn't mean that they exhibited the behaviors that equate with success in the role. There's a huge difference between experience and behavior. As self-made billionaire inventor James Dyson writes, "At Dyson, we don't particularly value experience. Experience tells you what you ought to do and what you'd do best to avoid. It tells you how things should be done when we are much more interested in how things shouldn't be done. If you want to pioneer and invent new technology, you need to step into the unknown and, in that realm, experience can be a hindrance."[7]

Trail Blazes

The Talent Scorecard evaluates people in three areas:
1. Technical capability: the knowledge and skills to complete the tasks of their responsibilities
2. People leadership: clarification of roles, exhibiting emotional intelligence, creating accountability, and providing the right level of support in achieving the group's goals
3. Executive skills: the ability to set direction, execute strategies, and effectively collaborate to deliver on initiatives

Five talent traps to avoid:
1. Rationalizing continuous underperformance
2. Uncertainty on how to behave
3. Making one-off exceptions on a regular basis
4. People unwilling to invest time and effort in their development
5. Allowing a first impression to be a permanent perception

An initial step in succession planning is role assessments. Identify the key roles by name and then add the following categories of information: knowledge, skills, responsibilities, metrics for success, and "other" for additional topics germane to the role.

Separate out the assessment of the "Difference Maker" roles—those critical to the organization's success.

A quantitative comparison of several candidates for the same role includes
identifying 5 to 10 primary success factors, a weighting of the factors on
relative importance to the role, and then a rating of the candidates on
each of the success factors.

CHAPTER 12

Innovation

"Ideas are gifts from the universe. Every time I have them, I capture them right then. The more that you write it down and pay attention to them, the stronger the gift and the connection will become. And you will start being flooded with more and more ideas."
—Sara Blakely, self-made billionaire and CEO of Spanx

When we hear the term "innovation," we tend to think of a cool new product or technology that's going to change the world. But that isn't really what most innovation entails. A recent three-year study on innovation found that only 13% of the world's leading consumer product companies introduced a breakthrough innovation.[1] Most innovation tends to come in incremental doses, even for companies known for innovation. Amazon founder Jeff Bezos said, "I bet 70% of the innovation we do focuses on slightly improving a process. That incremental invention is a huge part of what makes Amazon tick."[2] And this coming from the company that has been awarded a patent for a giant flying warehouse that acts as a launchpad for delivery drones.

The challenge with innovation is that it can be overwhelming. Try to find a word that carries with it more daunting expectations. The key is to transform this abstract blob of innovation into a practical approach to the business. The first step in this mental transformation is to see innovation's true meaning: to create new value for customers. When we use this lens of "creating new value for customers," innovation moves from the seemingly abstract to a more practical perspective. Customers may be internal, such as the sales force, or external, as in a channel customer

or end consumer. When is the last time you and your team created truly
new value for your customers?

> **Rocket Burn:** Innovation is defined as creating new value for customers.
> Innovation is sparked by an insight: a learning that leads to new value.

Insight

The common core of both strategy and innovation is insight. An insight
results from the combination of two or more pieces of information or
data in a unique way that leads to a new approach, new solution, or new
value. Mark Beeman, professor of psychology at Northwestern University,
describes insight in the following way: "Insight is a reorganization of
known facts taking pieces of seemingly unrelated or weakly related
information and seeing new connections between them to arrive at a
solution."[3] Simply put, an insight is learning that leads to new value.

A study of more than 5,000 executives showed that the most important innovation trait for managers in high-performing organizations is
the ability to come up with insights.[4] Unfortunately, the research also
showed that only 35% of global executives believed their strategies are
built on unique insights.[5] And only 25% of managers believe their companies are good at both strategy and innovation.[6]

Innovation is the continual hunt for new value; strategy is ensuring
we configure resources in the best way possible to develop and deliver
that value. Strategic innovation can be defined as the insight-based allocation of resources in a competitively distinct way to create new value
for select customers. Too often, strategy and innovation are approached
separately, even though they share a common foundation in the form of
insight. As authors Andrew Campbell and Marcus Alexander write, "The
fundamental building block of good strategy is insight into how to create
more value than competitors can."[7]

When insights—learnings that create new value—do appear, it's
important to record them. You never know when the idea will germi-
nate. At the beginning of his filmmaking career, George Lucas was working on the draft of a science fiction movie while he was mixing sound
for his 1973 film *American Graffiti*. During one of the sound mixing

sessions, the Academy Award–winning film editor and sound designer Walter Murch asked Lucas for Reel 2, Dialogue 2, which he said in its abbreviated form, "R2-D2." Lucas took note of the pleasant-sounding phrase, and it later became the name of the resourceful astromech droid in the Star Wars franchise.[8]

One of the common threads woven among great contributors throughout history is the discipline to record their insights, typically in notebooks. Pablo Picasso, Charles Darwin, Marie Curie, Ludwig van Beethoven, Isaac Newton, Thomas Jefferson, Benjamin Franklin, Beatrix Potter, Rosalind Franklin, Thomas Edison, Louisa May Alcott, and Mark Twain are just a few of the highly significant contributors who fastidiously recorded their insights. Leonardo da Vinci, the prolific Renaissance inventor, sculptor, painter, engineer, scientist, and architect, accumulated more than 20,000 pages of notes containing his thinking and insights. If anyone ever questions the value of recording ideas, they can reference the $30.8 million that Microsoft founder Bill Gates spent to purchase one of da Vinci's notebooks—the Codex Leicester.

The act of physically recording an insight triggers us to observe what's happening around us and reflect on those observations in order to transform them into something meaningful. In Matt Fitzpatrick's case, he transformed his 13 years of copious notes into the 2022 U.S. Open Men's Golf Championship. Following every shot he performs in both practice and competition, he records detailed information that can be analyzed to enhance performance that day and referenced in future situations. While he records standard information such as the club he hit, wind conditions, and where the ball landed, he also records things that even a high-processing computer couldn't track, such as where he intended to hit the shot versus the actual result. Reflecting on his disciplined process, Fitzpatrick says, "I just think: find the 1% somewhere where I can improve . . . having all that data, it just makes it more reliable."[9]

While we may not be earning a living reading a putt on the 18th green to win a check for $1 million, it's intriguing to think about applying someone's process who does. What if after every significant interaction during the day—one-to-one meetings, team meetings, presentations, and so on—you took five minutes to think, reflect, and record your insights on the interaction? Would that make you a higher performer?

A comment by Abraham Lincoln, "It is indispensable to have a habit of observation and reflection," reveals a powerful truth: taking time to stop and think will differentiate you from the majority of people living in a perpetual state of reactivity.

> **Off Course:** If you are not recording your insights, then they don't exist, at least not in a meaningful and applicable way.

There are many fascinating origin stories from entrepreneurs regarding the insights that led to their success. Whether it was Dan Stookey's botched glass experiment in 1952 that led to the creation of the Gorilla Glass used on today's smartphones, or Sara Blakely's frustration with the discomfort and appearance of women's undergarments leading to her creating the multibillion-dollar company Spanx, innovation is spawned by challenges. Finding ways to overcome these challenges are where insights enter, and challenges can become the seeds of strategy.

Solving Challenges

A challenge is a difficulty or dissatisfaction with an activity, task, or the status quo that is stimulating to one engaged in it because the solution leads to progress. Progress manifests itself in the new value produced by helping those you serve solve their problems. If you want to move out of a reactive mode, you must help your customers solve their current challenges. Entrepreneur James Dyson spent decades working on a vacuum technology to help people with the very common challenge of cleaning. He said, "I like frustration. I like seeing things in everyday life that don't work very well and try to make them better."[10]

One effective way of innovating, or creating new value, is to look at your market, customers, competitors, and own company, and ask, "What are the primary challenges people face?" Consider functional activities, tasks, processes, internal and external aspects. If you feel your group is too caught up in the feature/benefit battle with competitors, come back to the key challenges or problems and how to solve them in ways that introduce new value. Before revolutionizing the vacuum with his cyclone technology and see-through, bagless canister, James Dyson solved a problem many of his British neighbors who worked in their yards felt: wheelbarrows getting their tires stuck in the mud. Instead of a "wheel" barrow, he introduced the Ballbarrow, which used a ball in place of the wheel to solve the problem of the wheels getting stuck in the mud.

To effectively use challenges as part of your toolkit to develop new value for customers, I've designed a four-step process to identify and prioritize the challenges in your business:

1. **Challenge funnel:** Begin by creating a list of challenges that would enter the top of the funnel and then whittle down from there to approximately six or fewer based on their relevance to solve. Consider both external challenges (market trends, competitive activity, customer changes, etc.) and internal challenges (silos, unclear decision making, too many priorities, etc.).
2. **Challenge filter:** Graph the challenges using two criteria: probability of solving and importance to the business. Use the framework to discuss and determine the priority of challenges.
3. **Challenge map:** For the primary challenge identified, examine it and articulate the causes, effects, relevance, and outcomes.
4. **Solutional thinking:** Describe the main challenge that needs to be addressed, specify the relevance (who this is important to and why), identify the gap between the current state and desired state, generate a range of three to five mutually exclusive options for solving the challenge, including the pros and cons of each, and finally capture the direction or recommended action plan in the form of the goals, objectives, strategies, and tactics.

Biomimicry

What do humpback whales, fireflies, and kingfishers have in common? They are all members of the animal kingdom that have inspired solutions to challenges we face. Biomimicry is the conscious use of "design inspired by the way functional challenges have been solved in biology."[11] The reality is that nature has provided solutions to many of the same challenges we encounter, including transportation, architecture, energy, and more. Despite this fact, research demonstrates that when comparing nature's solutions with our patent database, there's only about a 10%

overlap in similar solutions. As American biologist Edward Wilson writes, "Nature holds the key to our aesthetic, intellectual, cognitive, and even spiritual satisfaction."

Humpback whales have tubercles or bumps on their fins, which provide them with an 8% improvement in lift, 32% reduction in drag, and a 40% increase in angle of attack versus flippers that are smooth. The design of their fins is being used to create wind turbines with increased efficiency and also has the potential to enhance the efficiency and safety of airplanes and fans. The lanterns on fireflies have asymmetrical microscopic projections (microstructures) that release light. Researchers have added these microstructures to the surface of LED lights, which allows more light through, improving light extraction by 90%.

High-speed bullet trains have dramatically decreased travel times for millions of people in dozens of countries around the world. Their current success can be traced back to a solution inspired by a bird called the kingfisher. The first bullet trains could travel in excess of 120 mph but when they exited tunnels, a loud boom was heard. This was due to a wall of wind that accumulated at the front of the train and then collided with the air outside of the tunnel, causing the loud noise. The noise pollution generated was a cause for concern and needed to be addressed.

Fortunately, one of the engineers tasked with solving this challenge was also a bird enthusiast. He observed that when kingfishers dove into the water at high speeds to catch fish below the surface, their entry hardly disturbed the water due to the knife-blade shape of their bills. His team replicated this design for the front of the bullet train, which eliminated the loud noise and also increased their fuel efficiency by 15% and their speed by 10%.[12]

An effective means of leveraging biomimicry to generate innovative solutions to challenges is to biologize the question. In this technique, we're transforming the challenge into a biologically driven question. If the challenge you face is, "How do we adapt to the changing competitive landscape in order to maintain market share?" then biologizing the question creates the following: "How does nature adapt to changing conditions?" Perhaps we note that certain animals, such as the Arctic fox, are able to shift the color of their fur from brown in the summer to white in the winter to maintain effective camouflage. We can follow this thread by asking how we can modify or adapt our offerings to different types of customers or the various purchasing seasons during the year.

With Amazon alone shipping approximately 1.6 million packages per day, drones are increasing in number and are on the precipice of becoming a standard method of delivery. One of the drawbacks is the potential for damage caused by the rotating blades during collisions. Inspired by the pufferfish's ability to inflate by ingesting water when feeling threatened by a potential predator, the PufferBot was developed to enable the drone to deploy a collapsible plastic shield around itself at a moment's notice, diminishing the damage when the aerial robot collides with another object. To inspire this train of thought, you could begin with the question, "How does nature protect itself?" The prolific Renaissance creator Leonardo da Vinci writes, "Human subtlety will never devise an invention more beautiful, more simple, or more direct than does nature because in her inventions nothing is lacking, and nothing is superfluous."

Using biomimicry to inspire novel solutions to challenges introduces the broader concept of domain jumping. Domain jumping involves the mental leap over the walls of the current discipline into unrelated fields to hijack their approaches to solve our challenges. Dan Cathy, CEO of Chick-fil-A, is a strong proponent: "When it comes to creativity and innovation to lead in any industry, the most valuable lessons we learn are going to come from other related industries, not necessarily the particular one that we're competing in."[13]

Domain Jumping

Research demonstrates that domain jumping is a powerful innovative thinking technique. A study was conducted with roofers, rollerbladers, and carpenters to find ways to make gear safer for each of the activities. Ironically, the groups were far better at coming up with innovative safety gear solutions for the groups they were not a part of than for their own arena. The further the distance between the challenge and the original domain perspective, the greater the creativity of the solutions. For instance, rollerbladers were more effective at generating ideas than roofers for improvements in convenience and comfort of carpenters' gear.[14]

The following steps can help you domain jump to solve your challenges:

1. Identify the challenge. Let's use the following example to walk through this process: Our time to service clients is too slow, causing defections.
2. Develop a list of 5–10 professions (e.g., surgeon, detective, teacher, etc.) and explore the question: How would this professional approach this challenge? A surgeon has a preoperative team that handles logistics and key activities to prepare the patient for surgery. What if we added a dedicated team to do preparatory work prior to our interaction with the customer to speed up our service?
3. Develop a list of 5–10 companies (e.g., Marvel Comics, Airbnb, Uber, Spanx, Porsche, SpaceX, etc.) and explore the question: How would this company approach this challenge? What if we took Porsche's approach and invested a disproportionate amount of our resources in world-class design of our customer service process—what could that look like?
4. Create a list of 5–10 places (e.g., Disneyworld, Apple retail store, museum, hospital, etc.) and explore the question: What if this situation was like this place? What if we used a museum as a template for our customer service process, with an information desk or kiosk at the entry point, automated audio and video experiences along the journey to provide deeper level information, and an IMAX movie experience to further educate and engage our customers?
5. Create a list of 5–10 items (e.g., Dyson vacuum, electric keyboard, telescope, etc.) and explore this question: What if this situation was like this item? What would it take to redesign our customer service process, so it was like a Dyson vacuum in that it offered greater transparency, was much simpler than the competition's process, and didn't require burdensome attachments?
6. Create a list of 5–10 arenas or disciplines (e.g., sports, reality TV, astronomy, biology, engineering, etc.) and explore the question: What if we used this arena's/discipline's perspective to address the challenge? What would it look like to reengineer the customer service process, beginning with the ideal outcomes and working backward to eliminate points of friction and replace them with points of greater personalization?

Catalyzing Questions

Embedded in the various innovation techniques described is the root of new thinking: the question. Consider the most fascinating conversations, movies, or companies you've experienced and it's quickly apparent that they were fueled by an intriguing question or questions that sparked your interest. What if we moved to the West Coast? What if an alien lifeform visited earth and hunted only by sound? What if you could have 100 million songs in the palm of your hand?

> **Rocket Burn:** Spend more time generating insightful questions. Thoughtful questions are the true spark of innovation because they transform challenges into attackable situations.

It's clear how powerful questions can be to transport us to mental oases to inspire innovation and solve challenges. Why, then, do we invest so little time in them? Research shows that between the ages of 3 and 5, the average child asks approximately 100 questions per day. By the age of 12, the number of questions a child asks plummets to nearly zero.[15] This trend infiltrates adulthood and the workplace as well. The next time a challenge or issue arises on your team, clock the amount of time spent on coming up with the solution versus the question. In many workplaces, the ratio is 90:10, which is the opposite of what great thinkers such as Albert Einstein espouse: "If I had an hour to solve a problem, I'd spend 55 minutes thinking about the problem and 5 minutes thinking about solutions."

It takes a confident leader to invest a larger chunk of time exploring the right question to frame the challenge because knocking around questions can appear inefficient to the group. There can be a strong prevailing meeting wind to "just get on with it" and move to the solution portion of the conversation, which feels more productive, and representative of progress being made. However, it's exactly that extra time required to create and ponder questions that enables us to bring together disparate and distant ideas that form the basis of the combinatorial thinking at the heart of innovation. Examples of combinatorial thinking can be found in the DNA of companies such as Spotify, which is a combination of a radio station, library, and subscription health club, and Airbnb, which is a combination of a B&B (bed and breakfast), travel agency, and social media hub.

Here are several techniques that may be helpful in developing your ability to use questions to innovate:

1. **Create a question log.** As you move throughout your day, record questions that come to mind or you're exposed to through others that stimulate productive thinking. Invest time at the end of the week or month to review the questions in your log, refine them, and begin putting them into categories (e.g., competitor questions, customer questions, culture questions, etc.) for future reference.

2. **Question storming.** When you're in a group meeting to review a challenge or issue, have people take five minutes individually and record 10–20 questions regarding the subject at hand. Then have people share their questions and identify 3–5 questions to drive the remainder of the conversation.

3. **SCAMPER.** Apply the SCAMPER acronym to the situation using the following questions.[16]

> Substitute: What can be substituted? (Automated Teller Machine [ATM] for bank teller)
> Combine: What can be combined? (Theatre + circus = Cirque du Soleil)
> Adapt: What can evolve into something new? (CVS into CVS MinuteClinics)
> Magnify: What can be made larger or more important? (Delivery speed: Amazon Marketplace)
> Put to other use: How else can things be used? (Butcher's disassembly line for auto assembly line)
> Eliminate: What can be eliminated or removed from this? (Dyson vacuum removing the traditional bag)
> Reverse/rearrange: What could we reverse or rearrange? (Enterprise Rent-A-Car will pick you up instead of you picking up the car)

Look through the lists of companies' values and populating a majority of them is "innovation." To be a true company value, innovation should be viewed by all employees through the lens of creating new value for customers. Just as important, an organization's culture must support the positive results and unintended consequences of people performing activities that involve risk.

Innovation is spawned by insight: a learning that leads to new value. While we typically use an insight at the beginning—to create a new initiative or project—insights can also be discovered at the end. Intentionally investing time individually and collectively at the conclusion of an initiative can create a virtuous cycle of insight. Jony Ive, former chief design officer at Apple, agrees: "I've always thought there are a number of things that you have achieved at the end of a project. There's the object, the actual product itself, and then there's all that you learned. What you learned is as tangible as the product itself, but much more valuable, because that's your future."[17]

Trail Blazes

Innovation is creating new value for customers.

An insight results from the combination of two or more pieces of information or data in a unique way that leads to a new approach, new solution, or new value.

A challenge is defined as difficulty or dissatisfaction with an activity, task, or the status quo that is stimulating to one engaged in it because the solution leads to progress.

Biomimicry is the conscious use of "design inspired by the way functional challenges have been solved in biology."

An effective means of leveraging biomimicry to generate innovative solutions to challenges is to biologize the question. In this technique, we're taking the challenge and transforming it into a biologically driven question.

Domain jumping involves the mental leap over the walls of the current discipline into unrelated fields to hijack their approaches to solve our challenges.

Catalyzing questions are the true spark of innovation because they transform challenges into attackable situations. Consider these three techniques:
1. Question log
2. Question storming
3. SCAMPER

PART IV

Communication Fitness

*"The strategy dialogue went on at all levels of the organization. . . .
The ongoing discussion helped keep the strategy on track and helped
give the CEO insights into the strategic capabilities of his leaders."*
— A.G. Lafley, former CEO, Procter & Gamble

"Houston, we have a problem." The most well-known words on navigation in American history were actually never said by the Apollo 13 astronauts. Well, not exactly. The exact communication first said by Apollo 13 Command Module Pilot John "Jack" Swigert, and then repeated by Mission Commander James Lovell, was, "Houston, we've had a problem here," in response to the explosion of oxygen tank number 2. This also resulted in the failure of the number 1 tank, leading to the command module's loss of electricity, light, and water. Their original communication was shortened in the name of artistic scripting for director Ron Howard's film *Apollo 13*.

CHAPTER 13

Strategy Conversations

"Conversations are the way workers discover what they know, share it with their colleagues, and in the process, create new knowledge for the organization. In the new economy, conversations are the most important form of work."

— Alan Webber, co-founder, *Fast Company* magazine

Imagine last year's record-breaking sales performance has earned representatives from the different functional areas of your company—marketing, sales, account management, operations, HR, and IT—an awards trip to a tropical island. As the plane descends toward its destination, mechanical troubles require an emergency water landing (yes, you should have been paying attention to the flight attendants when they showed how to inflate the life vest under the seat). All passengers swim safely to different islands around the plane: marketing managers to one island, sales managers to another island, and so on. However, with no operable electronic devices, you are unable to communicate with your colleagues on the other islands. How does this story end?

It doesn't.

While physical islands don't separate managers, conceptual ones certainly do. Research with 880 managers shows that only 35% are aware of other functional groups' strategies within their own company! Why? Less than half of managers set aside time on a regular basis throughout the year to think about and discuss strategy with their colleagues. The result is that many managers reside on "Islands of Insight"—secluded beaches of great ideas that go unshared, unnoticed, and unused by others in the organization. These Islands of Insight are perhaps the greatest source of untapped potential in an organization. The good news is that the key to unlocking this potential doesn't require new capital, equipment, or people. All it requires are conversations.

A business is only as good as its conversations. Think about it for a moment: every step of progress your business takes, from establishing purpose in the form of mission, vision, and values, to creating a new product offering, to servicing customers, all flows through conversations. When we think of ways to improve the business, how often does "have higher-quality, more efficient conversations" factor in? Rarely. But it should.

A strategy conversation is defined as a verbal interchange of thoughts that result in new insights on how to achieve a goal. The goal may be quantitative, qualitative, or problem solving in nature. The interchange, or giving and receiving of ideas reciprocally, represents the intersection of thoughts, opinions, and assumptions that begins to create a shared understanding of the situation. Strategy conversations are valuable in internal situations such as setting strategic direction, gaining insight into one another's functional area strategies, and innovating for competitive advantage. They are also of value in external situations such as developing strategic partnerships with customers, strengthening relationships with suppliers, and understanding market dynamics.

When it comes to internal development of strategic direction, strategy conversations are the main gear that makes each phase go (Figure 13.1). A physical gear is a part with cut teeth that meshes with the teeth of other parts to transmit or receive force and motion, often permitting driven machinery to run in either direction. In much the same way, strategy conversations are used to transmit or receive thoughts moving in either direction, resulting in insights that generate progress toward one's goals in each phase of the strategy development process. As author Gary Hamel notes, "Strategizing depends on creating a rich and complex web of conversations that cut across previously isolated pockets of knowledge and create new and unexpected combinations of insight."[1]

The barriers to internal strategy conversations include the following:

- **Silos:** Departments and levels are not on the proverbial same page, because they are unaware of each other's strategies.

Figure 13.1   Strategy Conversation Gear.

- **Lack of buy-in:** This results in inability to influence commitment without authority across functions.
- **Fire drills:** People are constantly reacting to the urgent but unimportant matters that pop up.

Do you notice any of these barriers to strategy conversations within your group?

From an external perspective, strategy conversations are instrumental in the profitable growth of the business. Often, the key to gaining a greater share of a customer's business is your ability to understand the customer's goals and then configure resources to deliver superior value toward those goals. This flies in the face of a typical sales approach of your goals masquerading as the customer's goals in hopes of shortcutting the real effort to finding common ground through conversation. Too often, a company's promise of being a "strategic partner" to the customer is nothing more than lip service.

The barriers to external strategy conversations include the following:

- Transactional versus a partner relationship with customers, resulting in price-focused interactions
- Inability to ladder up within a client or account, leaving you stuck working with non-decision-makers
- Selling product instead of facilitating the exchange of value, causing you to be shut out of future opportunities with key customers because you aren't bringing anything new to the table

Are any of these barriers to strategy conversations with customers negatively affecting your business?

As you prepare to embark on the journey of integrating strategy conversations into both your internal processes and work with external customers, keep the following principles in mind:

- Be candid, sincere, and free from reservation or disguise.
- View others as teachers and be willing to learn and change positions.
- Engage the intellect and emotion by considering how people will think and feel, including the topic, invitation to participate, setting, and so on.
- Maintain a host mentality by making people feel welcome and safe to contribute.
- Expect the tension of trade-offs: strategies require saying no to people and engaging in activities that may create anxiety and discomfort.

Regarding the last principle, keep in mind what Reed Hastings, CEO of Netflix, said: "If you are not genuinely pained by the risk involved in your strategic choices, it's not much of a strategy."[2]

Rocket Burn: Utilize the Strategy Conversation Framework to guide your important conversations. The three elements are Dialogue, Discussion, and Direction.

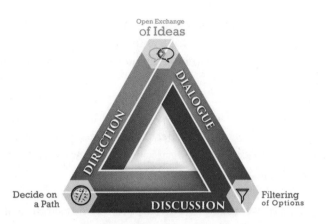

Figure 13.2 Strategy Conversation Framework.

To move strategy conversations from concept to reality, I created the Strategy Conversation Framework (Figure 13.2) to provide a guide to leading strategy conversations internally with your teams and externally with your customers. Strategy conversations involve three elements: Dialogue, Discussion, and Direction.

Dialogue

The intent of the Dialogue phase is to create a forum for the free flow of meaning, resulting in a shared understanding of the key issues. It is through dialogue that we learn of each other's assumptions, ideas, and opinions, not so we can judge them, but so we can observe them to create something new. To that end, the mindset in the dialogue phase is exploratory, with the intent of "thinking together," as opposed to the serial monologues that tend to dominate many conversations.

The characteristics of the Dialogue phase include the following:

- Explore common ground: instead of immediately fixating on areas of disagreement, participants look to see where there is unity.
- Reveal assumptions: openly express what each person takes for granted regarding the situation at hand.
- Reexamine all positions: loosen the fixation on individual positions to open one's mind to other possibilities.

- Look for the value in others' ideas: make an effort to see the benefits of others' thoughts and attempt to build on them.
- Discover new options: combine elements of one another's ideas to create something new.

When earnestly applied to the situation at hand, these characteristics of dialogue can shape the team's behavior in new, productive directions. To effectively navigate the Dialogue phase, here are three guideposts to check off on the journey:

1. **Frame the conversation.** Develop a brief description of the context of the given situation (e.g., product sales decline due to changing market demographics in the northeast region) and then articulate the goal of the strategy conversation (e.g., identify a new account management approach to boost sales). The goal of the strategy conversation is what you are trying to achieve by engaging with one another in this conversation.
2. **Think together.** For some groups, thinking together is a completely new concept because they've been conditioned to constantly defend their positions and attack others. Thinking together can be accomplished by selecting the appropriate strategic thinking questions or tools for the topic under consideration and then recording people's insights in graphic form. For instance, if the goal is to disrupt the market with innovation, the team would benefit from using a framework such as the Norm Deviation Matrix to visually lay out new ideas on how to break with industry norms to create new value for customers.
3. **Listen.** To give one's full attention to another for the sake of understanding their perspective is a true gift. In today's world where the average person checks their mobile phone every ten minutes, listening requires effort and discipline. To listen effectively requires that we be still to quiet our minds to understand others' words and the silence between them. It also demands that we suspend judgment to allow new ideas some air before we choke them off with our preestablished positions and opinions.

Off Course: Multitasking derails effective communication because we miss both verbal and nonverbal cues that could stimulate insights. Put the phone away during any type of in-person communication—it will still be there when you're finished.

To engage in the Dialogue phase, begin with the following starter questions:

• How would we describe the situation at the heart of this strategy conversation?
• What are we trying to achieve—what's our goal or desired outcome?
• What strategic thinking questions or tools will catalyze the conversation and generate insights?

As you move through this phase, keep in mind the four Dialogue Don'ts:

1. Don't judge ideas: suspend opinion to see the value in others' thoughts.
2. Don't fixate on positions: uproot assumptions to allow new ideas space to grow.
3. Don't limit options: bring an exploratory mindset without bounds.
4. Don't make decisions: keep an open mind and don't seek immediate answers, solutions, or closure.

As author Ram Charan wrote, "Dialogue can lead to new ideas and speed as a competitive advantage. It is the single-most important factor underlying the productivity and growth of the knowledge worker."[3]

Discussion

The intent of the Discussion phase is to explore options to achieve the goal established for the strategy conversation. The word "discussion" can be traced to the Latin *discutere,* meaning "a shaking apart, to break up."[4] It is in the Discussion phase that we are decomposing the ideas generated through dialogue to examine them at a more granular level to determine how they can contribute to the achievement of the goal we've established. Here we are beginning to determine the pool of alternatives for reaching our goal by breaking down groups of ideas into potential pathways to move the situation forward.

The characteristics of the Discussion phase include the following:

- Surface issues: slay sacred cows and dispel myths that chain you to the past.
- Clarify alternatives: clearly articulate the options that have been created to reach the goal.
- Conduct premortems: look at alternatives from a future state to see what can potentially derail them.
- Encourage differences: ask for divergent assessments to create a holistic perspective.
- Seek closure: move the participants toward a decision.

As a funnel icon suggests, the Discussion phase is intended to take all the ideas generated during Dialogue and whittle them down into productive alternatives to address the situation and reach the goal. To effectively navigate the Discussion phase, here are three guideposts to check off on the journey:

1. **Advocacy and inquiry.** First introduced by professors Chris Argyris and Donald Schon, the concept of advocacy and inquiry espouses a give and take of points of view.[5] Based on their accompanying rationale, it also encourages the mental agility to shift one's opinion when warranted. Advocacy involves voicing one's point of view on the topics at hand while sharing the thinking behind that view. Balancing advocacy with inquiry requires the sincere interest to find out others' point of view through thoughtful questions and active listening. Taking the initiative to invite others' questions also helps them feel comfortable in exploring the unknown. This element of the strategy conversation helps surface hidden issues, assumptions, and agendas by actively engaging each party in the exchange of the items on their mind.

2. **Create the "and."** In the world of improvisation, the rule of "Yes, and . . ." is an important one. It means that whatever the other improv player gives you ("Help! It's an alien from outer space!"), you have to

build on or add to their statement ("Yes, and take me to your leader."). The idea is that you don't disagree with them ("I'm not an alien"), you go with their flow ("I'll blast you with my ray gun!").

In a strategy conversation, it's easy to fall into the either/or trap, where you look at each option as separate from the next. However, looking for opportunities to build aspects of one alternative onto another can yield some new and exciting ideas. Instead of viewing the customer's demands for faster service and a lower price as a one or the other proposition, you would explore with them ways to create their ideal "and": speed and low cost.

3. **Assess options.** One of the reasons sales representatives and account managers fail to grow their business is that they are unable to create a range of solutions that are desired by the customer. They limit their thinking to the tactics they've used in the past and this creates an anchor that prevents them from seeing newer options on the horizon. The same issue ensnares managers involved in the annual strategic planning process. Their approaches to growing the business are confined to the tried and true, not the different and new. A good list of options spans from the status quo ("do nothing") to the evolutionary ("What if we . . .?") to the revolutionary ("No one has ever tried . . ."). It also includes a brief assessment of the pros and cons of each.

To engage in the Discussion phase, begin with the following starter questions:

- Here's what I think and why I think it. What are your thoughts? What do you see differently?
- How can we combine several of these ideas to go from "either/or" to "and"?
- What are three to five mutually exclusive options for achieving our goal and the pros and cons of each?

As you move through this phase, keep in mind the four Discussion Don'ts:

1. Don't get stuck in dialogue: move the conversation toward options to achieve the goal.

2. Don't stay macro: discussion demands a breaking down of the issues to a micro-level.
3. Don't fail to combine: look for opportunities to combine ideas to find the "and."
4. Don't shield ideas: actively invite questions so everyone understands the options.

Discussion harnesses the disparate insights, puts them under a microscope, and asks, "How can we combine these ideas to create new options to achieve our goal?"

Direction

The intent of the Direction phase is to provide a clear path forward to achieve the goal of the strategy conversation. The word "direction" comes from the Latin word *direction,* meaning "arranging in line, straightening."[6] The Direction phase takes the input and insights generated through dialogue and discussion and configures them into a decision on which course of action to pursue. This decision takes the form of a strategic framework designed to communicate the chosen alternative to others and provide instruction on its implementation.

The characteristics of the Direction phase include the following:

- Cut things off: the decision makes clear what you will and will *not* do.
- Commit resources: the decision does not become reality until time, people, and budget are allocated.
- Shape direction: the decision should provide guidance to all involved on where they are headed.
- Communicate focus: the chosen option should help people determine which activities to invest their time in.
- Develop accountability: the action plan sets the *who, what,* and *when* for execution.

The Direction phase draws the strategy conversation to a close. The decision to pursue a course to achieve the goal or intent established at the outset has been made and it's now incumbent upon the participants to ensure the appropriate steps for implementation are taken. For an internal process like strategy development, the direction phase may include the design of a StrategyPrint, or two-page blueprint for the business, to be customized by each functional group and for each level of the field sales force. For an external customer strategy conversation, the direction phase might include a plan to introduce an innovative new service strategy that addresses the customer's goals and fits with the company's capabilities. Either way, talk has moved to action.

To effectively navigate the Direction phase, here are three guideposts to check off on the journey:

1. **Make a decision.** Selecting the strategy—how to achieve the goal—requires trade-offs. Trade-offs mean not attempting to do everything. Choose one path, and not the other. Inherently, trade-offs mean decisions. The decision to achieve the goal established at the outset of the strategy conversation is based just as much on what you have chosen *not* to do, as it is on what you will do. Too often, managers are unable or unwilling to cut things off from their time and attention to focus on the new actions. Their attempt to keep all the plates in the air, instead of putting a few down, will sooner or later result in some broken dishes. Once you've made your decision, determine what will no longer receive time, people, or budget.

2. **Create the strategic framework.** Whether you're developing an internal strategic plan or an external customer account value map, it's important to visually depict your strategy. Start by identifying three to five key strategic themes—the hubs of resources that will drive differentiated value—and the supporting activities of each, represented like the spokes of a bicycle wheel. This graphical representation of the strategy is a great communication tool with internal colleagues or external customers to ensure everyone is working in the same direction.

3. **Develop the action plan.** A great cause of frustration in organizations is conversation-filled meetings on a weekly basis that generate no substantive changes in the business. Ensure that your strategy to achieve the goal becomes reality by drafting a brief action plan. The action plan should outline roles, responsibilities, activities, outcomes, and time frames. It's also important to build in time for periodic strategy tune-ups to assess how the plan is coming and any changes that need to be made.

To engage in the Direction phase, begin with the following starter questions:

- Which alternative have we decided to select to meet our goal and why?
- What are the three to five strategic themes that best represent where we will focus our resources to enable our strategy to reach our goal?
- What are the roles (who), activities (what), outcomes (why), and time frames (when) associated with this plan?

As you move through this phase, keep in mind the four Direction Don'ts:

1. Don't waver on your decision: make a clear decision on the best option to move forward and don't continually rehash it.
2. Don't fail to cut things off: new initiatives require active disengagement from less important ones.
3. Don't settle on words alone: create a visual strategic framework to communicate the direction.
4. Don't forget accountability: ensure everyone is clear on the *who, what, why*, and *when*.

As former Intel CEO Andrew Grove said, "Clarity of direction, which includes describing what we are going after as well as describing what we will not be going after, is exceedingly important."[7]

Strategy conversations will transform the internal Islands of Insight in your organization into a powerful Insight Ecosystem where people's best thinking is shared and leveraged on a regular basis. They will span the silos between functional areas and levels, create greater commitment to one another's strategies, and extinguish a culture of fire drills. From an external perspective, strategy conversations will create a common ground of value from which you, your customers, and your suppliers can all benefit. They will shift your customer's perspective of working with you from that of a transactional vendor to a real strategic partner.

If you see gaps in how your organization functions, it's likely that the central gear of strategy conversations is missing. Without that gear, silos will stand, assumptions will go unchecked, and potential customers will be lost. Converse now, or forever hold your peace.

Trail Blazes

A strategy conversation is defined as a verbal interchange of thoughts that result in new insights on how to achieve a goal.

The barriers to internal strategy conversations include the following:
- Silos: Departments and levels are not on the proverbial same page, because they are unaware of each other's strategies.
- Lack of buy-in: This results in inability to influence commitment without authority across functions.
- Fire drills: People are constantly reacting to the urgent but unimportant matters that pop up.

The barriers to external strategy conversations include the following:
- Transactional versus a partner relationship with customers, resulting in price-focused interactions
- Inability to ladder up within a client or account, leaving you stuck working with non-decision-makers
- Selling product instead of facilitating the exchange of value, causing you to be shut out of future opportunities with key customers because you aren't bringing anything new to the table

Strategy conversations involve three elements: Dialogue, Discussion, and Direction.

Three keys to effective dialogue:
1. Frame the conversation
2. Think together
3. Listen

Three keys to effective discussion:
1. Advocacy and inquiry
2. Create the "and"
3. Assess options

Three keys to effective direction:
1. Make a decision
2. Create the strategic framework
3. Develop the action plan

CHAPTER 14

Collaboration

"When I was a kid, there was no collaboration; it's you with a camera bossing your friends around. But as an adult, filmmaking is all about appreciating the talents of the people you surround yourself with."
—Steven Spielberg, film director,
writer, and producer

As one's responsibilities increase and the pressure to achieve goals and reach financial targets heightens, it's common to descend into a mental foxhole and lose sight of the power of collaboration. To collaborate is to work with others willingly and agreeably for a common purpose. Taking a page from Spielberg's script for success, are we actively aware of and tapping into the talents and insights of those around us on a regular basis in order to drive toward our destination?

Several studies suggest we have an opportunity to shorten our paths to success by engaging in effective collaboration. Why is this relevant? The majority of leaders and their direct reports are involved in collaborative activities a whopping 85% of their time.[1] A survey by Human Capital Media Research found that 58% of cross-functional groups within organizations do not effectively align their strategies with one another.[2] And when collaboration is occurring, it's not always achieving its intended effects. Research shows that a meager 6% of people collaborating through cross-functional groups think that they are regularly achieving outstanding results and less than 10% report that information is shared effectively.[3] How, then, can we realize the full potential of collaboration?

> **Off Course:** Only 1 out of 10 managers believe that information is shared effectively in their organization.

Enhancing Collaboration

We can begin by scooching up a little closer to one another—literally. An interesting study of an engineering firm found that "the communication between two engineers was a direct function of the number of meters between their cubicles in the building: the closer the cubicles, the more communication there was. When the cubicles were twenty-five meters apart, the communication dropped to almost nothing."[4]

Additional research with scientists found that those who worked next to their colleague were three times more likely to collaborate on technical scientific topics than scientists who were seated 30 feet away.[5] With the increase in the number of people operating in hybrid mode and working remotely at least part of the time, leaders must take an active role in shortening the physical or virtual distance between those who would benefit from greater collaboration. Common techniques for bridging these potential gaps are daily huddles, weekly check-ins, and technology platforms such as Microsoft Teams, Slack, Hive, Canva, Google Slides, Dropbox Paper, and Zoom, to name a few.

> **Rocket Burn:** Decreasing the physical distance between people increases their level of communication and collaboration. In a hybrid environment, what additional techniques could you employ to reduce the virtual distance and increase collaboration?

Culture plays a significant role in the cultivation or curtailing of collaboration. Since culture is manifested through a system of shared behaviors based on core values, it's helpful to examine the organization's primary behaviors to determine their impact on collaboration. Are people rewarded for helping others achieve their goals, or is the more prevailing attitude best summed up by the character Norm Peterson from the TV show *Cheers*: "It's a dog-eat-dog world and I'm wearing Milk Bone underwear."

Research involving students from Stanford University demonstrated the power of language on collaboration. Using a prisoner's dilemma concept for the game, students were offered the choice of working with or against their classmates. When the game was described as the "community game," 70% of students chose to cooperate with one another. When the game was described as the "Wall Street game," indicating market competition, those choosing to cooperate with others dropped to 30%.[6] The findings suggest that the language a leader uses to communicate can have a significant impact on people's collaborative behaviors—in this case, whether people within the same organization choose to collaborate or compete with one another. A popular mantra to clarify the distinction is "collaborate internally and compete externally."

The following questions can serve as a starting point in examining the environment for collaboration in your organization:

- What factors have inhibited collaboration?
- What factors have facilitated collaboration?
- Identify the mindsets, behaviors, and actions that can foster future collaboration for your group.

A subtle but powerful technique to turbo charge collaboration is to work alone. Say what? While the idea of working by oneself to collaborate more effectively is counterintuitive, research demonstrates its value. Dozens of studies show that during idea generation sessions, those people who worked in silence to think about and record their ideas prior to talking with others produced higher-quality and significantly more ideas than those who immediately jumped into conversations.[7]

Beginning a session by having people work individually to write down ideas allows for more original thoughts to surface because people aren't immediately influenced by the first thing that comes out of their colleague's mouth. Working alone to start also spreads accountability for ideas across the entire group, preventing the mental drafting that some do to avoid having to contribute. Finally, studies show that in idea generation sessions, individual thinking prior to group conversation generates a higher quality and quantity of ideas than initiating the session with collective brainstorming.[8]

Collaboration can be enhanced through skillful facilitation. An effective facilitator creates rhythms of conversation, fluctuating between divergence and convergence. Typically, divergent thinking sets the stage through open dialogue designed to generate lots of ideas and options on the topic at hand in a nonjudgmental fashion. Convergent thinking then sweeps up the ideas, sorting them into categories for deeper evaluation where options are assessed and judgments made.

If you have teams that are struggling with collaboration, here is an agenda that may help grease the wheels for more productive cooperation:

Goal: Identify principles and practices to foster high-level collaboration between your teams.

Pre-Work: Please review the following questions and come prepared to discuss your ideas:

- *Collaborate* is defined as "to work with others willingly and agreeably for a common purpose." How would you describe the common purpose for your teams?
- Consider two examples from your past where excellent collaboration occurred. What were the key factors that created the high-level of collaboration? How could those factors be applied to your teams?
- What challenges or issues could hinder high-level collaboration between your teams?
- A principle is defined as "a guiding rule of conduct." What principles do you believe would help guide strong collaboration between your teams?
- What action steps would you recommend to ensure high-level collaboration between your teams moving forward?

The results generated from the agenda outlined can then be captured by following these steps:

1. Identify the "What" for both teams: their primary goals and objectives.
2. Record the "How" for both teams: the strategies and tactics they have designed to achieve their goals and objectives.
3. Determine the "Who" for both teams: identify which people and which roles will be explicitly involved in the collaborative effort.
4. Be explicit on timelines for the "When."

It's ironic that business strategy is designed to clarify a group's direction, but the sessions to discuss it can often be muddied, disjointed, and result in greater confusion. One study showed that 80% of senior executives' meeting time is spent on issues that account for less than 20% of the company's long-term value.[9] The researchers also found that only 12% of executives "believed that their top management meetings consistently produced decisions on important strategic or organizational issues."[10] This doesn't have to be the case. In my experience facilitating strategy sessions with hundreds of executive leadership teams, I've developed principles and techniques to ensure your collaboration sessions are as effective and efficient as possible.

For example, consider your most recent strategy session and answer these five questions comprising the Strategy Facilitation Assessment to see how your team is faring:

1. The facilitator of the meeting is not the leader in the meeting because these are two different and conflicting roles.

   True   False

2. The facilitator does not have a stake in the decisions being made in the meeting.

   True   False

3. The meeting outcomes have been identified prior to the session in the agenda.

   True   False

4. The meeting attendees have been carefully chosen to include only the people whose interaction is required on the topics.

   True   False

5. The meeting has been organized around topics and questions for conversation, not a series of presentations.

   True   False

How many "False" answers did you have? Three or more would indicate there's a great opportunity to raise the bar of your strategy sessions.

To complete the full complimentary 20-question Facilitation Quiz, visit https://www.strategyskills.com/strategy-facilitation-assessment/.

The Facilitation Framework gives you a concrete way to improve your team's sessions and it involves three *P*s: Purpose, People, and Process.

Facilitation Framework

Purpose

One of the first things to consider is the purpose for the session, and here I'm not just referring to the generic agenda. What is the desired outcome of the session? There's a big difference between an agenda that lists topics to be discussed and one that includes the desired outcome for the session. Is the desired outcome a new strategic framework, identification of the company's core competencies, or creation of competitive strategies to neutralize a new player in the market?

When designed strategically, executive leadership team sessions can also serve the following purposes: provide an opportunity to build relationships, stimulate people to think differently, create a shared understanding of the business, develop greater commitment to priorities, and get on the proverbial "same page." Start by ditching the traditional format of the agenda, the one with time slots on the left and topics on the right. Placing time frames on each topic (9:00 a.m.–9:15 a.m. Develop Mission; 9:15 a.m.–9:45 a.m. Develop Vision; 9:45 a.m.–10:30 a.m. Save the Planet) is a sure way to limit people's thinking and conversation. A good facilitator will have the approximate time frames estimated on their facilitator's guide, but these aren't shared with the group. Why? Because if it's 9:43 a.m., people mentally check out of the current topic and move on to "Save the Planet," which starts at 9:45 a.m., even though they may just be discovering an important new insight.

Replace the traditional agenda format with the following items: desired outcome for the overall session, total time frame (e.g., 8:00 a.m.–4:00 p.m.), topics, desired outcome for each topic, and person responsible for leading the conversation. Be prepared for pushback from someone wanting more specific time frames attached to each topic. This is typically the multitasker looking to schedule their duck-out time—don't give it to them.

As you design the agenda, keep in mind that studies show the most important meeting items do not necessarily receive the greatest amount of time and attention. Be sure to place the most important topics of the conversation at the beginning of the session, as they tend to receive a disproportionate amount of time and attention. Before you move from one topic to the next, take the important step of jotting down the outcome for that topic and next steps.

Another key aspect of purpose is to discern what relevant information should be shared *before* the session, and what should be discussed *during* the session. Research shows that 40% of meeting time is spent sharing information that could be delivered before the meeting.[11] To add insult to injury, 65% of meetings were *intentionally* set up to be status updates or information sharing.[12] It's shocking to see how much of an executive team's time is completely wasted by having eight people sit around a conference room table for a half-hour listening to someone else's update. If it's an update, send it out prior to the session for people to review and then facilitate questions and comments on the update during the session.

People

In considering the people, think about both the facilitator and attendees. The facilitator's role is to lead the group through a series of conversations to reach the desired outcome. In doing so, the facilitator needs to possess both business acumen and emotional intelligence. Emotional intelligence can be overlooked, but a person's ability to read the room, listen actively, ask provocative questions, and then modify their approach accordingly, is critical.

Here are some guidelines for consideration when choosing a facilitator:

- Not the leader in the meeting. The facilitator's role and the leader's role are different and need to be kept separate. A leader attempting to facilitate the strategy session risks steering the conversation to their point of view and will limit the input of the team, especially those not willing to provide ideas that oppose those of the boss.
- Does not have a stake in the decisions being made. A facilitator can't lead a strategy conversation around the reallocation of resources if their resources are on the table as well.

- No internal political affiliations that will influence the outcome of the conversation. This is relevant both during the meeting and afterward. Company cultures that allow backchannel conversations after the meeting do themselves no favors because these one-to-ones leave other people with less information and open leaders up to claims of favoritism.
- Expert in the process of strategic thinking. Unfortunately, in some organizations, the use of exercises in strategy sessions is eerily similar to the game of pick-up sticks. A series of random, unrelated strategic thinking tools are tossed onto the flipchart with no rationale about their actual practical application or sequencing. "Hey, let's do a SWOT Analysis, then a Gap Analysis, and wrap up with a Five Forces of Competition Model." People leave the session with a frustrated, unfulfilled sense of having done some thinking, but in a very unproductive way. An expert strategist understands which of the 100-plus strategic thinking tools is appropriate for their specific situation, and just as important, which tools would be a waste of time.

Off Course: If a leader is going to be a contributor to a session, they cannot also serve as the facilitator because it can skew the input and bias the output.

A facilitator can come from within the organization or outside the organization as long as they meet the criteria outlined. When you add up the salaries in the room for a two-day offsite strategy session and think about how the executive team's entire approach toward the business can be strengthened or deflated, you can see why the selection of a facilitator is such an important factor.

The other aspect of people to think through are the attendees. Let's start with the numbers. Research shows that 20% of meeting attendees should not be there in the first place.[13] If a person is not going to actively contribute insights during a session, they should not be there. Anyone in the room who is not a knowledgeable, active contributor is going to slow the session down. Additionally, for every person in the meeting beyond seven, the probability of making decisions drops by 10%. The researchers conclude, "By the time you get to 17 people, the chances of your actually making a decision are zero."[14]

Process

Once you've determined the purpose of the session and the people attending, it's time to outline the process. Innovative thinking exercises can be an excellent way of starting the session. These exercises help executives think differently about the business to discover ideas that may lie in other domains, combine elements in new ways, and break the normal way of doing things. When we view innovation as "creating new value for customers," a floodgate of insights can be opened with the right question or exercise.

Typically in executive leadership sessions, decisions should be made. It's helpful to understand at the outset who has the ultimate decision rights for each decision to be made. While this sounds obvious, it's not often clear even at the executive level who is actually responsible for certain decisions. Once the decision rights have been determined, steps include identifying the decision at hand, establishing criteria for the solution, exploring options, weighing the risks and benefits of each option, and soliciting input from the group.

The other aspect of process that often gets overlooked is the selection of an activity to reach the desired outcome for a particular topic. It's not enough to simply put a topic on the agenda and then hope the conversation leads down a path that appropriately addresses the issue. For each topic, a specific activity should be identified to get to that outcome. As an example, your strategy session topic may be succession planning. The desired outcome is to identify the number-two person behind each functional area vice president. The activity to reach that desired outcome is to work through the Nine-Box Talent Model as a team.

There are a host of other facilitation process techniques, including a variety of voting methods, prioritization tables, and decision-making

---

Rocket Burn: Effective strategy sessions are guided by topics, activities, and outcomes.

frameworks. If you've chosen wisely, your facilitator will have these items at their disposal and prescribe the appropriate ones to reach the desired outcome. At the conclusion of the session, be sure to create a brief action plan encompassing the *what*, *who*, and *when* to ensure accountability for next steps.

When making a large financial investment in a new product or piece of capital equipment, great care is taken to ensure the money is spent wisely. The same cannot be said for many executive leadership team meetings, even though there's a similar level of investment when adding up people's time and salaries over the course of a year. Too often, these sessions are either the "same old, same old," or a haphazard mishmash of unrelated agenda items unattached to a real purpose. If you apply the Facilitation Framework and practice the three *P*s of purpose, people, and process, you'll see a dramatic improvement in the way your team collaborates about the business. If not, you can always break out a game of pick-up sticks.

In addition to providing people with the opportunity to contribute their insights in a collaborative setting, it's equally important to share with everyone why a certain option has been selected or decision made. People don't have to agree with the choice or the rationale behind the *why*. The important thing is they want to know what the selection is and why. In essence, they need the "because," as in "We're doing X, because Y." That's it.

Research in the social sciences shows that people are much more likely to fulfill a request in a collaborative manner if you simply give them a reason for doing so. One such study featured a person in line waiting to make copies at a Xerox machine. If the person asked the study participant in line ahead of them, "Excuse me, I have five pages. May I use the Xerox machine?" they were granted permission to go ahead 60% of the time. When the request was modified to include rationale—"May I use the Xerox machine because I'm in a rush?"—the permission rate jumped to 94%. While the reason "I'm in a rush" is fairly nebulous, it was prefaced by the magic word "because."[15]

 Rocket Burn: You can increase commitment to your initiative, project, or strategy by more than 30% if you simply talk with the team about why you're doing what you're doing.

Collaboration is fueled by mindset, language, and behaviors. The quality and quantity of collaboration is embedded in an organization's DNA, consisting of the values and principles by which people work. If you don't believe that collaboration is optimal among your people and their teams, start by identifying the types of words, activities, and principles that would foster it and introduce them into everyday interactions. Ensure that culture and financial incentives are supporting collaboration and share both external and internal examples of successful collaboration and the benefits they have yielded. Even in highly competitive companies and business arenas where a "survival of the fittest" mentality presides, recall the other words of the author of that theory, Charles Darwin: "It is the long history of humankind and animal kind, too, those who learned to collaborate and improvise most effectively have prevailed."

Trail Blazes

To collaborate is to work with others willingly and agreeably for a common purpose.

Research shows that decreasing the distance between people increases the likelihood of communication and collaboration.

Collaboration can be fueled by people working individually first to generate ideas and then coming together to discuss with one another.

An effective facilitator creates rhythms of conversation, fluctuating between divergence and convergence.

Divergent thinking sets the stage through open dialogue designed to generate lots of ideas and options on the topic at hand in a nonjudgmental fashion.

Convergent thinking then sweeps up the ideas, sorting them into categories for deeper evaluation where options are evaluated and judgments made.

The Facilitation Framework gives you a concrete way to improve your team's sessions and it involves three *P*s: Purpose, People, and Process.
1. Purpose: what is the desired outcome for the session?
2. People: who is qualified to facilitate the session and who should attend?
3. Process: what is the flow of the session, including topics, activities, and decisions?

Effective strategy sessions are guided by topics, activities, and outcomes.

Research in the social sciences shows that people are much more likely to fulfill a request in a collaborative manner if you simply give them a reason for doing so.

CHAPTER 15

Customers

"I've learned that people will forget what you said, people will forget what you did, but people will never forget how you made them feel."

—Maya Angelou, author, poet,
and civil rights activist

The Sherpa are a Tibetan ethnic group populating areas of the Himalayas, Nepal, and Tingri County best known for their navigational abilities and skillful mountaineering, often in service of others. Their excellence helping others climb the Himalayas and Mount Everest has fostered the use of the term "sherpa" as a generic descriptor for a skilled guide on any type of journey. While a guide doesn't typically select the destination, they have the ability to show people how to reach it. In business, customers determine their destination and we, in a sense, act as sherpas to help them reach it. Do you and your team have a clear and consistent understanding of your customers' destination? How effectively are you guiding them toward it?

When we hear the word "customers," it's natural to first think of the external customers who purchase our offerings. After all, without the influx of revenue, a business becomes a hobby. However, insightful leaders realize the power of treating employees like customers by providing them with a high level of development and support so as to maximize the value they can bring to external customers. Herb Kelleher, cofounder and former CEO of Southwest Airlines, explains, "I was criticized at business schools. They would try to pose a conundrum, 'Who

comes first, your employees, your customers, or your shareholders?'
I would say, wait a second, it's not a conundrum, your employees come
first . . . .You treat them well, they treat your customers well, the customers come back, and the shareholders love the results."[1] Let's begin by
reviewing techniques to serve internal customers.

Internal Customers

When we describe a leader as someone who sets direction and serves
others to achieve goals, it's clear to see how important the internal customers or employees are to fulfilling this function. As Herb Kelleher
described, many of them are the conduit to external customers and the
source of profitable growth that an organization needs to flourish over
the long term. A key link in this chain of service is employees at all levels
understanding how their work contributes to achieving the organization's goals and translating the strategies to their daily activities. Research
suggests that many leaders take this integral step for granted.

One study of companies performing near or at the top of their markets that had stated their strategies publicly found that less than 30% of
their employees could correctly select their firm's strategy from six
choices.[2] Another study of 4,000 managers revealed that less than 30%
could identify at least three of their company's key strategies.[3] These
findings suggest that more than 70% of executives are not acting by the
defining nature of a leader in that they are failing to set direction, or
effectively communicate that direction, to their employees.

In failing to set and communicate direction, leaders are then unable
to serve their internal customers because there's confusion on what
they're collectively trying to achieve and how to go about achieving it.
This underscores the importance of having a tool such as the StrategyPrint
(explained in Chapter 1) to put goals and strategies in writing, providing
clarity for direct reports on what should and should not be the areas of
focus and resource allocation. It also enables them to create their own
one- or two-page blueprint for their strategic direction and the activities
that they'll employ to achieve them. This consistent format for capturing
and communicating priorities throughout the team gives the leader a
highly efficient means of reviewing each area of the business and is also
an effective tool for one-to-one meetings.

One-on-Ones

One-on-ones are a commonly used meeting format for leaders and their direct reports to catch up and download on activities and progress. Research with 250 managers involved in one-on-ones with their leader found that nearly 50% rated these sessions not as valuable as they potentially could be.[4] There are three techniques for ensuring your team's one-on-ones rate much more favorably and create a mutual intersection of value.

1. **Ditch the nightly news.** A meeting—even involving only two people—still needs to meet the criterion of "collective interaction." If the session is simply a report where the business update is presented like it's being read off a local newscast teleprompter, look to move from the static to the dynamic. Have the direct reports provide the StrategyPrint or a one- to two-page business update in written form to their leader two days prior to the one-on-one meeting. This will give the leader time to process it, identify areas of focus, and prepare key questions for the discussion.
2. **Own it up.** If a leader is truly serving the people they lead, then it's helpful to have their direct reports own the agenda by creating it based on the issues that they'd like to ask questions about, receive counsel on, and discuss in depth. They should share the agenda with their leader at least two days prior to the one-on-one meeting so that the leader can review both the agenda and the written update and prepare accordingly. Leaders should provide regular feedback on the agenda topics and flow to help their direct reports enhance this important use of time.

Years ago, Starbuck's CEO Howard Schulz's efforts to eliminate the pouring out of leftover milk by baristas centered on modifying the steaming pitchers to include lines indicating exactly how much milk should be added to make the different size cappuccinos and lattes.[5] Establishing similar lines of demarcation clarifying how deep or far a direct report should go on activities and issues can be useful so that there's a clear understanding of where their ownership begins and where it transitions to someone else. Unchecked or faulty assumptions, just like spilled milk, can cause tears.

3. **Prioritize and calibrate.** In addition to providing valuable insights into people's business, the one-to-ones are an opportunity to develop and strengthen relationships. While important business issues may come up, the one-on-one sessions should not be the first thing to cancel on your calendar. Canceling these sessions even periodically sends a message that can be interpreted that the direct report and/or their needs aren't really that important. It's easy to rationalize canceling the one-on-one meetings as schedules get busy, but each cancellation takes a tiny piece out of that relationship. It's also important to gauge these interactions to determine the appropriate cadence and time allotment and calibrate up or down based on how well the meetings are fulfilling each party's needs.

> **Off Course:** It's easy to cancel one-on-one meetings with direct reports when other seemingly more important issues come up. It's also a mistake. Showing commitment to the relationship by honoring the meetings will build a stronger relationship in the long run.

Research shows that a weekly meeting lasting 30 minutes provides the most satisfaction and stimulates the greatest level of engagement. This average investment of 25 hours per year in meeting one-to-one with a direct report should pay dividends in the long run because of the dual benefits of advancing business and professional development.[6] There may be value from a relationship development standpoint to schedule a one-on-one each quarter over lunch or dinner to break the script and allow the different venue to catalyze the conversation. Survey your direct reports at least twice a year for their assessment of the one-on-one meetings to gain their perspectives on what's working, what's not working, and any changes they think would be of mutual value.

Managing Up and Laterally

While it's common when thinking about serving internal customers to focus on direct reports, research indicates the importance of focusing on your colleagues at the same level and the person or board of directors to whom you report. One study concludes, "Managing up and laterally is 50% more important than managing subordinates for business success and twice as important for career success."[7] As one's direct reports can actively seek the investment of a disproportionate amount of a leader's time, it's essential for their development and the leader's growth to ensure they are spending enough time with colleagues and their boss.

> **Rocket Burn:** Investing more time with your colleagues and boss than your direct reports may seem counterintuitive, but research shows it will result in greater business and career success.

When it comes to interaction with colleagues at the same level, several of the primary challenges observed are the territorial nature of guarding resources and information along with an overly competitive approach. A leader must be clear and set both qualitative and quantitative expectations that people are to act in the best interest of the organization, not their divisional, departmental, or functional area.

The keys to managing up, whether to a C-suite leader or the board of directors, are to be clear, be concise, and put it in writing. Be clear means explaining complex issues and technical matters in ways that are easily understood by the leader. It also means providing transparency to the real issues and problems the business is facing, so the leader is never caught off guard and surprised by challenges. Be concise means to provide only the salient background on situations, and not waste the leader's time with information that is not on point. It also means thinking through challenges to generate a range of three to five options to solve them before talking with the leader, so the leader isn't required to do their work too.

Put it in writing means to share business updates in a consistent one-to two-page written format that the leader can review prior to in-person conversations. This transforms one-on-one meetings from presentations to question-fueled conversations with a greater focus on the most important topics to cover. It also makes a leader's time much more efficient because they are able to view all of their direct reports' business landscapes from the higher-level written plateau as opposed to starting every conversation slogging away at ground zero. Finally, the written updates instill a sense of confidence that issues aren't falling through the cracks and frees up mental bandwidth because the leader doesn't have to keep every detail in their head.

It can be helpful to categorize your internal interactions with direct reports, colleagues, and bosses into three discrete networks: growth, insight, and execution. A **growth network** comprises those people who directly contribute to your development, from a knowledge, skill, and opportunity perspective. These individuals may be internal mentors, coaches, or others from whom you can gain valuable enhancements in your competencies and capabilities, making you more valuable to the business.

An **insight network** describes the people who help you understand the context of the business, articulate challenges, creatively ideate solutions, and design strategies to achieve your goals. These people are often in roles close to the external customer, in centralized market research or competitive intelligence positions, and may also include external resources such as consultants, vendors, suppliers, industry thought leaders, and other subject matter experts.

An **execution network** consists of those individuals who are instrumental in accomplishing your priorities in the form of activities, projects, strategies, and tasks. These individuals may include people who are solid line direct reports, dotted line direct reports, individual contributors, and colleagues. Taking notes on the key players in your networks and your interactions with them can maximize your relationships and advance your ability to get things done.

External Customers

The adage "the customer is always right," should be modified today to "the right customer is always right." There's a long list of companies that have tried to be all things to all customers, and a few of them are even still in business. Many recognize that at some point, sacrificing current and potential customers for greater profit can be an effective approach.

When Disney CEO Bob Iger came back to run the organization the second time, he assessed the situation and determined the company needed to stop pursuing subscribers at any cost for its Disney+ streaming service. Instead, he said, "We have to start chasing profitability. It will be demanded of us."[8] Harvard Business School professor Michael Porter shares a roadmap for this approach: "A company can usually grow faster and far more profitably by better penetrating needs and customers where it is distinctive than by slugging it out in potentially higher growth arenas in which the company lacks uniqueness. So the first place to look for growth is to deepen your penetration of your core target of customers. The common mistake is to settle for 50% of your target segment when 80% is achievable. You can shoot for true leadership when the customer target is properly defined not as the whole industry, but as the set of customers and needs that your strategy serves best."[9]

The ironic aspect of trying to be all things to all customers is that the lack of trade-offs (e.g., price/quality, custom/generic, scale/boutique, etc.) makes the offerings less appealing across the board. When the value proposition has been watered down to appease the full spectrum of customers, there is no factor on which the spike in value is particularly high and engaging enough to attract and keep customers. As the saying goes, the only thing in the middle of the road are yellow lines and roadkill. A good place to start is to perform a Customer Assessment.

The Customer Assessment (Table 15.1) is a tool designed to provide a simple evaluation of how well a customer fits with your business. The framework lists the customer, their primary needs, and their profit/

Table 15.1 Customer Assessment.

Customer	Primary Needs	Profit/ Value (1-5)	Strategic Fit (1-5)	Maintain Or Prune	Next Steps
Acme	General digital services	3	4	Maintain	Create awareness for additional services
Technobody	Advanced and customized data solutions	5	5	Maintain	Leverage current work for multi-year contract
Costazon	Basic data management at low prices	2	1	Prune	Refer to low-cost rival

value rating using a 1–5 scale, where 1 = low and 5 = high. The next dimension examined is strategic fit using the same 1–5 scale. For the strategic fit factor, a customer is rated on how well their needs match with your offering's distinct benefits, such as service levels, brand appeal, and convenience.

The next area for consideration is whether to maintain the customer or prune them from the business. A quick and cost-effective way to improve the bottom line is to prune unprofitable customers from the business. While this sounds like a no-brainer, it doesn't happen nearly as often as it should because people are wed to the "more customers, more market share, more everything," mentality. The final consideration is appropriate next steps based on the analysis, so that it doesn't result in a purely conceptual exercise.

Once you've clarified which customers to maintain and develop, it's helpful to dive into the individual decision maker's mind and understand their goals. The Customer Goal Assessment (Table 15.2) is a simple way to determine the fit between an individual customer's goals and how well your group is positioned to meet those goals.

For instance, the individual customer we're serving may be the vice president of procurement and supply chain. Through conversations with her and meetings with members of her team, we identify her goals and their importance. We then determine our ability to support those goals. The first step is to chart these factors.

Table 15.2 Customer Goal Assessment.

Customer Goal	Importance to Customer	Your Ability to Support
Maintain independence	9	1
Build strong brand in community	4	4
Increase business acumen of team	6	7
Reduce product costs	7	5
Be seen as strategic leader	9	7
Increase level of convenience	6	4
Create culture of innovation	5	3

Next, we use the Customer Goal Matrix (Figure 15.1) to visualize her goals, the importance of those goals to her, and our ability to support them. Laying out the goals visually relative to one another based on the criteria of importance and ability to support provides a helpful framework for discussion and identification of which ones to focus on to enhance the relationship. Validating these goal ratings through conversations with the customer then provides a seamless transition to review with her the corresponding objectives, strategies, and tactics, or GOST Framework. This is an effective process for changing one's lens from a "my agenda first" perspective to ensuring that you're meeting the customer where they are and helping them navigate to where they want to go.

In working with external customers at all levels of the organization, there will naturally be many requests as part of the working relationship. The default mode in some organizations is to respond by immediately acquiescing to each and every request, whether reasonable or

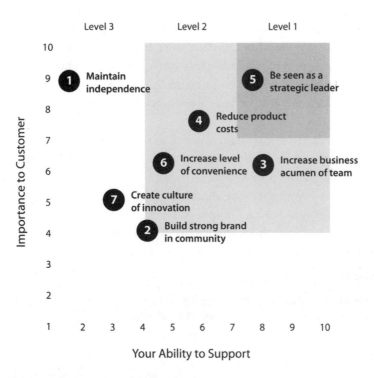

Figure 15.1   Customer Goal Matrix.

unreasonable. In other organizations that believe in the principle "great strategy is as much about what you choose not to do," they will muster the discipline to say no to customer requests that are unreasonable and don't fall within the scope of the relationship. However, there is an effective technique bridging these two approaches referred to as "Yes, and . . ." that we briefly touched on earlier in a slightly different context.

The phrase "Yes, and . . ." is a foundational principle in the art of improv comedy. When two or more comedic actors are involved in an improv sketch, no matter what statement is made or question asked, the initial response should be "Yes, and . . ." This means that they agree to accept each other's initiating remarks and are committed to building on them, which effectively moves the action forward. The same results can be had in customer interactions in a business setting. When a customer shares a request such as "Time is not on our side. We'll need you to turn this order around and have it to us by tomorrow," we can respond with one of several options:

- "Sure, we'll get right on it." Your team will be upset by another fire drill from the client that continually refuses to plan ahead and hijacks the time of a team of people that were working on other priorities.
- "No, that time frame is outside of our agreement." The client will be upset because the issue is now stalled, you haven't taken action to move it forward, and created a perception that you're not providing good service.
- "*Yes*, we can turn this order around and have it to you by tomorrow, *and* it will cost an additional 40% because it's outside of the agreed upon delivery window, and we're happy to do it for you because you're a valued customer." You've shared a positive response by agreeing to move their issue forward, and at the same time educated them that a rush request today and in the future will require a higher fee to compensate your business for the fire drill.

> **Rocket Burn:** Instead of telling external customers "no" when they have unreasonable requests, consider using "Yes, and . . ." followed by the conditions under which you can take care of their request.

Management guru Peter Drucker said, "The purpose of a business is to create and keep a customer," which might be enhanced to read, "The purpose of a business is to create and keep a *profitable* customer."[10]

Board of Directors

For C-suite leaders in public companies and some private and nonprofit organizations, a key stakeholder is the board of directors. A board of directors is the governing body of an organization, weighing in on and making key decisions in the areas of significant investments, mergers and acquisitions, strategic direction, dividend allocation (public companies), setting compensation, and hiring and firing of senior executives. If directors are going to perform these duties effectively, they must build a strong foundation of knowledge on the industry and the organization's business. Unfortunately, this is rarely the case. Research with more than 1,500 directors of boards found that only 10% of board members felt that they had a comprehensive understanding of the industry and market dynamics and only 20% believed they fully understood the company's strategy.[11]

> **Off Course:** Only 2 out of 10 board of directors members fully understand the company's strategy and only 1 out of 10 believe they have a strong understanding of the industry and market dynamics in which the company operates.

Directors are often appointed to boards because they bring new and different perspectives, which means in many cases they come from different industries. These new and different perspectives can be valuable if they are quickly complemented by a thorough understanding of the company's business and the industry in which it operates. However, if a company's senior executives are continuously having to educate directors on fundamental business dynamics and spend time in board meetings answering questions about basic principles of the business, then changes need to be made. If these issues ring true, several approaches to these changes should be considered.

If a director has been onboarded with the appropriate background information on industry dynamics, and fundamentals of the business, and has been on the board for at least a year, then it's fair to test their knowledge. Have each director take an industry and company business assessment on an annual basis to ensure that they possess a baseline level of knowledge. Directors who don't pass the test should be removed.

Directors should also be evaluated annually on their overall contribution to the board by their peer directors. One technique is to have each director write down the names of five other directors whom they believe add considerable value and should remain on the board. If a director does not appear on anyone's list, they should be removed. Richard Parsons, former chairman of Citigroup and CEO of Time Warner, cites a *Fortune* 50 CEO when he writes, "It impacts other directors if you tolerate a weak board member. It's hard, but you have to step up to the plate."[12]

> **Rocket Burn:** Assess the knowledge and value of board members on an annual basis and remove directors who are not contributing significant worth.

A survey of more than 1,000 corporate directors showed that the number-one reason for the success or failure of CEO appointments was alignment on strategic direction between the board of directors and the CEO.[13] Therefore, a key consideration for many C-suite leaders is how to engage with their boards on strategy. Are you engaging the board of directors in unscripted conversations fueled by provocative questions that are generating insights based on their experience and expertise? Or are you and your team spending hundreds of hours a year preparing scripted presentations that are robotically rubberstamped by the board for approval? David Pyott, CEO of Allergan, said, "Boards need to have strategy discussions with management and the CEO all year long. It can't be a 'once and done' event—strategy needs to be discussed at literally every meeting."[14]

A powerful forum for executive team and board of director interaction is to conduct a biyearly offsite meeting on the key challenges facing the organization in the next three years. It's important to prepare three to five thought-provoking questions as pre-meeting work so that participants have an opportunity to think deeply and descend below the surface of the business to the core issues. An external facilitator can add value to these sessions because of their neutrality, which enables all of the executive leadership team members and board of directors to share their full perspectives without having to appear impartial to the outcome. A board of directors can be an invaluable source of insights and guidance for the executive team, or they can be a never-ending sinkhole of wasted time and energy. Choose wisely.

Trail Blazes

A leader can serve both internal and external customers.

A StrategyPrint, or two-page blueprint for the business, can provide clarity for a leader's direct reports on where they should be focusing their time and talent.

Three techniques for improving one-on-one meetings:
1. Think dialogue, not monologue updates.
2. Have direct reports own and create the agenda.
3. Don't cancel the meetings when fire drills ring.

Research shows that a weekly one-on-one meeting lasting 30 minutes provides the most satisfaction and stimulates the greatest level of engagement.

While many leaders focus a disproportionate amount of time on their direct reports, research shows that their ability to manage laterally and up is significantly more important to both business and career success.

It can be helpful to categorize your internal interactions with direct reports, colleagues, and bosses into three discrete networks: growth, insight, and execution.

The Customer Assessment is a tool designed to provide a simple evaluation of how well a customer fits with your business.

Invest time discovering what the goals and strategy are for your external customers.

A board of directors is the governing body of an organization, weighing in on and making key decisions in the areas of significant investments, mergers and acquisitions, strategic direction, dividend allocation (public companies), setting compensation, and hiring and firing of senior executives.

Directors should be evaluated annually on their industry knowledge and overall contribution to the board by their peer directors.

CHAPTER 16

Meetings

Meeting (mee-ting), noun: the act of people coming together to rehash topics they've been talking about for five months, check their mobile phones every 10 minutes for anything more interesting than the meeting they're in, and agree to things they have no intention of following up on.

While this definition isn't the one in the dictionary, it's likely a more accurate description of what's happening in organizations than the official version. Let's face it, most meetings, either in-person or virtual, are wasting people's time and the company's money. Who says? The research.

The average professional invests approximately 21.5 hours per week—more than half the average work week—in meetings, which equates to more than 1,075 hours per year.[1] Unfortunately, managers rated more than half the meetings they were involved in (in-person or virtual) as "ineffective." Nearly 85% of senior executives surveyed stated that their meetings were not a good use of individual or group time.[2]

When you start to calculate the number of hours spent in unproductive meetings across all the people in your organization, the amount of time, money, and energy being wasted is staggering. For example, at one multibillion-dollar organization, a weekly review meeting involving a group of managers cost more than $15 million per year.[3] Would you invest that amount of money in a physical product that was broken? Not likely. You would either fix it or get rid of it. And that's what you need to do with your meetings: fix them or get rid of them.

Off Course: 85% of executives described their meetings as a waste of time.

Where do we begin to right these wrongs? Let's start with what a meeting should be: a gathering of two or more people featuring collective interaction and engagement using conversations to make progress toward a purpose. Note the use of the words "interaction" and "conversations" in the definition. If you find yourself in meetings and especially videoconferences on a regular basis where the format is primarily a one-way presentation, there's ample opportunity to improve your situation. Jamie Dimon, chairman and CEO of JPMorgan Chase, says, "Very rarely do I allow a presentation. It's all pre-reads and recommendations. We prepare in advance so that we're using meeting time to make decisions."[4]

Research with senior executives in nearly 200 companies showed that the majority of meetings (65%) were not designed to reach decisions but rather were vehicles for basic information sharing.[5] If one person in a meeting is speaking more than 50% of the time, it's not a meeting, it's a monologue. Information sharing and updates should be done in writing or video and distributed at least 24–48 hours prior to the meeting so people can review, digest, and formulate questions to drive the meeting conversation.

As with most improvement efforts, it's helpful to begin with a brief assessment of the "as is" situation. Prior to an initiative to improve your meetings, it may be helpful to gain insights from your team on what's working and what's not. Here are 5 sample questions from the 20-question Meetings Quiz to identify strengths and areas for improvement for the meetings you typically attend:

1. Relevant information is sent out prior to meetings to avoid one-way presentations during the meetings.

    Yes   No

2. Meetings start at their scheduled time.

    Yes   No

3. People are fully attentive and not engaged in multitasking (e.g., checking phones).

    Yes   No

4. People leave meetings with a clear understanding of who is doing what and by when.

Yes   No

5. I decline meeting invitations when the purpose and/or agenda have not been communicated.

Yes   No

In this brief sample, a score of three or more "No's" indicates an opportunity to dramatically improve the efficacy and productivity of your meetings. You and your team can take the complimentary 20-question Meetings Quiz at https://www.strategyskills.com/meetings-quiz/.

Strategic Meeting Framework

A helpful tool to ensure your meetings are not a series of monologues is the Strategic Meeting Framework (Figure 16.1), which provides an outline to improve the efficacy and efficiency of your approach to collective interactions in three core areas.

1. **Intent.** The intent or purpose of the meeting should clearly answer why people are investing their time in this interaction. Intent should

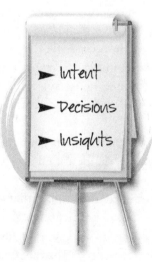

Figure 16.1 Strategic Meeting Framework.

also capture the desired outcome that the meeting is designed to produce. Especially when it comes to virtual meetings, intent is often assumed or overlooked. The absence of intent begets a routine of video-conferences where nice-to-know information is passed along verbally, when it could have been communicated in a much more efficient manner. Patricia Frost, chief human resource officer of Seagate Technology, says, "Every time there's a meeting, I make sure the leader's intent is in that invite. If you can't give me that, we shouldn't be having the meeting."[6]

Notice that intent is not the equivalent of agenda. An agenda is typically a list of topics to discuss. While some of the items on the agenda may move the group toward a desired outcome, the agenda itself is not the purpose or desired outcome but should have the purpose clearly called out in writing. If the purpose is identified beforehand, it enables people who won't add or gain value from participating to appropriately decline the meeting invitation. The reality is that despite the fact that roughly 33% of managers want to skip irrelevant meetings, the majority don't. The research shows that 83% accept the invitation and less than 15% decline.[7]

When I facilitate strategy workshops for intact teams or executives from cross-functional areas, managers are expected to share the intent at least a week prior to the meeting to give potential attendees an indication of whether the intent matches up with their goals. Research shows that up to half of the content of meetings is not relevant to participants and 20% of meeting participants should not be there in the first place.[8] If you have meetings at which a leader and their direct report are both present, the question needs to be asked: Do both really need to be there?

Intent Question: For the meetings on your calendar this week, has the intent for each one been clearly identified on the agenda?

2. **Decision.** A survey of executives found that 88% did not believe that their executive leadership team meetings generated decisions on key organizational and strategy-based topics.[9] One of the primary reasons so many meetings waste people's time is that they continue to talk about the same issues over and over, without moving things forward.

The feeling of "meeting déjà vu" that you've experienced this meeting before is not an illusion, because you actually have experienced it before! The tsunami of multitasking that goes on during meetings often occurs because the session leader did not think through in advance what decisions the group needed to make, so progress grinds to a halt.

Meetings often occur because clear decision rights are not in place or people believe that every decision should be through group consensus. It's important that the people involved in the meeting are all clear on the decision rights and responsibilities for the topics being discussed. Just as a sales representative or account manager is not going to spend most of their time talking to a potential customer who can't make the purchase decision, strategic executives are not going to have multiple meetings without identifying the decision makers and providing them with the input required to move things forward.

Once a decision has been made, it's important to remember the premise behind trade-offs that we reviewed earlier: the Latin origin of *decision* is *decidere*, or "to cut off." Once you decide to do something, the group should also clearly identify what you will be "cutting off" from your time, attention, and budget. If you fail to cut things off from future meeting agendas, your team will soon be drowning in too many priorities, projects, and tasks.

Decision Question: For your next in-person or virtual meeting, what decisions have been identified for the group to make?

3. **Insights.** Perhaps the most overlooked aspect of meetings should occur in the final 5–15 minutes. It's at this point of the session that the team reviews their learnings or takeaways from the interaction. Instead, people are checking their phones to see what their next meeting is or banging out emails and texts. Meanwhile, the entire group has missed an opportunity to get better by recording their insights.

Rocket Burn: Carve out the final minutes of a meeting for people to record their insights and assign action steps.

Leaving a meeting without checking to see what insights have been cultivated contributes to the vicious cycle of talking about the same issues week after week, month after month. The meeting facilitator should give participants a few minutes to record their individual insights. They then ask people to share their takeaways to see what the range of insights include along with appropriate action steps. The leader can then capture this new reservoir of learnings to build the group's bank of collective expertise. If at the end of a meeting people don't have any new insights, this is a signal to the leader that changes need to be made to the meeting design or the meeting itself may no longer be useful.

Meeting Insights: What were the top three insights from your most recent meeting?

A final action item from the Strategic Meeting Framework is represented in the motto "Kill One to Create One." If someone in your group or another group proposes a new regular meeting, first see if the "Intent—Decision—Insights" criteria are being met. If so, the group should then decide which regularly scheduled meeting should be terminated: kill one to create one.

The potential money you can save by running more effective meetings is startling. Let's take an example using the fictitious company Technobody, featured in the strategy graphic novel *StrategyMan vs. the Anti-Strategy Squad: Using Strategic Thinking to Defeat Bad Strategy and Save Your Plan.*[10] The company has 166 managers. If the average managerial salary is $80,000 (an industry average based on Glassdoor data) and 40% of their time is spent in meetings, then roughly $32,000 per manager is spent on meetings during the year.

If 50% of meeting content is irrelevant and ineffective (conservative estimate based on research), then $16,000 (50% × $32K) is wasted per manager each year in bad meetings. If we then multiply $16K in waste per manager by 166 managers, we see that a conservative estimate of wasted meeting cost for Technobody is $2.65 million per year. This number does not even include the time spent preparing for meetings or the wasted meeting time of the 900-plus independent contributors who report to these managers. You can use the process described above with the number of managers in your group and average salary to see just how much bad meetings are costing your team.

Strategic Approach to Meetings

There are five steps you can follow to help your organization take a more strategic approach to meetings:

1. **Conduct a meetings audit.** Before a doctor prescribes a medication, they first diagnose the patient's condition. In the same spirit, before you prescribe new meeting guidelines, it's helpful to first baseline what's happening today. When conducting a meetings audit, look at factors such as the types of meetings, frequency, length, intent, participants, and outcomes. Closely examine the reasons these meetings exist and if there are any meetings that are unnecessary. Once the audit is complete, it provides a bounty of useful information to shape the future state of meetings. Another powerful way to assess meetings in real-time is to score them. For each meeting you attend, rate the session on a scale of 1–3, with 3 = high value and 1 = low value. At the end of the week or month, evaluate the meetings and their scores to determine which are adding value and which are not. For those meetings that are scoring low on value, decide if there's a way to enhance the value by modifying them, or eliminate them altogether.

2. **Identify current meeting mistakes.** Meeting mistakes occur in three phases: pre-meeting, in-meeting, and post-meeting. They can be categorized as either leader mistakes or participant mistakes. For example, a common in-meeting mistake by the leader is failing to rein in off-track conversations. A common in-meeting mistake by participants is multitasking, which conveys a lack of interest in the topic and/or a lack of respect for the person speaking at the time. There are approximately 25 mistakes to look for in the three phases to ensure that the group is not sabotaging their own efforts at improvement. Here is a sample checklist of post-meeting mistakes:

   ☐ Failure to end the meeting at the scheduled time
   ☐ Lack of accountability and time frame on topics for follow-up
   ☐ Agreeing to things in the meeting but not following through on what was agreed upon
   ☐ Undersharing: failure to share the meeting insights/summary with people who are impacted by the outcomes but did not attend
   ☐ Oversharing: emailing the meeting insights/summary to people who are not impacted by the outcomes

3. **Educate managers on what good looks like.** Begin this step by collecting the current best practices being used by managers within the organization. Then look externally to see what principles and guidelines are being used by other organizations within and outside your industry as it relates to meetings. For instance, organizations such as Amazon and Stripe begin many meetings in silence, reading a thoughtfully written document on the meeting topic, so that everyone is beginning from the same place and can formulate key questions.[11]

   Another technique gaining traction is to designate a day of the week when no meetings are to be held. In theory, these large chunks of time can be dedicated to individual work without interruption. Preliminary study has shown that keeping one day a week free of meetings has a number of benefits. Professor Benjamin Laker summarizes the findings of his research: "When one no-meeting day per week was introduced, autonomy, communication, engagement, and satisfaction all improved, resulting in decreased micromanagement and stress, which caused productivity to rise."[12]

4. **Utilize meeting tools.** One of the keys to leading effective and efficient meetings is aligning the goals of the meeting with the appropriate tools and processes to get there. If you're leading a strategy development meeting, there are more than 100 different strategic thinking tools you can choose from to help your team think and plan strategically. The key is selecting the handful of tools that make the most sense based on the context of the business, goals and objectives, competitive landscape, and so on. Be clear on your meeting goals and then choose the process and tools to get there. A solid meeting design begins by identifying the topics to be discussed, the goals of each topic, and the activities that can be used to guide the team through the session. For example, if the meeting topic is succession planning, the goal may be to identify the number-two person for each functional VP, and the activity would be to work through a nine-box talent model.

5. **Develop meeting checklists.** Research in the social sciences on habits shows that in order to effectively change people's behaviors, it's helpful to provide physical or environmental triggers. One such effective trigger is the use of meeting checklists. These physical reminders

ensure that teams across the organization are aware of the basic meeting principles, techniques, and tools to optimize their meeting time. However, the checklists are only valuable if they are accompanied by the corresponding discipline to utilize them on a consistent basis. Following is a sample of items from the Meeting Preparation checklist:

- ☐ Invite the right people, not all people.
- ☐ Disseminate information and data prior to the meeting.
- ☐ Have a clear topical agenda, allowing for flexibility.
- ☐ Identify the decisions to be made.
- ☐ Start on time, even if not everyone is there.

Meetings are often a reflection of the organization's culture and take on the tone of their leader's approach to the business. Apple co-founder Steve Jobs led meetings that have been described as friction-filled and painfully to the point, based in part on an experience he had growing up.

Jobs's neighbor introduced him to his rock tumbler, which transformed the rough rocks they found in their backyards into smooth stones. The transformation occurred after a day of the rocks banging around in the tumbler machine with liquid and grit powder. Jobs said, "Through rubbing up against each other, creating a little bit of friction, creating a little bit of noise, had come out these beautiful, polished rocks. And that has always been my metaphor for a team working really hard on something that they are passionate about. That is through the team, through that group of incredibly talented people bumping up against each other having arguments, having fights sometimes and making noise, and working together they polish each other, and they polish the ideas and what comes out are these really beautiful stones."[13]

The e-commerce company Shopify has taken a disciplined approach to improving productivity with their approach to meetings. They canceled many recurring group meetings to the tune of more than 12,000 events from employees' calendars, which freed up 95,000 hours. Shopify also put strict guidelines around meetings of 50 or more people and instituted a no-meetings Wednesday policy. Kaz Nejatian, Shopify's chief operating officer, wrote to employees, "We're starting the year fresh with some useful subtraction: freeing ourselves from an absurd amount of meeting time, and unlocking an incredible amount of maker time."[14]

Keep in mind that your meetings reflect your organization's culture and leadership. How would you describe the efficacy, efficiency, and tone of your meetings? Effective meetings can be energizing forums to help your team set direction, make decisions, and unify efforts. Ineffective meetings can be anchors that weigh people down with irrelevant information, didactic presentations, and unclear priorities. Which type do you attend today? Do you think it will be different tomorrow?

Trail Blazes

A meeting is defined as the act of people coming together to rehash topics they've been talking about for five months, check their mobile phones every 10 minutes for anything more interesting than the meeting they're in, and agree to things they have no intention of following up on. (Just kidding.)

A meeting is a gathering of two or more people featuring collective interaction and engagement using conversations to make progress toward a purpose.

The Strategic Meeting Framework provides an outline to improve the efficacy and efficiency of your approach to collective interactions in three core areas: Intent, Decisions, Insights.

The intent or purpose of the meeting should clearly answer why people are investing their time in this interaction and capture the desired outcomes.

Identify the decisions to be made at meetings so certain items are cut off from future time and attention in order to focus on new areas.

Do not add a new regularly scheduled meeting without considering an existing meeting to eliminate.

Five steps to a more strategic approach to meetings:
1. Conduct a meetings audit.
2. Identify current meeting mistakes.
3. Educate managers on what good looks like.
4. Utilize meeting tools.
5. Develop meeting checklists.

CLOSE

People crave competence, capability, and clarity. Competence is the knowledge to perform at high level. Capability embodies the resources and skills to transform expertise into value. And clarity is seeing and selecting the right direction to reach your destination. Are you ready to lead people from confusion, uncertainty, and reactivity to competence, capability, and clarity? Are you ready to be strategic?

A young woman was hiking a mountain trail she had never explored before. About 30 minutes into the hike, she passed several older women who waved and said, "You're hiking awfully fast. Why not slow down and enjoy the scenery?" So the young woman slowed her pace. Thirty minutes later, she came upon two older men seated on a large rock. They smiled and said, "You better pick up the pace if you want to get to the top and back down before dark." So the young woman hurried along. An hour later, as she was nearing the top of the mountain, she spotted a young man on a different path above her and he said, "Why are you walking down there? The view is much prettier up here." So the young woman changed course and took the higher path.

She finally reached the beautiful, breathtaking mountain summit and soaked in the spectacular view. As she was about to hike back, she encountered a monk seated on the edge of the cliff, finishing his meditation. "My child," said the monk, "You seem rushed. Sit here, breathe in the fresh air, and become one with the mountain." So the young woman sat down, closed her eyes, and meditated. When she finished, night had fallen, and it was pitch black. She got up and walked straight off the edge of the cliff. She did indeed, become one with the mountain.

There will always be people telling you, "Go this way, not that way . . . go faster . . . no, go slower . . . stop here, no . . . stop there," critiquing your every move. While you should be aware of what others say to gain relevant insights, you'll want to rely primarily on the greatest navigational instrument ever designed: your mind. If you chart your course by continuing to develop the four areas of strategic fitness—strategy, leadership, organization, and communication—and use these skills as your compass, then your journey will be as fulfilling as your destination.

ARE YOU TACTICAL OR STRATEGIC?

What's Your SQ?

Take the Strategic Quotient™ (SQ) Assessment to measure your strategic capabilities as exhibited through your mindset and behaviors, with a focus on the critical disciplines for being strategic:

• Acumen (Thinking): The generation of insights to create new value

• Allocation (Planning): Focusing resources through strategic trade-offs

• Action (Acting): Prioritizing and executing initiatives

Are you strategic? Take the assessment today and find out.

The Strategic Fitness System

The Strategic Fitness System™ (SFS) is an online platform for leaders to develop key business skills in the areas of strategy, leadership, organization, and communication. It contains more than 200 tools and forums for you to continuously learn and practice your skills, including:

• 50 Strategic workouts and exercises

• StrategyPrint® strategic action plan template

• Strategic Journal to record insights and structure your thinking

Find these additional resources and sign up to receive the free Strategic Thinker newsletter to help you achieve executive excellence along with more videos, articles, and guidance for your strategic journey at: **www.StrategySkills.com**

NOTES

Introduction

1. Richard Pyle, "Amelia Earhart case leaps to life in diary," *Los Angeles Times*, April 1, 2007.
2. Ibid.
3. Ibid.
4. *AmeliaEarhart.com*, accessed December 6, 2022.
5. National Museum of American History, Smithsonian Institution, timeandnavigation .si.edu, accessed December 6, 2022.
6. *History.com*, accessed December 6, 2022.
7. *AmeliaEarhart.com*, accessed December 6, 2022.
8. *Dictionary.com*, "navigate," accessed December 7, 2022.
9. Andrew Johnston, Roger Connor, Carlene Stephens, and Paul Ceruzzi, *Time and Navigation: The Untold Story of Getting from Here to There* (Washington, D.C.: Smithsonian Books, 2015).
10. ANNEX 25: *Guidelines for Voyage Planning*, International Maritime Organization Resolution A.893(21), November 25, 1999.
11. Christopher Dann, "The Lesson of Lost Value," *strategy + business*, issue 69.
12. Chris Gagnon, Elizabeth John, and Rob Theunissen, "Organizational Health: A Fast Track to Performance Improvement," *McKinsey Quarterly*, September 17, 2017.
13. Jim Clifton and Jim Harter, *It's the Manager* (New York: Gallup Press, 2019).
14. Sarah Krouse, "Robert Iger Returns to Disney Facing Radically Different Landscape," *Wall Street Journal*, November 22, 2022.
15. Chip Cutter, "Hilton's CEO Sees a New Golden Age for Travel," *Wall Street Journal*, December 19, 2022.
16. *Merriam-Webster's Dictionary*, "strategic," merriam-webster.com, accessed December 7, 2022.
17. Robert Kabacoff, "Develop Strategic Thinkers Throughout Your Organization," *Harvard Business Review*, February 7, 2014.
18. Ibid.
19. Patricia Sellers, "The Queen of Pop," *Fortune*, September 28, 2009.

20. David Yoffie and Michael Cusumano, *Strategy Rules* (New York: HarperCollins Books, 2015).

21. "Corporate Board of Directors Survey," *Chief Executive* magazine, November–December 2011.

22. Brook Manville, "Want to Be a CEO? Five Essential Qualities Boards Look For," *Forbes*, April 10, 2016.

23. Cal Henderson, "It's Easy to Get Lost in the Weeds," Fast Company, December 2018–January 2019.

24. James Kouzes and Barry Posner, Great Leadership Creates Great Workplaces (San Francisco: Jossey-Bass, 2013).

25. David Welch, "At Mary Barra's GM, It's Profit Before All Else," Businessweek, May 18, 2017.

26. Dorie Clark, "Pointless Meetings Are the Worst. You Can Avoid Them," Wall Street Journal, May 7–8, 2022.

27. Scott Anthony, Paul Cobban, Rahul Nair, and Natalie Painchaud, "Breaking Down the Barriers to Innovation," *Harvard Business Review*, November–December 2019.

Chapter 1

1. Martin van Creveld, *The Art of War: War and Military Thought* (London: Cassell, 2000).

2. Meg Whitman, "Bidding on Success," *Rotman* magazine, Spring–Summer 2005.

3. Lawrence Freedman, *Strategy: A History* (New York: Oxford University Press, 2013).

4. Rich Horwath, "The Strategic Mindset: Applying Strategic Thinking Skills for Organizational Success," *Chief Learning Officer*, Strategic Thinking Institute, www.strategyskills.com/pdf/The-Strategic-Mindset.pdf, 2018.

5. Freedman, *Strategy: A History*.

6. *Dictionary.com*, "essence," accessed August 28, 2020.

7. Tim Mullaney, "A Master Class in the Magic of Success from Disney CEO Bob Iger," CNBC.com, May 9, 2017.

8. Paul Carroll and Mui Chunka, "7 Ways to Fail Big," *Harvard Business Review*, September 2008.

9. Ozan Varol, *Think Like a Rocket Scientist: Simple Strategies You Can Use to Make Giant Leaps in Work and Life* (New York: Hachette Book Group, 2020).

10. Freedman, *Strategy: A History*.

11. Sun Tzu, *The Art of War*, James Clavell, ed. (New York: Delacorte Press, 1983).

12. Chris Zook and James Allen, *Repeatability: Build Enduring Business for a World of Constant Change* (Boston: Harvard Business School Publishing, 2012).

13. Alan Deutschman, *Change or Die* (New York: Regan, 2007).

14. Matthew Olson, Derek van Bever, and Seth Verry, "When Growth Stalls," *Harvard Business Review*, March 2008.

15. Josh Tyrangiel, "Tim Cook's Freshman Year," *Businessweek,* December. 6, 2012.

16. Donald Sull, "Why Strategy Execution Unravels—and What to Do About It," *Harvard Business Review*, March 2015.

17. Michael Porter and Nitin Nohria, "How CEOs Manage Time," *Harvard Business Review,* July–August 2018.

18. Leslie Perlow, Constance Noonan Hadley, and Eunice Eun, "Stop the Meeting Madness," *Harvard Business Review*, July–August 2017.

19. Michael Mankins, Chris Brahm, and Gregory Caimi, "Your Scarcest Resource," *Harvard Business Review*, May 2014.

20. Kerri Anne Renzulli, Cybele Weisser, and Megan Leonhardt, "The 21 Most Valuable Career Skills," *Money* magazine, June 4, 2020.

21. Horwath, "The Strategic Mindset."

22. Michael Birshan, "Creating more value with corporate strategy," *McKinsey Quarterly*, 2011.

23. Austin Carr, "Punk, Meet Rock," *Fast Company*, April 2014.

Chapter 2

1. Meg Whitman with Joan O'C. Hamilton, *The Power of Many: Values for Success in Business and in Life* (New York: Crown Publishers, 2010).

2. Stephen Hall, Dan Lovallo, and Reinier Musters, "How to Put Your Money Where Your Strategy Is," *McKinsey Quarterly*, March 2012.

3. Michael Gibbert, "In Praise of Resource Constraints," *MIT Sloan Management Review*, Spring 2006.

4. Bill DeMain, "How Malfunctioning Sharks Transformed the Movie Business," *Mental Floss*, June 20, 2015.

5. Donald Sull, "How to Thrive in Turbulent Markets," *Harvard Business Review*, February 2009.

6. Hall, Lovallo, and Musters, "How to Put Your Money Where Your Strategy Is."

7. Sull, "Why Strategy Execution Unravels."

8. Ibid.

9. Adi Ignatius, "We Need People to Lean into the Future," *Harvard Business Review*, March–April 2017.

10. Udo Kopka, "From Bottom to Top: Turning Around the Top Team," *McKinsey Quarterly*, November 2014.

11. Stephen Hall, "How to put your money where your strategy is," *McKinsey Quarterly*, March 2012.

12. Hall, Lovallo, and Musters, "How to Put Your Money Where Your Strategy Is."

13. Tim Ferris, *Tools of Titans: The Tactics, Routines, and Habits of Billionaires, Icons, and World-Class Performers* (New York: Houghton Mifflin Harcourt, 2016).

14. *Porsche Corporate Marketing Collateral*, September 2014.

15. Kevin Plank, "My Formula for Innovative Design," *Inc.*, July–August 2014.

16. Leigh Buchanan, "The Psychology of Productivity," *Inc.*, March 2015.
17. Chris Zook and James Allen, *The Founder's Mentality: How to Overcome the Predictable Crises of Growth* (Boston: Harvard Business Review Press, 2016).
18. Betsy Morris, "What Makes Apple Golden," *Fortune*, March 17, 2008.
19. *Dictionary.com*, "decide," accessed December 7, 2022.
20. Olivier Sabony and Dan Lovallo, "Strategic Decisions: When Can You Trust Your Gut?" *McKinsey Quarterly*, March 1, 2010.
21. Sull, "Why Strategy Execution Unravels."
22. Rik Kirkland, "Cisco's Display of Strength," *Fortune*, November 12, 2007.
23. Morten Hansen, "How to Succeed in Business? Do Less," *Wall Street Journal*, January 12, 2018.
24. Kathleen Chaykowski, "Instagram's Big Picture," *Forbes*, August 23, 2016.

Chapter 3

1. Elena Lytkina Botelho, Kim Rosenkoetter Powell, Stephen Kincaid, and Dina Wang, "What Sets Successful CEOs Apart," *Harvard Business Review*, May–June 2017.
2. Ibid.
3. Amos Tversky and Daniel Kahneman, "The Framing of Decisions and the Psychology of Choice, *Science*, January 30, 1981.
4. Amos Tversky and Daniel Kahneman, "Judgment Under Uncertainty: Heuristics and Biases," *Science* (185): 1124–30.
5. Gary Neilson, Karla Martin, and Elizabeth Powers, "The Secrets to Successful Strategy Execution," *Harvard Business Review*, June 2008.
6. Michael Mankins, "Strategies for a Changing World," *Harvard Business Review*, June 2010.
7. Scott Amyx, "Why Innovation Benefits from Dissent," *Forbes*, June 24, 2019.
8. Whitman, *The Power of Many*.
9. Scott Stawski, *The Power of Mandate: How Visionary Leaders Keep Their Organization Focused on What Matters Most* (New York: McGraw-Hill, 2019).
10. Jeff Bezos, introduction by Walter Isaacson, *Invent and Wander* (Boston: Harvard Business Review Press, 2021).
11. Ibid.
12. Bradley Staats, *Never Stop Learning: Stay Relevant, Reinvent Yourself, and Thrive* (Boston: Harvard Business School Press, 2018).
13. Julian Birkinshaw and Jordan Cohen, "Make Time for the Work That Matters," *Harvard Business Review*, September 2013.
14. *Dictionary.com*, "delegate," accessed December 7, 2022.
15. Kevan Hall and Alan Hall, *Kill Bad Meetings: Cut 50% of Your Meetings, Transform Your Culture, Improve Collaboration, and Accelerate Decisions* (London: Nicholas Brealey Publishing, 2017).

Chapter 4

1. Melissa Schilling, *Quirky: The Remarkable Story of the Traits, Foibles, and Genius of Breakthrough Innovators Who Changed the World* (New York: Public Affairs, 2018).
2. *Dictionary.com*, "compete," accessed December 8, 2022.
3. Gavin Kilduff, "Driven to Win: Rivalry, Motivation and Performance," *Social Psychological and Personality Science* 5(8), 2014.
4. John Legere, "T-Mobile's CEO on Winning Market Share by Trash-Talking Rivals," *Harvard Business Review*, January–February 2017.
5. Ese Erheriene, "Watchmakers Reset Due to Apple," *Wall Street Journal*, November 19, 2018.
6. Freek Vermeulen, "Stop Doubling Down on Your Failing Strategy," *Harvard Business Review*, November–December 2017.
7. Austin Carr, "Blockbuster CEO Jim Keyes on Competition from Apple, Netflix, Nintendo, and Redbox," *Fast Company*, June 8, 2010.
8. Jesper Sorensen and Glenn Carroll, *Making Great Strategy: Arguing for Organizational Advantage* (New York: Columbia Business School Publishing, 2021).
9. Niraj Dawar, *Tilt: Shifting Your Strategy from Products to Customers* (Boston: Harvard Business Review Press, 2013).
10. Kurt Eichenwald, "Microsoft's Lost Decade," *Vanity Fair*, August 2012.
11. Michael Porter, "The Five Competitive Forces That Shape Strategy," *Harvard Business Review*, January 2008.
12. David Yoffie and Mary Kwak, *Judo Strategy: Turning Your Competitors' Strength to Your Advantage* (Boston: Harvard Business School Press, 2001).
13. Jigoro Kano, "The History of Kodokan Judo," United States of America Traditional Kodokan Judo, usatkj.org, accessed December 8, 2022.
14. Grand View Research, "Bottled Water Market Size, Share & Trends Analysis Report By Product, By Distribution Channel, By Region, and Segment Forecasts, 2022–2030," Grandviewresearch.com, April 8, 2022.
15. Eatbigfish, "Challenger Brands to Watch in 2021," MarketingSociety.com, January 2021.
16. Jim McKelvey, *The Innovation Stack: Building an Unbeatable Business One Crazy Idea at a Time* (New York: Portfolio, 2020).
17. Michael Dell with Catherine Fredman, *Direct From Dell: Strategies that Revolutionized an Industry* (New York: Harper Business, 1999).
18. Michael Raynor and Mumtaz Ahmed, "Three Rules for Making a Company Truly Great," *Harvard Business Review*, April 2013.
19. Peter Thiel with Blake Masters, *Zero to One: Notes on Startups, Or How to Build the Future* (New York: Crown Business, 2014).
20. Bruce Henderson, "The Origin of Strategy," *Harvard Business Review*, November–December 1989.

21. Michael Raynor and Mumtaz Ahmed, "Up in the Air," *Conference Board Review*, Spring 2013.

22. Nina Kruschwitz and Knut Haanaes, "First Look: Highlights from the Third Annual Sustainability Global Executive Survey," *MIT Sloan Management Review*, Fall 2011.

23. Zook and Allen, *Repeatability*.

24. Hal Gregersen, *Questions are the Answer: A Breakthrough Approach to Your Most Vexing Problems at Work and in Life* (New York: HarperBusiness, 2018).

25. Scott Kaufman and Carolyn Gregoire, *Wired to Create: Unraveling the Mysteries of the Creative Mind* (New York: TeacherPerigee, 2015).

26. Michael Porter, Robert Hof, "How to Hit a Moving Target," *Businessweek*, August 21–28, 2006.

27. Zook and Allen, *Repeatability*.

28. Hall, Lovallo, and Musters, "How to Put Your Money Where Your Strategy Is."

29. Chris Bradley and Eric Matson, "Putting Strategies to the Test," *McKinsey Quarterly*, January 1, 2011.

30. Sally Blount, "Why Are We Here?" *Harvard Business Review*, November–December 2019.

31. Kevin Coyne, "Sustainable Competitive Advantage," *McKinsey Quarterly*, November 1984.

32. Bruce Chew, "The Geometry of Competition," Monitor Group (2000).

Chapter 5

1. Kouzes and Posner, *Great Leadership Creates Great Workplaces*.

2. Ibid.

3. Reed Hastings, "An Explanation and Some Reflections," *Netflix Media Center*, September 18, 2011.

4. Garry Kasparov, *How Life Imitates Chess: Life's a Game. Play to Win.* (New York: Bloomsbury, 2007).

5. *Dictionary.com*, "context," accessed December 8, 2022.

6. Anthony Mayo and Nitin Nohria, "Zeitgeist Leadership," *Harvard Business Review*, October 2005.

7. Donald Sull, "Fast Fashion Lessons," *Business Strategy Review*, Summer 2008.

8. J. Randel, H. Pugh, and S. Reed, "Methods for Analyzing Cognitive Skills for a Technical Task," *International Journal of Human-Computer Studies* 45 (1996): 579–97.

9. Travis Bradberry and Jean Greaves, *Emotional Intelligence 2.0* (San Diego: TalentSmart, 2009).

10. Per-Ola Karlsson, Martha Turner, and Peter Gassmann, "Succeeding the Long-serving Legend in the Corner Office," *strategy + business*, Summer 2019.

11. Bradberry and Greaves, *Emotional Intelligence 2.0*.

12. Whitman, *The Power of Many*.

13. Sophie Oberstein, *10 Steps to Successful Coaching,* 2nd ed. (Virginia: ATD Press, 2020).
14. Kouzes and Posner, *Great Leadership Creates Great Workplaces.*

Chapter 6

1. Rachel Bachman, "Mikaela Shiffrin Reaches Pinnacle of Alpine Skiing," *Wall Street Journal,* January 10, 2023.
2. Anders Ericsson and Robert Pool, *Peak: Secrets from the New Science of Expertise* (Boston: Houghton Mifflin Harcourt, 2016).
3. Ibid.
4. Jeff Bezos, introduction by Walter Isaacson, *Invent and Wander.*
5. Andre Agassi, *Open: An Autobiography* (New York: Vintage Books, 2009).
6. Doug Lemov, Erica Woolway, and Kati Yezzi, *Practice Perfect: 42 Rules for Getting Better at Getting Better* (San Francisco: Jossey-Bass, 2012).
7. Joseph Grenny, Kerry Patterson, David Maxfield, Ron McMillan, and Al Switzler, *Influencer: The New Science of Leading Change* (New York: McGraw-Hill, 2013).
8. Bob Bowman with Charles Butler, *The Golden Rules: 10 Steps to World-Class Excellence in Your Life and Work* (New York: St. Martin's Press, 2016).
9. David Rubenstein, *How to Lead: Wisdom from the World's Greatest CEOs, Founders, and Game Changers* (New York: Simon & Shuster, 2020).
10. Laine Higgins, "This Swimmer Does It Differently," *Wall Street Journal,* July 30, 2021.
11. Tim Grover with Shari Lesser Wenk, *Winning: The Unforgiving Race to Greatness* (New York: Scribner, 2021).
12. Staats, *Never Stop Learning.*
13. Francis Greene, "Why Entrepreneurs Don't Learn from Their Mistakes," *Wall Street Journal,* December 1, 2019.
14. Ferris, *Tools of Titans.*
15. Ibid.
16. Ibid.
17. Rubenstein, *How to Lead: Wisdom from the World's Greatest CEOs, Founders, and Game Changers.*
18. David Ferry, "Is Sleep the Ultimate P.E.D.?" *Men's Health,* November 2019.
19. Ibid.
20. Steven Kotler and Jamie Wheal, *Stealing Fire: How Silicon Valley, the Navy SEALs, and Maverick Scientists are Revolutionizing the Way We Live and Work* (New York: Dey Street, 2017).
21. Dan Bigman and Ted Bililies, "Benioff's Way," *Chief Executive* magazine, Fall 2022.
22. Rachel Bachman, "Who's That Meditating Under the Goal Post?" *Wall Street Journal,* November 25, 2022.
23. Mayo Clinic Staff, "Water: How Much Should You Drink Every Day?" mayoclinic.org, accessed December 15, 2022.

Chapter 7

1. Mark Williams and Tim Wigmore, *The Best: How Elite Athletes Are Made* (London: Nicholas Brealey Publishing, 2020).
2. Brad Gilbert and Steve Jamison, *Winning Ugly: Mental Warfare in Tennis—Lessons from a Master* (New York: Touchstone, 2013).
3. Josh Peter, "LeBron Touts Benefit of Athletes' Mental Fitness," *USA Today*, December 11, 2019.
4. Geoff Smart and Randy Street, *Who: Solve Your #1 Problem* (New York: Ballantine Books, 2008).
5. Ferris, *Tools of Titans*.
6. Fran Simone, "Negative Self-Talk: Don't Let It Overwhelm You," *Psychology Today*, December 4, 2017.
7. Kilduff, "Driven to Win: Rivalry, Motivation and Performance," *Social Psychological and Personality Science*.
8. Michelle Malia, "A Winner Never Quits," *Men's Health*, March 2016.
9. Sofia Viranyi and Virginia Morell, "From Wolf to Dog," *Scientific American*, July 2015.
10. Daniel Coyle, *The Talent Code: Greatness Isn't Born. It's Grown. Here's How.* (New York: Bantam Books, 2009).
11. Ann Graybiel, "The Basal Ganglia and Chunking of Action Repertoires," *Neurobiology of Learning and Memory* 70, 1998.

Chapter 8

1. Heike Bruch, "Beware the Busy Manager," *Harvard Business Review*, February 2002.
2. Jack Flynn, "20 Vital Smartphone Usage Statistics [2023]," Zippia.com, October 20, 2022.
3. Eyal Ophir, "Cognitive Control in Media Multitaskers," *Proceedings of the National Academy of Sciences* 106(37), 2009.
4. Gary Keller with Jay Papasan, *The One Thing: The Surprisingly Simple Truth Behind Extraordinary Results* (Austin, Texas: Bard Press, 2012).
5. Julie Jargon, "Overcome Multitasking Madness," *Wall Street Journal*, May 2, 2022.
6. Dan Bigman, "What Matters Most," *Chief Executive* magazine, September–October 2018.
7. Steven Bertoni, "Turn On, Tune In, Tick Off." *Forbes,* April–May 2022.
8. Bruce Daisley, "Nine Easy Steps to a Better Day at Work," *Wall Street Journal*, February 22, 2020.
9. Keller with Papasan, *The One Thing*.
10. Kevin Kruse, *15 Secrets Successful People Know About Time Management* (Philadelphia: Kruse Group, 2015).
11. Andrew Blackman, "The Smartest Ways to Use Email at Work," *Wall Street Journal*, March 12, 2018.

Chapter 9

1. Adrian Bejan, "The Constructal Law of Organization in Nature: Tree-Shaped Flows and Body Size," *Journal of Experimental Biology*, May 1, 2005.
2. Ibid.
3. Garin Pirnia, "LEGO Genius Built a Fully Functioning Claw Machine with More Than 13,000 Bricks," *Mental Floss*, August 8, 2019.
4. Eugene Kim, "Microsoft Has a Strange New Mission Statement," *Business Insider*, June 25, 2015.
5. Stawski, *The Power of Mandate*.
6. Danny Meyer, *Setting the Table: The Transforming Power of Hospitality in Business* (New York: Harper, 2006).
7. Hugh McCutcheon, *Championship Behaviors: A Model for Competitive Excellence in Sports* (Chicago: Triumph Books, 2022).
8. Reed Hastings and Erin Meyer, *No Rules Rules: Netflix and the Culture of Reinvention* (New York: Penguin Press, 2020).
9. Ibid.
10. Michael Kerr, *Hire, Inspire, and Fuel Their Fire* (Canada: Mike Kerr, 2018).
11. Zook and Allen, *The Founder's Mentality*.
12. Kathleen Chaykowski, "Instagram's Big Picture," *Forbes*, August 23, 2016.
13. Julia Kirby and Thomas Stewart, "The Institutional Yes," *Harvard Business Review*, October 2007.

Chapter 10

1. Zhenya Lindgart, Martin Reeves, George Stalk, and Michael Deimler, "Business Model Innovation, *BCG*, December 2009.
2. Geoff Colvin, "Your Business Model Doesn't Work Anymore," *Fortune*, February 25, 2013.
3. Robert Kaplan and David Norton, "Having Trouble with Your Strategy? Then Map It," *Harvard Business Review*, September–October 2000.
4. Norman T. Sheehan, Nicolai J. Foss, "Exploring the Roots of Porter's Activity-Based View," *Journal of Strategy and Management* 2(3), 2009.
5. "IMARK Member Execs Share Perspectives on Business Planning," *IMARK Now*, Spring 2017.
6. Paul Leinwald, Mahadeva Matt Mani, and Blair Sheppard, "Reinventing Your Leadership Team," *Harvard Business Review*, January–February 2022.
7. Rich Horwath, *Elevate: The Three Disciplines of Advanced Strategic Thinking* (New York: Wiley, 2014).
8. "Winning Today's Race While Running Tomorrow's," *PwC's 26th Annual Global CEO Survey*, January 16, 2023.

Chapter 11

1. Chip Cutter, "Adobe's Chief Sizes Up the State of Tech Now," *Wall Street Journal*, January 9, 2023.
2. R.G. Tharp and R. Gallimore, R. "Basketball's John Wooden: What a Coach Can Teach a Teacher," *Psychology Today* 9(8), 1976, 74–78.
3. Jim Collins, *Good to Great: Why Some Companies Make the Leap . . . and Others Don't* (New York: HarperBusiness, 2001).
4. Stawski, *The Power of Mandate*.
5. J. E. Hunter and R. F. Hunter, "Validity of Common Methods for Predicting Job Success," *Psychological Bulletin*, 1984.
6. Chad Van Iddekinge, "Experience Doesn't Predict a New Hire's Success," *Harvard Business Review*, September–October 2019.
7. James Dyson, *Invention: A Life* (New York: Simon & Schuster, 2021).

Chapter 12

1. Eugene Foo, Kim Wagner, Andrew Taylor, and Hadi Zablit, "Setting a Foundation for Breakthrough Innovation," *BCG*, October 28, 2014.
2. Daniel McGinn, "The Numbers in Jeff Bezos's Head," *Harvard Business Review*, November 2014.
3. John Kounios and Mark Beeman, "The Cognitive Neuroscience of Insight," *Annual Review of Psychology*, August 30, 2013.
4. Katharina Herrmann, "Do You Have the Right Leaders for Your Growth Strategies?" *McKinsey Quarterly* 2, 2011.
5. Chris Bradley, "Have You Tested Your Strategy Lately?" *McKinsey Quarterly*, January 2011.
6. Barry Jaruzelski, "The Global Innovation 1000: Making Ideas Work," *strategy + business* 69.
7. Andrew Campbell and Marcus Alexander, "What's Wrong with Strategy?" *Harvard Business Review*, November–December 1997.
8. Brett and Kate McKay, *The Art of Manliness: Classic Skills and Manners for the Modern Man* (Cincinnati: How Books, 2009).
9. Andrew Braton, "Fitzpatrick is Golf's Best Notetaker," *Wall Street Journal*, July 14, 2022.
10. Steve Hamm, "The Vacuum Man Takes on Wet Hands," *Businessweek*, July 2, 2007.
11. Michael Pawlyn, *Biomimicry in Architecture* (Britain: RIBA Publishing, 2016).
12. David Goldenberg, "10 Technologies We Stole from the Animal Kingdom," *Mental Floss*, September 7, 2013.
13. Don Yaeger, "North Stars," *Chief Executive* magazine, Winter 2023.
14. Nikolaus Franke, "To Innovate Better, Find Divergent Thinkers," *Harvard Business Review*, June 2015.

15. Warren Berger, *A More Beautiful Question: The Power of Inquiry to Spark Breakthrough Ideas* (New York: Bloomsbury, 2014).
16. Bob Eberle, *SCAMPER: Games for Imagination Development* (England: Prufrock Press, 1996).
17. Rick Tetzeli, "Believe," *Fast Company*, September 2016.

Chapter 13

1. Gary Hamel, "Killer Strategies that Make Shareholders Rich," *Fortune*, June 1997.
2. Michael Copeland, "Reed Hastings: Leader of the Pack," *Fortune*, December 6, 2010.
3. Ram Charan, "Conquering a Culture of Indecision," *Harvard Business Review*, April 2001.
4. *Dictionary.com*, "discussion," accessed December 15, 2022.
5. Chris Argyris and Donald Schon, *Theory in Practice: Increasing Professional Effectiveness* (San Francisco: Jossey-Bass, 1974).
6. *Dictionary.com*, "direction," accessed December 15, 2022.
7. Andrew Grove, *Only the Paranoid Survive: How to Exploit the Crisis Points that Challenge Every Company* (New York: Currency, 1996).

Chapter 14

1. Rob Cross, "How to Succeed Quickly in a New Role," *Harvard Business Review*, November–December 2021.
2. Horwath, "The Strategic Mindset."
3. Sally Blount and Paul Leinwand, "Reimagining Effective Cross-Functional Teams," *strategy + business*, November 20, 2017.
4. Thomas Allen, *Managing the Flow of Technology* (Cambridge: MIT Press, 1977).
5. Grenny et al., *Influencer*.
6. Varda Liberman, Steve Samuels, and Lee Ross, "The Name of the Game: Predictive Power of Reputations versus Situational Labels in Determining Prisoner's Dilemma Game Moves," *Personality and Social Psychology Bulletin*, 30(9), 2004, 1175–1185.
7. Adrian Furnham, "The Brainstorming Myth," *Business Strategy Review*, January 2003.
8. Brian Mullen, Craig Johnston, and Eduardo Salas, "Productivity Loss in Brainstorming Groups: A Meta-Analytic Integration," *Basic and Applied Social Psychology* 12(1), 1991.
9. Michael Mankins, "Stop Wasting Valuable Time," *Harvard Business Review*, September 2004.
10. Ibid.
11. Hall and Hall, *Kill Bad Meetings*.
12. Mankins, "Stop Wasting Valuable Time."
13. Hall and Hall, *Kill Bad Meetings*.

14. Michael Mankins and Sue Shellenbarger, "The Plan to End Boring Meetings," *Wall Street Journal*, December 21, 2016.
15. Robert Cialdini, *Influence: The Psychology of Persuasion* (New York: Harper Business, 2021).

Chapter 15

1. McKelvey, *The Innovation Stack*.
2. Leonard Sherman, *If You're in a Dogfight, Become a Cat!* (New York: Columbia Business School Publishing, 2017).
3. Bernard Kummerli, Scott Anthony, and Markus Messerer, "Unite Your Senior Team," *Harvard Business Review*, November–December 2018.
4. Steven Rogelberg, "Make the Most of Your One-on-One Meetings," *Harvard Business Review*, November–December 2022.
5. Susan Berfield, "Howard Schultz versus Howard Schultz," *Businessweek*, August 17, 2009.
6. Steven Rogelberg, "Make the Most of Your One-on-One Meetings."
7. Thomas Barra and Patrick Barwise, "Why Effective Leaders Must Manage Up, Down, and Sideways," *McKinsey Quarterly*, April 2017.
8. Joe Flint, "Iger to Focus Disney on Profit Instead of Adding Subscribers," *Wall Street Journal*, November 29, 2022.
9. Joan Magretta, *Understanding Michael Porter: The Essential Guide to Competition and Strategy* (Boston: Harvard Business Review Press, 2012).
10. Peter Drucker, *The Practice of Management: A Study of the Most Important Function in American Society* (New York: Harper, 1954).
11. Chinta Bhagat, "Tapping the Strategic Potential of Boards," *McKinsey Quarterly*, no. 1, 2013.
12. Richard Parsons, "The Boardroom's Quiet Revolution," *Harvard Business Review*, March 2014.
13. Donley Townsend, "Engaging the Board of Directors on Strategy," *Strategy & Leadership* 35(5), 2007.
14. Sarah Cliffe, "The CEO View: Defending a Good Company from Bad Investors," *Harvard Business Review*, May–June 2017.

Chapter 16

1. Clark, "Pointless Meetings."
2. Perlow, Hadley, and Eun, "Stop the Meeting Madness."
3. Mankins, Brahm, and Caimi, "Your Scarcest Resource."
4. Carolyn Dewar, Scott Keller, and Vikram Malhotra, *CEO Excellence: The Six Mindsets that Distinguish the Best Leaders from the Rest* (New York: Scribner, 2022).
5. Hall and Hall, *Kill Bad Meetings*.

6. Dale Buss, "Leading Through Uncertainty" *Chief Executive* magazine, Winter 2023.
7. Matthew Boyle, "Useless Meetings Waste Time and $100 Million a Year for Big Companies, Bloomberg.com, September 26, 2022.
8. Hall and Hall, *Kill Bad Meetings*.
9. Mankins, "Stop Wasting Valuable Time."
10. Rich Horwath, *StrategyMan vs. The Anti-Strategy Squad: Using Strategic Thinking to Defeat Bad Strategy and Save Your Plan* (Austin, Texas: Greenleaf Book Group, 2018).
11. Alex Konrad, "Old Unicorn, New Tricks," *Forbes*, June–July 2022.
12. Clark, "Pointless Meetings."
13. Robert Shaw, *All In: How Obsessive Leaders Achieve the Extraordinary* (New York: HarperCollins Leadership, 2020).
14. Lauren Weber, "How Did a Company Get 95,000 Hours Back? Canceling Meetings," *Wall Street Journal*, February 2, 2023.

ABOUT THE AUTHOR

Rich Horwath's vision is to teach the world to be strategic. For more than 20 years, he has focused relentlessly on providing leaders with innovative concepts and practical tools to think, plan, and act strategically in order to set direction, create advantage, and achieve their goals. As founder and CEO of the Strategic Thinking Institute, Rich serves executive leadership teams as a strategy facilitator, strategic advisor, and executive coach. He has helped more than a quarter million people around the world develop their strategic thinking and planning capabilities.

Rich is the *New York Times* and *Wall Street Journal* bestselling author of eight books on strategic thinking and has been rated the number-one keynote speaker on strategy at national conferences, including the Society for Human Resource Management Strategy Conference. He has appeared on ABC, NBC, CBS, and FOX TV to provide commentary on the strategic aspects of current events and his work has appeared in publications including *Fast Company*, *Forbes*, and the *Harvard Business Review*.

A former chief strategy officer and professor of strategy, Rich has created more than 700 resources to help leaders at all levels maximize their strategic potential. He designed the Strategic Quotient (SQ) Assessment, a validated tool to measure how effectively a person thinks, plans, and acts strategically. Rich created the Strategic Fitness System as an online platform for leaders to practice the skills to effectively navigate all areas of their business, including strategy, leadership, organization, and communication.

In addition to this work, *Strategic: The Skill to Set Direction, Create Advantage, and Achieve Executive Excellence*, Rich's most recent books include *StrategyMan vs. The Anti-Strategy Squad: Using Strategic Thinking to*

Defeat Bad Strategy and Save Your Plan, the first-ever graphic novel on strategy and medal winner of the Axiom Business Book Award; *Elevate: The Three Disciplines of Advanced Strategic Thinking*, about which a leader at Intel proclaimed, "If you only read one book on strategy, this has to be that book!" *Deep Dive: The Proven Method for Building Strategy*, which was described by the director of worldwide operations for McDonalds as "the most valuable book ever written on strategic thinking." And *Strategy for You: Building a Bridge to the Life You Want* helps people apply the principles of business strategy to their overall life.

Rich earned an MBA with Distinction from the Kellstadt Graduate School of Business at DePaul University and has completed advanced coursework in strategy at the University of Chicago Booth School of Business and the Amos Tuck School of Business Administration at Dartmouth College. His free monthly publication, entitled *Strategic Thinker*, is read by thousands of business leaders and academicians. Rich resides in Barrington Hills, Illinois. For additional information, please visit StrategySkills.com.

INDEX